CARING and SHARING in the Foreign Language Class

A Sourcebook on Humanistic Techniques

Gertrude Moskowitz

Professor of Foreign Language Education
Temple University

Newbury House Publishers, Inc. / Rowley / Massachusetts

Library of Congress Cataloging in Publication Data

Moskowitz, Gertrude.
   Caring and sharing in the foreign language class.

   Bibliography: p.
   1. Language and languages—Study and teaching—
Problems, exercises, etc.   2. Education, Humanistic.
I. Title.
P53.M66   407   77-17518
ISBN 0-88377-098-9

Cover sketch by Ellen Greenland; cover design by Vinca,
augmented by Midge Block

Thanks from the author and publisher are extended to
Mr. Joseph Bricklin of The Bricklin Press for the
Hebrew typesetting contained in the Appendixes.

NEWBURY HOUSE PUBLISHERS, INC.

Language Science
Language Teaching
Language Learning

ROWLEY, MASSACHUSETTS 01969

Printed in the U.S.A.   First printing: April 1978
                                              5   4   3   2

This book is dedicated to my uncle,
Louis Sherman (1923-1970),
who was the epitome of a humanistic human being.

Acknowledgments

Every acknowledgment I've ever read by an author of a book has included a statement of how the final product would not have been possible without the help of many people. And now I see why this is so. Because I, too, couldn't have completed this publication without the encouragement, cooperation, and help of many friends, colleagues, and teachers.

From the earliest days, I have Wilga Rivers to thank. When I shared with her the ideas I had in mind for this book, her positive reactions and enthusiastic support encouraged me to follow its pursuit.

But when I had completely outlined the prospective book and had copious notes on what I proposed to write, I found myself stuck. The actual writing was tough for me to tackle. But an hour's time in the company of a very dear friend, Joyce Terwilliger, gave me the impetus to get going.

Once the first draft of four of the chapters and a part of the fifth was written, two other friends and professionals were extremely helpful—Jacqueline Benevento, a talented chairperson of foreign languages, and Don Miller, a psychologist and psychodramatist. They allowed me to send them the manuscript, which they critiqued. And so I profited from constructive feedback from representatives of the fields of foreign language and psychology.

The three appendixes containing special vocabulary and humanistic quotes in seven languages were quite an undertaking. The following foreign language educators were invaluable in either preparing, confirming, or adding to the translations. Josette Smith, who was the principal person, and Helene Bromberg translated the French materials, with Elaine Baer and Fred Silberstein adding recommendations. Gudrun Hull did the major work on the German materials, with Marianne Haug and George Williams also contributing. In Hebrew, Dr. Esra Shereshevsky did the translation, which was reviewed by Dr. Gershon Weiss, who also meticulously proofread the galleys. Further suggestions were given by Mouska Moston, and Naomi Soroka and Sarah Binor of Israel. Domenica Falcione was solely responsible for the Italian materials, with Dr. Robert Melzi providing some verification. The Latin was primarily translated by Rudolph Masciantonio, with some assistance from Domenica Falcione. Luz Díaz judiciously translated all the Spanish, which was confirmed by Patricio Concha, Dr. William Calvano, and Rodolfo Suárez. To all these dedicated people I owe a great deal of gratitude. These appendixes were extremely difficult to translate because of the delicacy of the meanings of many of the words and the quotes. Much thought and time were required to complete each translation—far more than one would imagine.

I am indebted to the people whose ideas for humanistic exercises have been used or adapted for use in this book. Their names are given where the exercises appear.

In the methods courses and workshops on humanistic techniques that I have given, the foreign language teachers that I taught were a splendid source of reinforcement. Their enthusiasm, feedback, and successful use of the techniques in their own classes made the convictions I had about the value of humanistic techniques in the foreign language class become even stronger.

Gloria Moskowitz and my daughters, Lynne and Jan, are entitled to many thanks for listening to me talk and talk about the book as it developed and for acting as sounding boards when I felt the need for an opinion related to it.

A big bouquet should go to Ellen Greenland for the sketch on the cover and to Midge Block for the layout of the cover design.

Although many people were involved in the book's production, the one who worked the hardest and most diligently of all was Rosalie Rodríguez, who typed the manuscript over and over and over. Her inordinate patience and willingness to help made the tremendous job of typing get done when deadlines seemed impossible to meet. Contrary to the typing of my doctoral dissertation, which was the worst experience in my whole doctoral program, Rosalie made me feel as though she considered my book *her* book as well. Whatever pressures I felt *she* felt, and many days she came to work extra early or stayed very late to get the work done.

Rupert Ingram, president of Newbury House Publishers, proved to be very humanistic and flexible to work with. He made any concerns I had disappear with his cooperativeness, promptness, and thoughtfulness.

And my appreciation would be incomplete without mentioning that my mother's patience and my father's perseverence, which rubbed off sufficiently well on me, most certainly contributed to the fruition of this book.

Gertrude Moskowitz

Philadelphia, Pennsylvania
March 1977

CREDITS

ART WORK IN THE PHOTOGRAPHS

Chapter 1:   ESOL poster—Grace Pacelli
                 German poster—Barbara Cavanaugh

Chapter 2:   Hebrew poster—Jan Cohen
                 French poster—Ellen Greenland

Chapter 3:   Self-Kit—Cathe Makem
                 Self-Collages (a), (b)—Students in a French class of Sylvia
                      Schenfeld, Northeast High School, Philadelphia, Pa.
                 Self-Collage (c)—Maryann Helferty, student in a Spanish class of
                      Anna Budiwsky, Notre Dame High School, Philadelphia, Pa.
                 Ad in English—Ellen Wiberly
                 Brochure in German—Barbara Cavanaugh
                 Trees: Italian—Elena Verzieri;
                           English—Susan Cohen;
                           Hebrew—Jan Cohen
                 Memorable Moments—Ruth Graves, Barbara Cavanaugh, Ellen
                      Greenland
                 Artistry in Feelings: English—Barbara Cavanaugh; Latin—Patricia M.
                      Miller; Italian—Renée Sadres and Marcy Yampell
                 Sculpture in Feelings: free—Ellen Wiberly; daring—Carl Boscia;
                      optimistic—Richard Reilly

Chapter 4:   Spanish poster—Ruth Graves
                 Latin poster—by the author of the book

Chapter 5:   German poster—Larry Sauppe
                 French poster—Ellen Wiberly
                 Hebrew poster—Jan Cohen
                 Transactional Analysis poster—Barbara Cavanaugh

Appendix C: ESOL poster—Talia Dunsky
                 Latin poster—Mary Conway Stewart
                 French poster—Ellen Greenland
                 German poster—Barbara Cavanaugh

Contents

Appendixes A, B, and C contain useful information in seven
languages: English, German, Latin, Spanish, French, Italian, and Hebrew.

ILLUSTRATIONS

CARING and SHARING in the Foreign Language Class

Man has a mind. Man has feeling. To separate the two is to deny all that man is. To integrate the two is to help man realize what he might be.

— George Isaac Brown
The Live Classroom, p. 108

Introduction

We live in times of great unrest—locally, nationally, and internationally. "Apathy" is a word commonly used to describe families, citizens, and nations.

Most teachers have been prepared to pass their subject matter along to pupils. But too often their young "enthusiasts" are receiving this wisdom and knowledge with apathy instead of enthusiasm.

The foreign language class has been depicted by many as having interaction that is too rote and automatic, too controlled and with too much parroting, with the teacher being viewed as a drill sergeant. But foreign language teachers are also known for expanding the horizons of students, increasing their awareness of other cultures, other people, other worlds—promoting cultural pluralism. Now is the time, however, for foreign language teachers to foster also the study and growth of *one* race—the *human* race.

Foreign language teachers have been reaching out, searching for more exciting ways of getting through to their students. Affective education holds promise for changing the stereotypes of the foreign language class and for humanizing it instead.

The purpose of this book is to provide some specific ways foreign language teachers can weave humanistic strategies into their already existing curricular materials. Since most teachers are given textbooks to "cover," the most realistic approach to including humanistic concepts is *not* total abandonment of what teachers are expected to teach, but supplementing these materials where appropriate. This book provides you with 120 strategies or techniques known as humanistic, affective, or awareness exercises. They are intended to enhance your foreign language program by bringing out the best in your students—the positive side. The exercises attempt to blend what the student feels, thinks, and knows with what he is learning in the target language. Rather than self-denial being the acceptable way of life, self-actualization and self-esteem are the ideals the exercises pursue.

The intent then is not simply to include humanistic activities in the foreign language class as a teaching device. It is to help build rapport, cohesiveness, and caring that far transcend what is already there. Primary aims of these materials are to help students to be themselves, to accept themselves, and to be proud of themselves.

What can you look forward to from using these awareness exercises? The activities are motivating, fun, and interesting to participate in, and encourage the students' desire to express themselves in the target language. They add variety to the class and hold appeal for all age levels. A cooperative spirit develops in the class as communication that is not superficial is exchanged. And the materials help satisfy the demands students make for relevance and more personalized contact in their learning.

Don't expect instant miracles. Do expect pleasant, rewarding results as your students feel an added warmth towards themselves, towards each other, and towards the foreign language class. These exercises help nurture in the student the feeling that he is a success in life by helping him achieve more of his potential. They develop his sense of personal worth by teaching such things as "I am important and so are you." Communication opens up, allowing the students to see the human side of each other as well as the teacher. When learning a foreign language, feelings of uncertainty, insecurity, and even fear often develop in the learner. Use of awareness exercises will help foster instead a climate of caring and sharing in the foreign language class.

This book is an accumulation of my past fifteen years. The exercises often evolved from workshops, conferences, and growth groups I've participated in, from course work in group dynamics, from people I've had contact with, from books I've read, from ideas I've tried out in teacher-training classes, and from myself—ideas I have modified or originated for the foreign language class. Tracking down humanistic or personal growth activities to their original sources can be as difficult as determining the creators of folklore or legends. The origin of some exercises is not traceable; they just seem to be handed down. Some activities are commonly used or found in print so often that their original sources appear unknown.

Wherever possible I have acknowledged the originator of an exercise. When the original source is unknown, I have stated this. If proper credit has been overlooked for anyone, it is unintentional. If the source given for an exercise turns out not to be the originator, this is because others have compiled personal growth exercises and may not have listed their source for the activity. In my own experience, I have made up original exercises only to discover later that a very similar or even identical one had been developed by someone else. In many cases

I have modified already-existing exercises and, in so doing, give credit to the original source of the idea, where the source is known, stating that this is an adaptation of the author's exercise. Where no credit is listed for an exercise, I authored the technique.

The topics in this book are sequenced to prepare you with what you need to know to start using humanistic techniques in your classes. Chapter 1 reveals some key ideas from humanistic education to be aware of before you begin. Chapter 2 gives pointers on how to conduct humanistic activities successfully. The humanistic exercises are presented in Chapter 3 and are spelled out with hints on getting the best results from each. Suggestions for developing your own tailor-made exercises, with examples of some created by teachers, are provided in Chapter 4. And although Chapter 5 relates to training teachers in humanistic techniques, it is intended for everyone to read, as many points in it are helpful to the classroom teacher who is on his own and not training others. To avoid redundancy, such ideas were not included in earlier chapters.

Appendixes A and B will get you started with supplementary vocabulary useful in a number of the exercises. Decorating the classroom "humanistically" is the purpose of the quotes given in Appendix C. These three appendixes have been developed in seven languages: English, German, Latin, Spanish, French, Italian, Hebrew. Appendix D consists of five parts, which summarize and act as a cross reference for information given earlier about each exercise. Refer to these charts to note the recommended time of year, level(s) of language, and linguistic goals for the exercises. Three bibliographies are provided as well. At the end of Chapter 1 are readings related to the theory and rationale of humanistic education. A list of references containing a number of humanistic exercises is given after Chapter 4. And a variety of additional suggested readings, books, chapters, and articles appears at the end of the book for your reading pleasure.

The techniques included in this book have been carefully selected and all have been tested in the classroom. There are exercises for all levels of language. I have experienced these strategies myself and know the benefits I have received. I have led workshops and classes in experiencing these activities, have guided teachers in their use, and have witnessed the overwhelming positive effects they have on developing human relations and increasing self-esteem. These foreign language teachers, in turn, have used the techniques in their classes and have been excited about the enthusiasm with which students receive them and the increased interest they show in the target language.

Let me share with you a couple of representative stories that were told to me. Six months after instructing a methods course on humanistic techniques, I approached an outstanding demonstration teacher who had taken it. Here is what she had to say:

First and foremost, the techniques are awakening an interest in the students that's not been there before. Their desire to learn to express themselves in the language has been stimulated and has led to greater creativity. They've said and written for me in Spanish what they haven't even done in English. The type of relaxed atmosphere we've established has made students not afraid or ashamed to share what they think and feel. I'm delighted with their enthusiasm and ecstatic about the depth they have shown about themselves.

She then referred to some of the unsolicited reactions of her students:

"This has got to be the shortest period of the day."

"This is so much better than just talking about the stories or dialogs."

"We have to do things we've never done before—ask questions, give our opinions, and think about important and everyday things."

She concluded our conversation by saying that because her students are happier, she's happier. She teaches in an inner-city school.

I spoke to this teacher again the following school year. She informed me that *one hundred percent* of the students in an upper level class she taught using self-awareness techniques had elected to continue Spanish the following year. She also said that her customary enrollment of fifteen in Spanish 4 had increased to twenty-eight since the previous year. The word had spread as to what they were doing in Spanish class. In another school, a French teacher using humanistic techniques told me that enrollments in her upper level classes also have increased.

Such reports are very encouraging. When given the opportunity to talk about themselves in personally relevant ways, students tend to become much more motivated. The result is that they want to be able to express their feelings and ideas more in the target language. They *want* to communicate. When this happens, growth becomes a reciprocal process: enhancing personal growth enhances growth in the foreign language.

Using humanistic techniques in teaching foreign languages is exciting for the teacher and the student. I have come to believe in these strategies because they do seem to work; they promote growth in the target language and in the areas of personal development and human relations, so vital to us all, yet so neglected in school.

I treasure the rewards I have found while working in the area of self-awareness and encourage you to enter it and do the same. What greater knowledge can we give students than knowledge of themselves? What better preparation for life can we provide than ways to make it more fulfilling?

Chapter 1

All About Humanistic Education

THE BIG GAP

The committee, furiously working on your school district's statement of philosophy, is grinding away at polishing up the document. The members go over it anxiously to be certain no critical elements have been overlooked. With the accreditation team breathing down their necks—the visit is only a few weeks off—things *must go smoothly*. At last the committee feels relaxed. The task is completed and the statement is beautiful. "More schools should have such a well-stated, carefully thought-out philosophy," they remark. And so time passes . . .

The day arrives and so does the accreditation team, armed with a thousand penetrating questions. They tour the school for several days. And all looks well. Classes are running smoothly. Bulletin boards look impressive. Students are participating in answer to the teachers' many questions. The Instructional Materials Center displays a harvest of offerings for every subject and taste. The hallway floors are newly waxed, the school lunches are especially tasty, and a special assembly for the week goes splendidly, ending with the students fervently chanting the alma mater. The administration and faculty are beginning to breathe easier now. How can they miss? Even *they* are impressed with their school.

The questioning is about to start. The team members, who have spent three days being whisked here and there by a variety of staff members, are now preparing for the interrogation. It begins.

"We admire your statement of philosophy," the person heading the team remarks. The staff, feeling reassured, beams. "Yes, it's a beautiful, detailed document and could well serve as a model for such statements." A noticeable glow of pride and confidence appears on the faces of the school's representatives. "But," he goes on, "we have some key issues of concern to us." The staff sobers up.

"For example, we note that your philosophy clearly acknowledges that one of the most important goals of the school is the social-emotional development of students, that is, the development of the 'whole child.' But as we visited classroom after classroom these past few days, we didn't find a single instance of this taking place. We observed teachers presenting facts about the subject matter and students reciting answers to questions, but this approach did not touch on the personal growth and development of students that you so admirably propound. Would you be good enough to tell us just how your teachers are implementing this lofty goal in their teaching?" the chairperson challenges.

An obvious silence ensues before the spokesman for the staff responds. "Well, you see," he sputters, "we feel that the total environment of our school promotes the social-emotional growth of students."

"Could you be more explicit, Mr. Caraway?" a team member inquires. More silence . . .

"Well, our students have elections of officers who have input into school functions," he replies.

"School functions. I see. What types of school functions?" one of the interrogators interrogates.

"Oh, they plan school dances, and ways to raise money to leave gifts to the school, and—and much much more," Mr. Caraway manages to eke out.

"Do the officers and student body meet with faculty to determine the rules and regulations of the school?" another evaluator asks.

After a deep swallow, Mr. C. gives a brief, "No. The school's rules were set up some time ago and we find they serve our needs."

"That's interesting," remarks the chairperson, "because we noticed the news clippings about the student protests you had only last year."

"Another basic goal listed in your fine philosophy was the development in students of their own self-worth," the leader continues. "We're very interested in how that comes about. Again we saw no tangible evidence of this happening during classroom instruction."

At this point several of the staff members quietly converse with each other and a new spokesman, Mr. Tillman, addresses the question. "Our teachers are sensitive, and in their dealings with students are kind and responsive to their needs." The team members now exchange glances, with some raising of eyebrows, eyes opened wide and knowingly, and lips turned downward.

"Still another part of your statement which puzzles us is that you believe students must learn to accept and understand one another. Somehow we also had difficulty discerning this goal being implemented in your classes," the investigator goes on.

"We have a well-rounded athletic program where students learn to have a cooperative spirit and to be good sports," Mr. Trumbull, the physical education director pipes up, with a half-hearted laugh.

"I'm afraid," the head of the team remorsefully proclaims, "that you are guilty of what most other schools also suffer from—knowing the words but not the music. The elegant and rather thick document you call your school philosophy quite lucidly says all the right things, but in the actual classroom setting you're only giving lip service to these notions. It is the opinion of our accreditation team that it's about time schools begin to *do* what they profess to. We're in desperate need of turning out students who believe in and understand themselves and others, who are responsible, caring people, and who can cope with their daily lives.

"And furthermore," the formidable team member continues, "we found a heavy emphasis on subject matter in the classroom, which is to be expected, since schools are intended to teach youngsters subject matter, but much of this was rote learning, factual, and mechanical. It was literally impossible to find any concrete ways in which the more esoteric goals of your school were being carried out in the many classroom-contact hours your students spend here each day. What we observed being stressed was content that was remote to the students' daily lives. The relevance students demand and yearn for was missing.

"Your staff, no doubt, truly believes in the goals you developed in your philosophy. What you don't understand is how to put them into operation!"

ANALYZING OUR EDUCATIONAL DILEMMA

The situation you have just witnessed regarding school philosophies is only too true. The fictitious part is that accrediting teams often overlook how social-emotional goals are implemented. The objectives of education that are blatantly encased in writing in school philosophies generally advocate that school and life should not be separated. In reality, the purpose of school tends to have remained singular—the learning of subject matter.

Signs of Stress in Youth

Obvious signs of stress in today's youngsters are evidenced by the continuous increase in school dropouts, drug abuse, vandalism, venereal disease, runaways, mental illness, and the suicide rate. A report in the 1970s placed suicide as the second highest cause of death among young people in the United States. Figures from Canada indicate a four hundred percent increase in the past two decades for those between fifteen to nineteen years of age.[1] A medical report in New York City revealed that, in this same age bracket, 210 died from using heroin in 1969, a three hundred percent rise over the previous year.[2]

At the same time, we know that the happy, well-adjusted person who understands himself, has a positive self-concept, is aware of his own feelings and those of others, and who finds relevance in his life is not likely to become one of the above statistics.

Today's youth cry for education that will help them make sense of their lives and the world around them. They want learning which is more personal and human. Evidence of their extreme dissatisfaction with the status quo was apparent during the late 1960s when there were countless student uprisings. Over 2000 protests occurred in secondary schools in the United States in a six-month period. Statistics such as these seem hard to ignore. Unfortunately, however, what students often encounter in school are many hours they consider a waste of time and unrelated to them.

The law mandates that youngsters attend school for a good part of the formative years of their lives. Education which is not responsive to the obvious strains on youth and society and does not provide saner, more wholesome approaches to living is archaic, derelict, and just plain wrong.

Are the Reasons for Learning a Foreign Language Evident?

To foreign language teachers, who know all the joys and benefits of learning a foreign language, justifying for students why they should study a foreign language may seem unnecessary. The reasons are so obvious. Yet how many times are foreign language teachers confronted with justifying their subject to students? Why should this lack of interest prevail?

If the benefits of learning a foreign language were obvious to students, we would not constantly be faced with that question or with dropping enrollments and retrenchment. This brings to mind an incident I observed in the class of an otherwise excellent teacher who first aroused and then frustrated the students' desire for personal interaction. He had planned a five-minute warm-up at the start of the lesson, in which he asked personalized questions of the students. Since there had been a school prom over the weekend, he asked the students several questions about the affair. They were enjoying talking about it, and when he told them to take out their books, their response was, "Oh, couldn't we talk about the dance some more?" He replied that they had a lot to cover and there wasn't enough time. The class begged him—to no avail—and then groaned as he began the content for the day. And we wonder why we have to defend learning a foreign language!

When students talk about what they want to and are interested and attentive, teachers often feel they are off the subject and must get back to the content. Yet when students *do* talk about what relates to them, there *is* increased attention.

Too Much Concern for the Cognitive?

Carl Rogers has aptly summarized this intense concern with the cognitive or "intellectual" part of learning:

> Each year I become more pessimistic about what is going on in educational institutions. They have focused so intently on the cognitive and have limited themselves so completely to 'education from the neck up,' that this narrowness is resulting in serious social consequences . . . As a consequence of this overstress on the cognitive, and of the avoidance of any feeling connected with it, most of the excitement has gone out of education.[3]

The dropout doesn't leave school because we didn't give him enough facts, but because he doesn't find any meaning in them for him.

A glance at any daily newspaper vividly illustrates how much we are in need of more than subject matter in our classroom instruction. The international, national, and local headlines reek of conflict, and our own daily lives may, as well. Schools are indeed in need of education for living.

The Reform of Education

There have been many critics who have written strong condemnations of our schools. Accusations have been made that schools are oppressive places governed by authoritarian rules, which suppress spontaneity and creativity and foster dependency and dehumanization. During the 1950s and 1960s, following Sputnik, much effort was put into curriculum innovation. Change took the form of updating materials and "retreading" teachers to use them properly. Emphasis was on the content—the cognitive.

But such curriculum reform did not reform the existing situation. The results we got were no different from what we were getting right along. Indeed, education is, if anything, in deeper trouble. And foreign language instruction is a leading contender. A major reason for this is that our focus is often out-of-focus. Such curricular innovations do not concentrate on or introduce change in the most critical area of all: the quality of human interaction in the classroom, that is, the way we relate to one another.

Psychologist Arthur W. Combs has wisely pointed this out to educators:

> Billions of dollars and billions of man hours are currently being expended in attempts to reform education. Unhappily much of this effort is foredoomed to be wasted because it concentrates on the wrong problem . . . Teachers have long been expert in providing information . . . Our major failures do not arise from lack of information. They come from . . . our inability to help students discover the personal meaning of the information we so extravagantly provide them . . . Our preoccupation with . . . information . . . has dehumanized our schools, alienated our youth, and produced a system irrelevant for most students.[4]

The post-Sputnik focus on content led to a severely unbalanced curriculum which does not respond to current social and interpersonal issues. Many students remain disenchanted with school and the subjects they take. Teaching still tends to consist of boring hours of listening and being expected to learn insignificant minutiae. And school has long been a place where many come to have a low regard for themselves as learners and subsequently as human beings.

True curriculum reform calls for more than considering the academic side of education and giving lip service to the personal aspect. We must consider that many of the problems *in* school are caused by the problems *with* school.

Our educational institutions must put into practice what they purport to do on paper: foster the positive psychological growth of students. Otherwise, the past and present growing dilemmas in education and society will only intensify with time.

THE GROWTH OF GROWTH

Fortunately, today there seems to be a shift in our society's focus from one of academic achievement to one of self-actualization. Developing fulfilling relationships, recognizing interdependence, expressing one's feelings, achieving one's potential, sharing oneself, and giving and receiving support are all parts of this new area of emphasis. Many well-adjusted people are seeking ways to grow and to reach more of their potential. It has become more and more recognized that the vast majority of us achieve only a small portion of our potential. As a result, many self-awareness groups have sprung up. Despite the outrageous cost of living that we complain about, people are finding the means to invest in sensitivity training, body and sensory awareness, biofeedback, encounter and growth groups, meditation, yoga, women's and men's consciousness-raising groups, re-evaluation counseling, transactional analysis, assertiveness training, parent effectiveness training, values clarification, psychosynthesis, and psychodrama. All these aim at achieving peace of mind and/or body and greater self-fulfillment.

Man's Pursuit of Becoming Human

Through the ages man has been striving to become more human. One way secondary schools and colleges believe this humanization can come about is by exposing students to a number of courses in the humanities. If students elect to take a foreign language in their humanities courses and then drop it as soon as they can, we have to face these questions: how are we humanizing youth through a foreign language and what is missing in these classes? Why, despite efforts to enhance interest in foreign languages, does this continue? Minicourses, individualizing instruction, cultural approaches, and multi-media courses are examples of efforts to increase student motivation and success.

The situation in ghetto schools has dramatically illustrated the effects on behavior, attitudes, and learning when the content is irrelevant. And today, the middle-class and upper-class students, too, are less and less willing to learn when they find no interest or value in the subject matter. Foreign language educators must face the reality that this is indeed a key reason why students discontinue studying foreign languages despite all the efforts at increasing their interest.

George Isaac Brown has some compelling thoughts on this subject:

> Are all classrooms dead? No, not all. But too damned many are . . . What is the difference between a dead and a live classroom? In the dead classroom learning is mechanistic, routine, over-ritualized, dull, and boring. The teacher is robotized, and the children are conceived as containers or receptacles whose primary function is to receive and hold subject matter . . . The live classroom . . . is full of learning activities in which students are enthusiastically and authentically involved . . . Each student is genuinely respected and treated as a human being by his teacher . . . the learning involves living.[5]

This approach to humanizing is quite different from that of imparting specific subject matter from designated fields.

THE GROWTH OF GROWTH IN EDUCATION

Youngsters today want change and they want it now. They are searching for their identity and are in need of self-acceptance. They complain of feelings of isolation and detachment.

A humanistic poster created to decorate an ESOL classroom.

Today there is an area of education receiving attention, and its spread seems related to this concern for personal development, self-acceptance, and acceptance by others, in other words, making students more human. The terms used to describe this type of instruction are "affective," "confluent," "psychological," "emotional," or "humanistic" education. All these try to accomplish similar aims: *combining the subject matter* to be learned with the *feelings, emotions, experiences, and lives* of the learners. Humanistic education is concerned with educating the whole person—the intellectual and the emotional dimensions. It has developed from a variety of sources, but is most directly related to what is referred to as the "third force," or humanistic psychology, and the human potential movement.

(German) Humanistic Poster: "A little laugh makes a big day."

Traditionally education has poured the content into the student. Affective education draws it out of the student. It recognizes that anyone who teaches is automatically dealing with students' feelings, which are always present. These are bound to affect learning and should be put to use in teaching. How you feel about what you learn as you learn influences how you learn. Customarily the feelings of students are overlooked or denied in learning. Think how often students are told, "You shouldn't feel that way."

Self-actualization as the Goal of Education

Humanistic education also takes into consideration that *learning is affected by how students feel about themselves.* A basic assumption made is that the better youngsters feel about themselves and others, the more likely they are to achieve. Arthur Combs explains:

> ... what a person believes about himself is crucial to his growth and development ... a person learns this self-concept from the way he is treated by significant people in his life. The student takes his self-concept with him wherever he goes. He takes it to Latin class, to arithmetic class, to gym class, and he takes it home with him ... Everything that happens to him has an effect on his self-concept.[6]

So the role of the self-concept in learning is viewed as crucial.

Cecil Patterson advocates as the purpose of education the development of self-actualizing persons, that is, human beings functioning to their fullest capacity. He sees this goal as congruent with man's own true purpose in life: "It is the single, basic, common motivation of the individual."[7] Patterson charges education to develop self-actualizing individuals—persons who are responsible and who understand, accept, and respect others and themselves. Producing persons who can think, feel, and act, based not only on their intellect but their feelings, is an outcome he expects from education.

Combs and Snygg concur with this line of thinking and suggest that self-actualization or self-enhancement is the "all inclusive human need which motivates all behavior at all times in all places."[8]

Abraham Maslow, one of the fathers of humanistic psychology, studied a number of people considered as outstanding examples of self-actualizing persons—those judged as living to their fullest capacities and making the best use of their potentials. He was searching for the characteristics common to these individuals that distinguished them from typical people. The following are some of the characteristics that Maslow identified. Self-actualizing persons accept themselves and others, are natural and spontaneous rather than conforming, have a mission in life and a strong sense of responsibility, are independent and look to themselves for their own growth, experience pleasurable, awesome feelings related to every-day life, have great empathy and affection for humanity, are not prejudiced, and are creative in their approach to things.[9]

In his work as a therapist, Carl Rogers concludes that underlying the whole realm of problems his clients present, there is one central theme: "Who am I, *really*? How can I get in touch with this real self, underlying my surface behavior? How can I become myself?" [10] He declares that the most important question an individual can ask is "Am I living in a way which is deeply satisfying to me, and which truly expresses me?" [11]

But what has all this to do with learning a foreign language? Suppose the target language is taught so that students develop more positive feelings about themselves and their classmates and find out more about what they are really like. Such an approach will help increase the esteem and understanding students have for themselves and others, thus facilitating growth in the direction of being more self-actualized. Since self-actualization is such a powerful inherent need in humans, as students see the subject matter as self-enhancing, it will be viewed as relevantly related to their lives. They will then become more motivated to learn to use the foreign language and, as a result, will be more likely to learn.

Basing Humanistic Programs on Needs

Maslow regarded satisfying the basic psychological needs of people as vital. Among these needs are dignity, respect, belongingness, love, and esteem. He found that drug addicts experience lives almost devoid of having any needs gratified.[12] He stated that agencies working with drug addicts contend that they will give up drugs when they find meaning in their lives. Maslow also referred to psychologists describing alcoholics as essentially depressed and bored.[13]

Maslow pointed out that life has to have some meaning and contain peak experiences of joy to be worthwhile. He stressed that schools seem to look down on children having a good time. He affirmed that schools can give students a sense of accomplishment and that teachers should be joyful and self-actualized themselves. Too often though, learning involves pleasing the teacher rather than thinking and enjoying. Maslow charged that teachers must not only accept students, but help them learn about what kind of persons they are. Healthy people are much clearer about their values, and schools can help students derive their values from a knowledge of themselves.

In keeping with the thinking of Maslow, Robert E. Valett feels that humanistic education should start with assessing the basic needs of humans and that these should be the foundation upon which instructional programs are built. He categorizes children's basic needs into six areas:[14]

1. Physical security—food, clothing, shelter, good health
2. Love—attention, encouragement, praise, physical contact, warmth, support
3. Creative expression—promoting sensory capacities, gaining pleasure in expressing oneself creatively, exploring new ways of expressing oneself
4. Cognitive mastery—achieving relative competency in basic skills

5. Social competency—acceptance and interaction with peers, getting to know and relate to peers better

6. Self-worth—strengths stressed and weaknesses played down

To have self-worth, Valett notes, the other needs must be somewhat satisfied.

In terms of foreign language learning, the basic needs advocated by Maslow and Valett seem equally desirable, compatible, and possible to aim for.

What Humanistic Education Is

Humanistic education recognizes that it is legitimate to study oneself. The content relates to the feelings, experiences, memories, hopes, aspirations, beliefs, values, needs, and fantasies of students. It strives to integrate the subject matter and personal growth dimensions into the curriculum.

In any learning situation, feelings are always present and should be drawn upon, as they exert an influential role. In humanistic education, it is a two-way street: feelings must be recognized in the learning process and information must be available as well. Hawley and Hawley put it this way:

> Learning cannot be carried on in an emotion- and value-free climate, . . . and personal growth education cannot be carried on in a vacuum of information. The two should be one.[15]

Affective education is effective education. It works on increasing skills in developing and maintaining good relationships, showing concern and support for others, and receiving these as well. It is a special type of interaction in itself, consisting of sharing, caring, acceptance, and sensitivity. It facilitates understanding, genuineness, rapport, and interdependence. Humanistic education is a way of relating that emphasizes self-discovery, introspection, self-esteem, and getting in touch with the strengths and positive qualities of ourselves and others. It enables learning to care more for ourselves and others. In addition to all this, humanistic education is fun.

As students find that their thoughts, feelings, and experiences are regarded as important in school, school becomes important to them. This type of growth and closeness comes gradually. It is *not* instant intimacy.

Students who fail in school never have had a chance to experience such things—to become aware of their own strengths and to share themselves with others. Those who drop out because of lack of interest do not do so because we haven't given them enough facts. It's just that the facts have no meaning for them.

What Humanistic Education Is Not

Beware of misusing or misconstruing humanistic education. It is just as important to know what humanistic education is *not*. It is not the latest fad or gimmick. It is not a form of therapy, though it may be therapeutic. It is neither sensitivity training, permissiveness or license, nor a confessional. It is definitely not a way to hold students' attention on difficult days, something to be taken lightly or, in our own case, a way to trick students into learning a foreign language.

Teachers Do Make a Difference

Often foreign language teachers feel they do not have enough impact on the lives of students. Seeing apathy and apparent boredom on students' faces is very discouraging to teachers who are teaching their discipline because of their own love for it. This book was written because of my own conviction that teachers *can* and *do* make a difference in the lives of their students. The trouble is that often teachers are not aware of what students actually have been learning from them, and it may be: it pays to apple-polish and compete; keep your feelings to yourself; school is a boring place where time is wasted; or get the right answers no matter how you do it.

A teacher actually may affect the entire course of a person's life. In my own case, my fourth grade teacher and a professor in graduate school—contacts early and later in my life—changed my future. We're never too young or too old to be influenced. Most of the time, though, such experiences are not communicated to us by students, so we don't realize our power to influence for better or for worse. An aim of this book is to harness that influence and to help make it work for you and your students in such positive ways that it will be visible and clearly evident.

Aren't Foreign Language Teachers Already Humanistic?

Two important questions frequently raised when talking about incorporating humanistic teaching in foreign language classes are: Don't we already have many teachers who teach humanistically? and Don't foreign language teachers already relate the language to their students' lives? Yes, many foreign language teachers are humanistic in their approach to dealing with students in their classes. But that is quite different from using humanistic exercises and activities to help teach the content of the language.

And it's true that for some time foreign language teachers have recognized the importance of personalizing the content being learned by asking students related questions about themselves. But humanistic education takes this to a deeper level of exploration. It goes far beyond studying a unit dealing with the family or the house and then asking such questions as "How many brothers and sisters do *you* have?" or "What furniture is in *your* bedroom?" In a sense, these "personal" questions are impersonal. They share factual, superficial data about students.

Affective questions dealing with these same themes might be: How does it feel to be the oldest (youngest, or middle) child? What advantages and disadvantages are there? What special object do you display in your room that gives you pleasant memories? What does it mean to you? What do you think of when you look at it? These kinds of personal questions share the person that really *is*.

Personalizing based upon the characters in the textbook or the filmstrip hasn't been good enough. Just think about the opportunity that has been overlooked for so long. The foreign language teacher can provide content that *is* truly interesting and meaningful to the student—the study of himself. Talking about his own growth and development, sharing what *is* important to him, and participating in personally reinforcing interaction seldom found in other parts of the curriculum are valued areas of *communication*: the very essence of language learning.

AFFECTIVE MODELS OF TEACHING

Many humanistic programs have been developed in recent years. John P. Miller has organized affective teaching into four models, each having a main focus: [16]

1. *The developmental model*—The teaching strategies are in keeping with the developmental stage of life in which the learner is. Erikson's eight emotional stages of man are useful in this model as is the work of Piaget. Examples of Erikson's stages are: identity versus identity diffusion during adolescence and intimacy versus isolation in young adulthood.

2. *The self-concept models*—Emphasis is on enhancing the self-esteem and knowledge of one's identity. Such strategies also involve discovering one's values and living according to them. The goal is to enable youngsters to live according to their own expectations and not only those of others; that is, to gain control over their lives.

3. *The sensitivity and group-orientation models*—These work on helping people become more open with and sensitive to others. Communication skills are stressed, as is empathizing with others.

4. *The consciousness-expansion models*—Such models are intended to increase the imaginative, creative, initiative capacities. Producing a relaxed but alert state of mind is attempted. Some components of these models are: integrating the mind and body, sensory awareness, guided imagery, and achieving higher or deeper levels of consciousness. Emanating from Eastern psychologies, these models have been increasingly accepted by the Western world as the desirability of heightened awareness of oneself and the environment has been discovered.

The humanistic exercises presented in this book are diverse and eclectic in nature. They draw upon these four models in terms of their goals.

Miller's book should be read by those interested in a thorough treatment of the theoretical base and rationale for the above models, their classroom applicability, and the long and short range effects to be expected.

A Model for Sharing

Humanistic techniques help create a warmer, more accepting climate, and a feeling of greater closeness among students. But how does this come about? To better understand the process, it is helpful to refer to a model called the Johari Window.[17] Its mysterious name was coined from the first names of the psychologists who developed it, Joseph Luft and Harry Ingham.

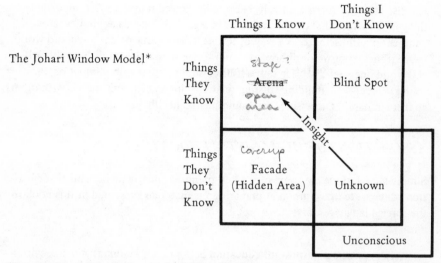

The Johari Window Model*

*Reprinted from John E. Jones and J. William Pfeiffer, eds., *The 1973 Annual Handbook for Group Facilitators.* La Jolla, Calif.: University Associates (1973). Used with permission.

    The model is viewed as a communication window through which information is given and received about oneself and others. It works this way. There are four areas in the window. The Open or Public Area contains information which I know about myself and you also know; it is therefore public knowledge. The Blind Spot consists of those things you know about me but that I am unaware of. The Facade or Hidden Area is just the reverse, those things about me that I keep to myself, that I do not want you to know. Perhaps I need to trust you more to reveal these things, or I may feel that you will think less of me if I let you know these parts of myself. The Unknown Area has data about me that neither you nor I am aware of. Some may be at the unconscious level.

    Now how does the model work? Ideally, the largest area should be the Open Area in which you and I know a good many things about me, while the other areas should be quite small. The way this can come about is through sharing and feedback. That is, the more I let you know about me, the smaller my Hidden Area will be and the larger the Open Area will grow. My Blind Spot will decrease if you give me feedback related to things I may not yet realize about myself.

    As I share things about myself with you and you give me feedback, I may develop some insights into myself that are in the Unknown Area. If I then share these insights with you, they revert to the Open Area. Therefore, through sharing and feedback the Open or Public Area increases, while the other three areas decrease. Humanistic techniques, then, aim at increasing the Open Area for everyone and, through the process of giving and receiving information about ourselves and each other, warmth and closeness develop as we truly get to know one another.

But just how essential is the process of sharing? Sidney M. Jourard, psychotherapist and teacher, spent many years in the scientific investigation of self-disclosure, or sharing oneself, because he viewed it as the most important thing in the world that can be studied. He regarded this area as vital because "authentic self-disclosure is a way of letting others know of one's self and world, to see if they approve or disapprove—and to see if one likes or dislikes this self and world one's self." [18] He saw self-disclosure as "that embodiment of 'the courage to be.' " [19] Building trusting relationships and sharing oneself with others go hand-in-hand as necessities for sound mental health.

ASSUMPTIONS OF HUMANISTIC EDUCATION

Simply stated, these are some of the key premises underlying humanistic education which were drawn upon in preparing the materials presented in this book for the foreign language class:

1. A principal purpose of education is to provide learnings and an environment that facilitate the achievement of the full potential of students.

2. Personal growth as well as cognitive growth is a responsibility of the school. Therefore education should deal with both dimensions of humans—the cognitive or intellectual and the affective or emotional.

3. For learning to be significant, feelings must be recognized and put to use.

4. Significant learning is discovered for oneself.

5. Human beings want to actualize their potential.

6. Having healthy relationships with other classmates is more conducive to learning.

7. Learning more about oneself is a motivating factor in learning.

8. Increasing one's self-esteem enhances learning.

The point of view taken here is that building language programs along these lines is essential in truly motivating the learner and in doing justice to him as a human being and as an individual.

FEARS ABOUT HUMANISTIC EDUCATION

A problem in incorporating humanistic activities in foreign language classes is that foreign language teachers are largely untrained and inexperienced in humanistic activities themselves. The whole notion is "foreign" to most foreign language teachers. And so they may have fears and be reluctant about going into this realm, even though it can be a deeper, more satisfying one for all.

Some of the fears expressed by teachers take the form of worrying that the foreign language teacher will take on the role of psychologist. In effect, teachers may already be in that role whether they admit to it or not. We all have the power to make others feel better or worse about themselves, but teachers, in particular, have this power with every sentence they utter. In using self-awareness techniques, teachers try to *enhance the student's personal growth* along with his growth in the target language. By doing so, they recognize that affective goals are a legitimate part of the curriculum. And there are certain procedures to follow when conducting humanistic exercises which help students feel better and avoid the cause for concern that teachers may have. These will be elaborated in the next chapter to help eliminate the basis for those concerns.

Arthur Jersild regards all teachers as practicing psychologists, whether or not they know it or accept it:

> Every teacher is in his own way a psychologist. Everything he does, says, or teaches has . . . a psychological impact. What he offers helps children to discover their resources and their limitations. He is the central figure in countless situations which can help the learner to realize and accept himself or which may bring humiliation, shame, rejection, or self-disparagement.[20]

Another fear some teachers have is that they may do some unintentional damage to students, since emotions and feelings are not areas customarily delved into. Their concern is generally unwarranted. The sensitive teacher will deal sensitively in most classroom situations, just as the insensitive teacher will be consistent with his own behavior patterns. George Isaac Brown, a well-known leader in the humanistic education movement, expresses his findings related to this worry very beautifully:

> We know of no students who have been harmed by our work. It has been our experience, working with large numbers of teachers at all levels of instruction, that teachers who are going to abuse their role will do so whether or not they have affective techniques available. If a teacher relates in a toxic or pathological way to his classroom content . . . this poison will out, no matter what the vehicle.[21]

Being innovative does indeed involve some risk-taking, but the need for innovation in the schools is quite pronounced. Generally, schools have not encouraged combining affective experiences with the learning of subject matter. This is no doubt one reason why many youngsters don't find the classroom a place where things that are important to their lives happen.

ACQUIRING EXPERIENCE IN HUMANISTIC TECHNIQUES

Actually humanistic techniques are good for the teacher as well as the students in expanding growth and self-awareness, getting in touch with feelings, and increasing creativity and potential. But how can you get the necessary experience to conduct humanistic activities in your own classes if you have no training in this area?

Today there are many workshops, in-service programs, and conferences at which humanistic exercises are being demonstrated. If none are available specifically for foreign language teachers, attendance at offerings for teachers in general can be of help. Many growth centers and human potential workshops for gaining some experience along these lines are also available.

A number of books have been published containing general humanistic activities. You will have to read widely, however, to locate those appropriate for the foreign language class, since many are not possible to handle in the target language. A little material is presently available for foreign language teachers. Such publications are available principally through humanistic education centers and primarily utilize values clarification and Gestalt exercises.[22]

And, then, this book was especially designed with *you* in mind. In Chapter 2 you will find the ins and outs and dos and don'ts of using humanistic activities in the foreign language class. Following this, Chapter 3 will take you step-by-step through numerous exercises which have been tested in classes and found to work. As you read them, "experience them" by doing what they ask of you. This will give you a "feel" for the activity and the experience behind it as you become aware of your own reactions. You can also try the exercises on friends, family, or colleagues to get responses and reactions.

After using tested techniques awhile, try making up some yourself. Chapter 4 will direct you on how to go about this and has samples of exercises foreign language teachers have written for you to try. And don't overlook Chapter 5. Although aimed at teacher trainers, many points made are intended for all readers.

GROWTH MUST BE TAUGHT

Humanistic education involves learning to be a better, more feeling human being. Educators have been notorious for assuming that social-emotional growth somehow just happens on its own. But if we don't teach for such goals, they just don't happen. We need a place in school where teachers and students can be human, get empathy, and take time to share. We must set our goals on teaching not only our target language, but also the language of "OKness."

Can this be done in the foreign language class? The answer is "Yes!" And that's what this book is all about. Won't you join me and find out?

NOTES

1. John P. Miller. *Humanizing the Classroom: Models of Teaching in Affective Education.* New York: Praeger (1976), p. 1.

2. Ralph L. Mosher and Norman A. Sprinthall. "Psychological Education in Secondary Schools: A Program to Promote Individual and Human Development." *American Psychologist.* 25 (October 1970), p. 911.

3. Carl R. Rogers. "Bringing Together Ideas and Feelings in Learning." Donald A. Read and Sidney B. Simon, eds. *Humanistic Education Sourcebook.* Englewood Cliffs, N.J.: Prentice-Hall, pp. 40-1. © 1975 by Prentice-Hall, Inc. Reprinted with permission.

4. Arthur W. Combs. "Sensitivity Education: Problems and Promises." *Educational Leadership.* 28 (December 1970), pp. 235-6. Copyright © 1970. Reprinted with permission of the Association for Supervision and Curriculum Development.

5. George I. Brown, Thomas Yeomans, and Liles Grizzard, eds. *The Live Classroom.* New York: The Viking Press (1975), pp. 1-2. Copyright © 1975 by George I. Brown. An Esalen Book. Reprinted by permission of The Viking Press.

6. Arthur W. Combs. "The Human Side of Learning." *The National Elementary Principal.* 52 (January 1973), p. 42. Copyright 1973, National Association of Elementary School Principals. All rights reserved. Used with permission.

7. Cecil H. Patterson. *Humanistic Education.* Englewood Cliffs, N.J.: Prentice-Hall (1973), p. 22.

8. Arthur W. Combs and Donald Snygg. *Individual Behavior.* New York: Harper & Row (1959), p. 38.

9. Abraham H. Maslow. "Self-Actualizing People: A Study of Psychological Health." Clark E. Moustakas, ed. *The Self: Explorations in Personal Growth.* New York: Harper & Row (1956), pp. 160-94.

10. Carl R. Rogers. "What It Means to Become a Person." Clark E. Moustakas. ed. *The Self: Explorations in Personal Growth.* New York: Harper & Row (1956), p. 196.

11. Ibid., p. 208.

12. Abraham H. Maslow. *The Farther Reaches of Human Nature.* New York: Viking Press (1971), p. 190.

13. Ibid., p. 188.

14. Robert E. Valett. *Affective-Humanistic Education: Goals, Programs, and Learning Activities.* Belmont, Calif.: Lear Siegler/Fearson (1974).

15. Robert C. Hawley and Isabel Hawley. *A Handbook of Personal Growth Activities for Classroom Use.* Amherst, Mass.: Education Research Associates (1972), p. 115.

16. John P. Miller. *Humanizing the Classroom.*

17. Joseph Luft. *Of Human Interaction.* Palo Alto, Calif.: Mayfield Publishing Company (1969).

18. Sidney M. Jourard. *Self-Disclosure: An Experimental Analysis of the Transparent Self.* New York: John Wiley and Sons, Inc., p. 188. Copyright © 1971, John Wiley and Sons, Inc. Used with permission.

19. Ibid.

20. Arthur T. Jersild. *In Search of Self: Exploration of the Role of the School in Promoting Self-Understanding.* New York: Teachers College Press. Copyright 1952 by Teachers College, Columbia University, p. 125. Used by permission of the publisher.

21. George I. Brown et al. *Live Classroom,* p. 298.

22. Refer to the first bibliography at the end of Chapter 2 for a listing of these publications.

READINGS RELATED TO THEORY OF
AND RATIONALE FOR HUMANISTIC EDUCATION

Brown, George I., Thomas Yeomans, and Liles Grizzard, eds. *The Live Classroom: Innovation through Confluent Education and Gestalt.* New York: Viking Press (1975).

Bugental, J. F. T. *Challenges of Humanistic Psychology.* New York: McGraw-Hill (1967).

Covington, Martin V., and Richard G. Beery. *Self-Worth and School Learning.* New York: Holt, Rinehart, and Winston (1976).

Crary, Ryland W. *Humanizing the School.* New York: Alfred A. Knopf (1969).

Curwin, Richard L., and Barbara Schneider Fuhrmann. *Discovering Your Teaching Self: Humanistic Approaches to Effective Teaching.* Englewood Cliffs, N.J.: Prentice-Hall (1975).

Eiben R., and A. Milliren, eds. *Educational Change: A Humanistic Approach.* La Jolla, Calif.: University Associates (1976).

Fairfield, Roy P., ed. *Humanistic Frontiers in American Education.* Englewood Cliffs, N.J.: Prentice-Hall (1971).

Heath, Douglas H. *Humanizing Schools.* New York: Hayden Book Co. (1971).

Jersild, Arthur T. *In Search of Self: An Exploration of the Role of the School in Promoting Self-Understanding.* New York: Teachers College Press (1952).

Klein, Thomas et al. *Spinach Is Good for You: A Call for Change in the American School.* Bowling Green, Ohio: Bowling Green University Press (1973).

Manning, Duane. *Toward a Humanistic Curriculum.* New York: Harper & Row (1971).

Maslow, Abraham. *Motivation and Personality.* New York: Harper & Row (1954).

———. *The Farther Reaches of Human Nature.* New York: Viking Press (1971).

———. *Toward a Psychology of Being.* New York: Van Nostrand Reinhold (1968).

Miller, John P. *Humanizing the Classroom: Models of Teaching in Affective Education.* New York: Praeger (1976).

Patterson, Cecil H. *Humanistic Education.* Englewood Cliffs, N.J.: Prentice-Hall (1973).

Purkey, William W. *Self-Concept and School Achievement.* Englewood Cliffs, N.J.: Prentice-Hall (1970).

Randolph, N., and W. Howe. *Self-enhancing Education.* Palo Alto, Calif.: Stanford Press (1966).

Read, Donald A., and Sidney B. Simon, eds. *Humanistic Education Sourcebook.* Englewood Cliffs, N.J.: Prentice-Hall (1975).

Ringness, Tom A. *The Affective Domain in Education.* Boston: Little, Brown & Co (1975).

Rogers, Carl. *Freedom to Learn.* Columbus, Ohio: Charles E. Merrill (1969).

———. *On Becoming a Person.* New York: Houghton Mifflin (1961).

Strom, Robert, and Paul E. Torrance. *Education for Affective Achievement.* Chicago: Rand McNally (1973).

Valett, Robert E. *Affective-Humanistic Education: Goals, Programs and Learning Activities.* Belmont, Calif.: Lear Siegler, Inc./Fearon Publishers (1974).

Weinberg, Carl, ed. *Humanistic Foundations of Education.* Englewood Cliffs, N.J.: Prentice-Hall (1972).

Weinstein, Gerald, and Mario Fantini, eds. *Toward Humanistic Education: A Curriculum of Affect.* New York: Praeger (1970).

Zahorik, John A., and Dale L. Brubaker. *Toward More Humanistic Instruction.* Dubuque, Iowa: Wm. C. Brown (1972).

Chapter 2

All
About
Humanistic Exercises

Well, look who's here! I'm glad you've come. I couldn't see writing a book encouraging humanism without being able to talk directly to you.

You're here to learn all about humanistic exercises so you can try them? Great! I'm delighted! Feel free to interrupt or ask questions as we go along.

WHAT ABOUT YOUR PRESENT INSTRUCTIONAL MATERIALS?

I see—the first thing you want to know is what are you supposed to do with the materials you already have and are expected to use in your foreign language classes. The answer—use them! Humanistic techniques can be included to supplement, review, and introduce your already existing materials. The reality of the situation is that almost every foreign language program uses commercially prepared materials, which are usually a large expenditure for the school district. The intention is not to discard these. Include an awareness activity wherever one relates to what the students are studying or where you find it appropriate.

Fitting In Humanistic Exercises

You'd like some examples of how to fit them in? All right. Suppose your class is reading a story in which exchanging gifts becomes central to the plot. Pick up the topic of gifts as a focus for an exercise. This is the theme in Exercise 73, "The Gift I've Always Wanted," found in Chapter 3. Basically, students respond to the question of what gift they would like more than anything in the world to have. The gift can be tangible or intangible. This notion then has many possibilities for further development and exploration.

Once students are taught to answer the question "How are you?" in the target language with the customary responses "I'm fine," "I'm not feeling well," and "So-so," give them a supplementary list of expressions. Oddly enough, curricular materials don't include much vocabulary for communicating how we really *do* feel. Appendix A contains a vocabulary list of words expressing feelings and emotions. Words from this list can be selected to expand the possibilities for answering. Then students can tell how they actually *do* feel when responding to this commonly asked question. You might ask the students what words they need to know to express their true feelings at a given time and supply them as well. Most of us use so few words to describe our feelings that this is useful vocabulary in any language, even our native tongue.

No, you needn't feel uneasy about introducing exercises related to feelings, values, and growth into the foreign language class. Although this is a new experience in most foreign language classes, affective education is "in" and accepted in other subject areas, and it's time we acknowledged it in our classes, too.

A WORD ABOUT GIMMICKS

You've heard some people say that humanistic exercises are gimmicks? Quite the contrary. You should believe in their true worth to use them. Let me share what can happen when these activities are perceived as gimmicks. In a methods course I taught for foreign language teachers on humanistic techniques, the teachers became very enthusiastic about these strategies and so did their students. The word spread in their schools and several other teachers heard about some of the exercises and tried them. In most cases these teachers did not get the same results at all.

You must have a basic understanding of each technique and how learning a foreign language fits in with it, know how to direct the activity and discussion, and make appropriate comments as needed. And you have to get involved in the activities yourself. Fritz Perls, Gestalt therapist, was reputed to have said that a gimmick is what a person calls a technique if he doesn't understand it. To use humanistic techniques and not understand their purposes or how to foster them will not achieve the intended benefits and results.

BUILDING A CLIMATE OF ACCEPTANCE

Yes, that's true. It's essential to establish a warm, supportive, accepting, and nonthreatening climate. As you use these techniques, you'll find that they are conducive to creating this very type of atmosphere. Your students will become more cohesive than you or they may ever have been before. You can develop an extraordinary rapport with students, beyond what you already have been doing successfully. The increased satisfaction in teaching that you can gain will astonish and reward you for your experimental efforts and your convictions.

ACCENTUATE THE POSITIVE

You'd like to know what are the most crucial things to be aware of when carrying out affective activities? I find that there are several and they are related. Let me ask you to try something first to help me make my point. Take a piece of paper and draw a line down the middle of the page. In the next two minutes (take longer, if you'd like) write down as many of the positive things about yourself as you can think of in one column and the negative things in the other column. Go ahead now, I'll wait . . .

How did you make out? . . . You got stuck on the positive ones after a few but had no trouble thinking up negative ones? Are you ever typical! This is frequently the case.

The point I was trying to illustrate is that, in my opinion, of key importance in using humanistic exercises is *focusing on the positive aspect.* Activities which emphasize identifying our strengths and those of others, developing a more positive self-image, giving and receiving positive feedback, and learning to understand ourselves and others better all contribute to this end. Such exercises act to enhance our self-concept and the ways we relate to others. They help develop powerful interpersonal skills which are often lacking in our communication but which can be learned. Building on the positive strengthens growth and can help students overcome some of their shortcomings.

You'd like an example of what I mean by positive focus? Here are a couple. If the students are in groups and each is asked to state something he particularly likes about the person on his right, that's focusing on the positive aspect. The students would not be asked to tell one thing they think the person to their right should change about himself. That would be emphasizing the negative. Or if students are sharing a pleasant experience or memory, don't ask them to share an unpleasant or unhappy memory.

Why Avoid a Negative Focus?

Although there are affective curriculum materials that do delve into negative aspects, I strongly advocate staying away from them. The feelings built up in the class will then be positive ones and not threatening for the teacher or the students to deal with. A far greater degree of skill in dealing with what arises must be had by the teacher before venturing into the negative aspect. Many teachers have not had sufficient training and experience in this area to adequately handle some of the unpredictable things which may come up otherwise.

But suppose the students want to deal with the negative side of things, you're wondering. This does tend to come up because we are so conditioned to seeing and hearing the negative, as our experiment a few minutes ago may have shown. It's likely to occur right after a rewarding activity in which the students have learned some positive things that the others think of them. One student may say, "Let's hear some negative things, too, so maybe we can change them," and others chime in, "Yeah, let's."

AVOID THIS LIKE THE PLAGUE. The trusting climate that was established (and enabled students to believe bringing up the negative was a good idea) will begin to diminish. Once you start including it, the door will be open for the negative to monopolize, which it will. Hearing one negative comment about ourselves acts to quickly wipe out all of the positive ones which were expressed.

The positive focus is a concerted effort to combat the overwhelming energy we spend putting ourselves down for what we think are our failings and inadequacies. We don't need to nourish the negative that we see in ourselves. We're already convinced of it. What we have to do is free ourselves of it by focusing on the good things in ourselves and others. Students can flourish and grow when the focus is on acceptance and approval.

And If the Negative Comes Up?

How do you deal with the negative when it comes up, then? To begin with, when you first introduce humanistic exercises, point out that the activities are going to deal with our positive sides and *not* the negative. Tell the class that as far as our negative qualities are concerned, we already know them only too well. After all, we're our own worst critics. What we hear and express far less is the positive side of how we think and feel and how we see others and others see us.

Explain that if we hear *many good* things about ourselves and *one bad* thing, we are likely to forget all the wonderful things which were said and dwell on the negative one. At some later point in time if the suggestion is made to go into something negative, review what you said previously. You can also point out that the very fact this has come up as a suggestion illustrates how accustomed we are to looking at the negative side.

Positive Focus Enhances Growth

You see, by stressing the positive, a bond of closeness begins to permeate the class and a feeling so necessary to youngsters—that of belonging—develops. We can encourage happier, better-adjusted students in our foreign language classes by helping to undo the negative things they feel about themselves—the ways they underestimate themselves. Feeling accepted reduces fears and builds trust. Expressing warmth is a powerful way to communicate in any language.

We all have strengths we aren't aware of. By discovering these we can see the best side of ourselves, increase our self-acceptance, sharpen our identity, and relate better to others. This approach then is an antidote for the isolated, detached, frustrated feelings students can get in school. It is an instrumental means of building friendships.

Don't forget that foreign language teachers are often in the role of providing negative feedback. They correct pronunciation and errors in speech and reading and writing. They give tests, mark papers, and issue grades. The opportunity for positive focus should be a welcome one to them.

You're convinced to deal only with the positive? Beautiful!

USE OF LOW-RISK ACTIVITIES

Now what's another thing I believe is significant when using awareness techniques? I can see you've really been listening. I recommend using low-risk activities: themes that are safe rather than threatening or overly personal.

An example of a low-risk activity would be sharing something you did recently which helped someone. A high-risk topic would be the reverse: something you did recently which hurt someone. It is the latter type of exercise I would avoid.

Here are some other themes which I would classify as high-risk or threatening:

Something I wish had never happened
What I dislike about myself
My saddest memory
My worst failure
Something I feel guilty about
A time I was taken unfair advantage of

Activities with such a focus are best avoided. These topics are not only high-risk but also deal with the negative side of things. The two often go together. Reversing the above themes changes them completely and makes them acceptable low-risk activities:

Something I'm glad happened
What I like about myself
My happiest memory
My greatest success
Something I feel proud of
A time I was treated very fairly

The idea of humanistic activities, as I view it, is that they should be enjoyable, thought-provoking, reinforcing, and not threatening. By using exercises that stress the positive and are low-risk, the fears that teachers may have that something too deep or too personal will come up and they won't be able to handle it properly can be put aside. Focusing on the positive aspect and low-risk activities helps safeguard against such situations.

SHARING LEADS TO CARING

What we are after is building a climate of trust where it is safe to share. The many personal benefits that can result from using affective exercises are possible only if sharing takes place. This means that students must share themselves: their feelings, experiences, interests, memories, daydreams, fantasies.

By sharing ourselves, others get to know us. When we don't know what others are like, rather than feeling acceptance towards them, we are more likely to feel neutral, ïndifferent, mistrustful, or disinterested. Sharing, then, enhances acceptance by others. As we come to feel that we are accepted by others, we can risk being ourselves. The discovery of finding we are liked as we are builds trust and self-acceptance. There seems to be a relationship among sharing, being accepted by others, and self-acceptance. We might say that sharing leads to caring.

(Hebrew) Humanistic Poster: "Happiness can be measured by how many people you love."

(French) Humanistic Poster: "In the garden of friendship I have gathered my friends."

A person who is more self-rejecting fears that if others get to know him, they won't like him. This type of individual often wears "masks" so others won't find out what he's like. Being accepted because of the masks he hides behind only causes further feelings of self-rejection. The convictions of such a person can be dissolved only when he actually shares his true positive side, lets others see what it's like, and discovers that he is accepted for just that. In trying to promote self-acceptance in the foreign language classroom, we are truly working on the social-emotional development of students. Psychologists agree that self-acceptance is crucial for mental health and growth. And it certainly can only enhance learning.

THE RIGHT TO PASS

When you're sharing, what if someone doesn't want to participate in an activity? That's a good question. A ground rule for all exercises which should be stressed is that anyone has the right to pass (not respond when it's his turn), if he prefers. This is to show respect for the students' feelings should some topic unexpectedly touch a sensitive area in someone. I've rarely seen anyone pass in exercises which are positive and low-risk, but the ground rule should be repeated enough so that students will know it's acceptable to keep to themselves whatever they prefer not to share.

Sometimes a student will pass because he can't think of something appropriate to share, or he may think what he has to say isn't important enough. Whatever the reason, this right should be respected. Be certain that the students understand that they are not to pass because they cannot say what they want to in the foreign language. Establish with the students that should they be having difficulty in expressing themselves in the target language, they should ask for help with what they want to say.

HELPING STUDENTS PERFORM IN THE FOREIGN LANGUAGE

You're wondering whether students can handle affective activities in the foreign language. In some ways it's like other topics in a foreign language class. Beginning levels will deal with a topic in a more elementary way than intermediate or advanced levels. Some exercises can be used at all levels, with the expectations of students differing according to their backgrounds in the language. Other exercises can be used only in upper levels of the language since, by their very nature, they require more complex thinking and expression. So activities are chosen to suit the level of the class.

With all levels, you'll probably provide students with a supplementary vocabulary for certain exercises. Most textual materials do not include an extensive enough vocabulary for what the students will want to express in some exercises. Additional vocabulary in the form of expressions, questions, and key responses will have to be given to the students to prepare them for the activity. Sometimes the vocabulary can be handed out in advance. At other times the students will have to ask you for specific terms they will need to know. Appendixes A and B are included to assist you along these lines for a number of the activities. The exercises in this book are intended to encourage expansion of the text and liberated expression at all levels of language.

Making Mistakes

You're concerned that the students will make lots of mistakes when they speak? Of course—*every time a student speaks in the foreign language, he risks making a mistake.* To help minimize errors, the teacher can structure the responses to fit specific patterns, for lower levels in particular. And don't forget that from the errors made, the teacher can gain insight into areas needing additional practice. The important thing is that the students will *want* to communicate, as these personalized activities are excellent motivators. And as the students do communicate, the teacher must have a certain tolerance for allowing errors. After all, we make errors too, in our daily communication in our native language.

Reverting to the Native Language

Be aware of the fact that the students can get so absorbed in an exercise that they will resort to the native language if they cannot use the target language. They may do this anyway so they can more easily express everything they want to say. If that happens, remind them that a primary reason for using the exercises is to learn the foreign language and to make it interesting and meaningful to them. You will help them if they need help with the language, but they are not to abandon the foreign language in doing an exercise. (There are occasions when you may wish to have them express their reactions in the native language at the end of an exercise if they cannot do so in the target language as yet.)

BUILDING A FEELING OF TRUST

As I said earlier, every time a student opens his mouth to speak the foreign language, he's taking a risk—that it won't be accurate, that he'll be corrected, that the class will laugh. In humanistic exercises, it's also very crucial for students to feel that they won't be made fun of because of what they share. This is why a climate of acceptance is necessary. As students find that what they contribute to the activities is accepted by their peers and that every word they say in the target language is not corrected, their trust and enthusiasm will grow.

Oh yes, trust builds slowly. Expect it to take a while. And don't expect miracles immediately. You and the students will need time to adjust, understand, accept, and respond to these new experiences.

SETTING GROUND RULES FOR EXERCISES

The way the teacher introduces an exercise will set the feeling tone for how the class will respond. The teacher should set general ground rules for behavior during the exercises and remind students of them if any are broken.

Yes, I agree, you're ready to hear these ground rules and some guidelines on how to get started. Here's an idea of how you could introduce humanistic techniques to a foreign language class. Of course, use your own style and words so it sounds like you.

"This year in our class you're going to be participating in some activities that will be quite different, sometimes unusual, and often fun. At first they may seem a little 'far out' to you, but as time goes on, you'll look forward more and more to them. They are new in foreign language teaching and teachers who have used them find their students really like and enjoy them.

"The main thing that's different about these activities is that they'll be dealing a lot with *you*—your feelings, experiences, values, hopes, and desires. We'll be sharing these in the class. I say 'we' because *I'll* be sharing *mine* with you, too. Through these activities or exercises we'll learn more about each other and more about ourselves.

"We'll get to know each other in less superficial ways than we usually do. And we'll see that the more we know about each other, the more we'll find we have in common and the more we'll understand and like each other. You'll even get to know better the people that you already know in class. These activities also will help us become more effective in how we act with people and get along with others.

"You know school isn't just a place to learn facts. It's a place to help you in your life. One important thing that can help all of us is knowing ourselves better.

"We'll be communicating in the foreign language about things we're interested in talking about and finding out. I'll always tell you what the purposes are as we do each exercise. There will be a purpose related to the language we're studying and a purpose in our getting to know ourselves and others, too. Often you'll be divided into small groups when we work on these activities. Sometimes you'll be moving around the classroom to carry out an activity.

"At the end of each exercise, we'll always discuss what happened, how we feel, and what we learned. As a rule, I'll ask you to write a few sentences about what you learned and your reactions to the activity. This will help me to know how to plan future lessons."

Everyone Gets Listened To

"There will be several very important ground rules we'll use when we carry out these exercises. If people forget them, you and I can remind them since the activities won't work if the rules are broken. First of all, we will listen to everyone in our group as each speaks."

No Put-downs

"Second, no one will be teased or laughed at for what he says. Remember we'll be sharing some things we feel or value or have experienced, and no one likes to be made fun of, especially when he's sharing something about himself. I know I don't. So this rule is very important—no put-downs."

Passing

"Third, if you have reasons for not wanting to respond to a particular question or to share an experience for a certain exercise, when it's your turn you can pass. Everyone will respect your right to do this and no one will ask you why.

"This does not mean you should pass because you are not certain how to say what you want to in the foreign language. If that's the case, ask the group to help you, or call me over. I'll be circulating from group to group during these activities. Is that clear, then? The right to pass means there's some reason you'd rather not share your feelings about a particular question. It may be that you haven't had enough time to think of a response. In that case, you can take your turn a little later."

FOCUS OF EXERCISES

"This does not mean that the questions or exercises will be snooping into very personal things that you don't want to talk about. Just the opposite. You'll probably want to be actively involved in the exercises. They will be dealing with the very positive and good things about all of us and not the gloomy or highly personal things we'd rather not discuss. But remember, if there is something you'd rather not answer, that's okay."

At this point you can ask whether there are any questions and call for a review of the ground rules. You might want to write them on the chalkboard as you go along, to help students remember them:

1. Everyone gets listened to
2. No put-downs
3. The right to pass
   a. No passes because you don't know how to say something in the foreign language

GETTING OFF TO A GOOD START

Then be prepared to jump right in with a sure-fire exercise that is fun and interesting, and go through the procedures you said you would. Your choice of a technique will be dependent on the level of language of the class and the time of the school year, which will affect how well the students already know each other. Appendix D-1 lists the time of year when each of the techniques in Chapters 3 and 4 is most appropriate. Those under the headings "First Few Days" and "Early in the School Year" are good exercises to start off with. Many serve as icebreakers and also initiate students into feeling greater warmth and empathy for one another. In addition, several of the strategies under the category "Discovering Myself" make good opening exercises. Note, in particular, Exercise 11, "Parts of Speech Like Me"; Exercise 17, "Suppose You Weren't You"; and Exercise 18, "Money Talks."

Be certain to be involved in the activity yourself, and give your responses before the whole group to set an example of the kind of sharing you want to encourage. This will help the class to follow suit. Get written feedback from the students afterwards so you'll know how the exercise was received. Ask a general question, such as "How did you feel about this activity?" or "What were your reactions to this activity?" Sometimes the written feedback is surprising and the students like the activity even more than we perceive.

PROCEDURES FOR PRESENTING ACTIVITIES

You're getting excited about this? I do, too, every time I talk about it! I think you're ready to hear how to present a humanistic technique. So here goes. There are certain procedures to follow to make each activity a learning experience. First of all, don't plunge the class into an exercise without preparing students for it. They should *know the purpose* of each activity and have an appropriate *introduction* to it. Directions for the exercise are then given, with *examples of responses* that might be made.

At the close of an exercise, students are asked *what they learned from the activity* and/or *feelings or reactions* they would like to share about the activity with the total class. This is called *processing the activity*; it is a very important phase in the learning and should not be overlooked. In this phase, students share insights they've gained about themselves and about the group or class and any feelings they've experienced. You can then *summarize the purpose and the learnings* for the class. You should also get constant written feedback, with the students' names on it, about the humanistic activities the classes experience, to get a good grasp on how each exercise is received. Although you can get an idea from the processing of how students react, I'm amazed at how much more I learn from having written feedback from each student. You can also see where each student is in his thinking and the extent he is growing.

An Example of the Process

You'd like me to illustrate these procedures for you step-by-step by going through a sample activity with you? Be glad to. I'll use Exercise 34, "I Like You—You're Different," and describe how I demonstrated it in my methods class. I *oriented* the class by saying: "Very often we feel it's important to be like other people, and we worry if we feel that we're different. At times it's fine to be like others, but it's also important to accept and be proud of our differences. There are many ways that we're like each other in this class, but there are also things about us that are not true of anyone else in this class."

The *assignment was given* to write down on a card three things about yourself that are not true of anyone else in the class—in other words, three things about you that make you different. (You could qualify this, if you want, by saying three things you feel good about that make you different from everyone in the class.) I then gave several examples, referring to myself: "I am the oldest person in this class, I won sixty silver dimes and a box of Forever Yours candy bars on a quiz show, and I was accidentally in a beauty contest once." (Encourage thinking creatively by including some unusual and humorous examples.) I told each person to put his name on the card but not to tell anyone what was on his card. I announced that I would collect the cards, read them aloud, and they would guess who each person was.

At the next class meeting, I restated the positive aspect of being different and read each card aloud, asking for guesses on the identity of each person. (The teacher should go over the cards first to correct any errors.) Based on all the names people guessed for each card, the class voted on whose card they thought it was. After each vote, I told them who the correct person was. Sometimes the right person's name was not among those guessed. In this case, I told them so after the vote, and they had to keep guessing until the correct person was identified.

We finished going through all the cards, including my own. (Remember that the teacher should be involved in the activities and share the things that students are expected to share.) As a follow-up to the activity I asked, "Who remembers something different about someone in the class?" The students then made statements such as, "Barbara lived in Cuba" and "Bob won an art contest." After a number of such statements were made, I had them ask questions about what they remembered. I gave some examples first: "Who has climbed Mt. Everest?" "Who can eat more ice cream than anyone else in the class?" "Who is the oldest of seven children?" Then the class asked similar questions of one another and responded in full sentences.

I then *processed the activity* by asking how they felt about it and what they learned. Comments made were that they found out many interesting and unusual things about each other, that it was fun to think about how we are different from others, that it felt good having others remember our differences, that it made people feel they wanted to know more details on some of these topics, and that they intended to ask one another for them. In fact, some asked questions right then as the person's identity was revealed.

To summarize, I mentioned that it can be a very nice feeling to be different. Sometimes we feel uneasy because we think we're different. Other times we feel discouraged when we think there's not much that sets us off as being different from others. Often people are interested in us *because of our differences.* We've just learned a number of new and interesting things about people in our class that makes us want to know even more about them. It was fun sharing our differences and hearing others impressed by them, and now we could probably think of many more ways in which we are different and are proud of it. I ended by referring to a poster on the bulletin board which showed two footprints talking to three footprints and saying, "I like you. You're different."

Importance of Starting and Ending Exercises

That's much clearer? Well, thank you. I just want to stress a few of the points I've made before going on. Don't just dive into an exercise without preparing the class adequately. Getting the students ready for each experience is important. Have a good introduction to the exercise—imaginative rather than mechanical. Tie it in at the end when you summarize, too. In your summary be sure to point out the purpose and meaning of the activity. Remember that insights and growth are key aims of these activities, so don't rush over or skip this phase.

Whenever possible, draw on what the students as groups or individuals have said, e.g., "Some of you, like Jonathan, feel . . . while others, like Marlene, feel . . . " You also can review and recall what was learned from previous exercises that relate to the one you're about to introduce or have just completed.

HINTS ON USING HUMANISTIC EXERCISES

Any particular hints I can pass along to you? Yes, here are a few. If it's the start of the school year, learn the students' names immediately—which you no doubt do anyway—and get the students to focus on learning them, too.

At first, gear the activities to those with high involvement. Select ones which help students feel closer to each other and foster an atmosphere of trust and sharing. Suggestions for specific exercises useful towards these ends were given earlier in this chapter under "Getting Off to a Good Start."

Don't plan too many activities for one period. They often will take longer than you think when students become interested in them.

Where the responses of students require some time and thought, assign the topic as homework first. Then they can use what they have written, either in total or as a guide, depending on the nature of the exercise. This type of homework is more motivating than the usual assignment. If a student does not do the assignment and finds he misses out on an interesting activity as a result, he may be more motivated to do it the next time.

Sometimes there are topics you will want students to think about or write about that are somewhat more personal but that you will *not* ask them to share. These will serve to trigger off other thoughts that they will be asked to discuss. Always make clear in advance what the students will and will not be asked to share, so they can approach their thinking on the topic with this in mind.

Working in Small Groups

That's right. Most of the exercises are intended to be done in small groups to allow maximum participation and involvement in using the foreign language and in getting the most out of the activity. Groups can be as small as two (dyads) or three (triads) or as large as seven. Beyond that the groups tend to get too large for most exercises and the more verbal students may take over. When first using humanistic techniques, it is wise to include a few in which students work in dyads, to focus on getting acquainted with only one person at a time and to get used to the process.

Smaller groups will save time with activities in which each student has several turns or is requested to respond at length. For activities in which the students give and receive positive feedback to each other, larger groups are desirable to maximize the input and impact each individual receives.

You're worried that by having your class working in groups they'll fool around and not stay on the topic? I know that's a real concern to teachers. You're also afraid that things will get out of control? As an aid, be certain to give some ground rules about working in groups, to prepare the class for it. Remember that they'll have more opportunities to speak the target language this way. Another way to overcome these worries is to choose activities that are so engrossing the students will really want to participate in them. And a third way is to convey to the class your trust in the process and your belief that it does work. You still may have to remind students to tone it down a bit if the neighboring classes are affected by the students in your class working in groups. Sometimes it does get exciting.

Is it as interesting to the class to be off by themselves in groups so much? Just because they're in groups doesn't mean that you don't deal with them as a total group as well. Don't forget that the processing part of each activity brings the class back together again. Also, some activities are conducive to having a round of answers in each group and then a few given for the total class to hear before repeating the next round in groups. It's enjoyable for each group to hear what other groups are coming up with in response to these exercises. And, of course, you will chime in from time to time with your own personal experiences and responses.

Getting the Class into Groups

Do I have any suggestions for getting students into groups? There are many different ways. Use them all.

A common way of forming groups is having everyone number off. If there are twenty-five in the class and you want five in each group, the students count off from one to five and then form groups with all those having the same number. Once an activity is over, new groups can be devised by asking the present groups to count off again. Different groups are formed, based on the new number each person now has. This means of dividing into groups leaves the formation up to chance.

However, ways also should be utilized that take advantage of other elements. One suggestion is to ask the students to find a partner or to form groups with others they do not know well or have not been in a group with as yet. Another idea is to tell those students who usually initiate choosing partners to wait to be chosen by those who generally don't initiate choosing. This latter technique allows students to reverse their typical role of "picker" and "pickee" to see how it feels.

In some of the activities, students can be regrouped based upon a response made in the exercise. In Exercise 3, "Lots in Common," the students find others with the same commonality. If they have sought out others with the same horoscope sign or favorite season of the year, let them remain with this group for a new activity. In Exercise 12, "The Shape I'm In," or Exercise 18, "Money Talks," each person makes a choice of a shape or a coin he identifies with himself. At the end of the activity, students can form new groups with others who made the same selections they did. The same thing can be done after Exercise 1, "Colorful Names," in which each person decides on a colored piece of construction paper for making a name-tag. When the exercise is concluded, the students can form a group with others who chose the same color as they did. Forming groups in these ways points out to students a common bond they share. They will like the idea of being grouped with others on the basis of their commonalities.

Here are two unusual alternatives for grouping students based upon choices they make:*

1. The students stand in a circle. Ask one third of the class to volunteer to step in the circle (state a number for them, such as eight or ten). Tell these volunteers to select someone in the outer circle whom they want to get to know better. Each of the students in the remaining third of the class then picks a group of two that has been formed and joins it to make groups of three. If you want groups of six, then two groups can combine.

2. The class stands in the middle of the room. Ask half the class to go to the front of the room and half to the back. Now tell each half to divide in half again, with some going to each of the two corners of their side of the room. At this point the class is divided equally in the four corners of the room. Next tell the class to form a fifth group in the middle, with a designated number that you give leaving the various corners of the room to do so. The class will now be divided into five groups.

These two alternatives give the students some opportunity for choice of a group they'll be in without encouraging cliques.

---

*Thanks to Don Miller for these two ideas for grouping students sociometrically.

The most important element is to constantly have different students working together in groups. The purpose is to have the students get to know *everyone* in the class. So mix the groups continually and often. The use of small groups also offers the shy and less verbal students more opportunity and greater safety in talking.

Getting Feedback from Students

You've been wondering about what different kinds of feedback to get? You certainly ask all the right questions! Not only should you get ongoing feedback about the exercises, but you can gather long-range data about their effects.

For example, administer a self-concept test early and late in the year to determine whether any changes occur. Keep track of whether there is any change in the students' achievement as the year progresses. And note whether the students are more willing to speak the foreign language and carry out homework assignments.

You also could do a more intricate study of the extent to which students accept each other in the class by making a sociogram. You do this by having your students respond to two or three questions in which they make choices. The students are told that they will be placed in groups for some forthcoming event, based upon their answers. Questions might be: "Whom would you like to work with on a school project?" "Whom would you like to sit with on the bus during the class's field trip?"

The questions should attempt to evoke different types of choices, as those above do, one a more task-oriented purpose and the other a more social one. Charts are made for everyone to determine the ranking of students, from those chosen the most all the way to those chosen the least. Students not selected at all are referred to as isolates. Make a sociogram or a sociomatrix of the class before you use humanistic strategies and compare it with one done after you have used them for an extended period of time. See whether the number of isolates is reduced and whether the status of students seldom chosen increases. Awareness techniques are intended to foster positive thinking and feelings of greater closeness among students as they get to know one another better. A sociogram will help measure whether they actually are bringing these about. A list of suggested references on sociometry is given at the end of the chapter.

Obtain other forms of feedback by asking students, from time to time, to respond in writing or by raising their hands to such questions as: "How many of you think you know more students in this class now?" "How many of you think you know students in this class better than you usually do in your classes?" To check that students are clear on the reasons they are using awareness activities, have them respond in writing to a question such as: "The main reasons we do these activities in our foreign language class are . . . "

As you get written feedback from students, you can share what the group is feeling with the class. It is important for students to realize that you take their input seriously and will act on it.

Saving Your Voice

With my soft voice how do I manage to be heard when the class is working in groups? I've found it extremely helpful to use a tape recorder set up to operate on PA. This makes the microphone into a public address system. I use it so that I can get the class's attention when they're in groups without raising my voice at all. I can also tell them, in a very soft voice which can easily be heard, to quiet down a little so we don't disturb others—if that seems to be a concern—and can give further instructions during an exercise. I strongly recommend using the microphone when the class is in groups.

And now it's up to you. You've been an ideal listener and have asked a number of pertinent questions, which I hope I've answered. So let me invite you to dig into Chapter 3, where you'll find a wealth of humanistic activities to pick from. They've all been tested in classes and are included here for you because they worked.

Read them over and select the ones that will fit the levels and abilities of your students. Decide where they can be worked into the materials you now use and what structures and vocabulary they can fit in with. Try them out on yourself and others. And then go to it. The rest will come with experience. Say listen, thanks for coming along. Just turn the page now and hang in there. The rewards are just ahead, waiting for you and your students, too . . .

REFERENCES ON SOCIOMETRY

Evans, Kathleen M. *Sociometry and Education.* New York: Humanities Press (1962).
Gronlund, Norman E. *Sociometry in the Classroom.* New York: Harper & Row (1959).
Jennings, Helen H. *Sociometry in Group Relations: A Manual for Teachers,* 2nd ed. Washington, D.C.: American Council on Education (1959).
Miller, Delbert C. *Handbook of Research Design and Social Measurement,* 2nd ed. New York: McKay (1970).
Moreno, Jacob L. *Sociometry and the Science of Man.* New York: Beacon House (1956).
Moreno, Jacob L. et al., eds. *The Sociometry Reader.* Glencoe, Illinois: The Free Press (1960).
Northway, Mary L. *A Primer of Sociometry,* 2nd ed. Toronto: University of Toronto Press (1967).
–––. *Sociometric Testing: A Guide for Teachers.* Toronto: University of Toronto Press (1957).
Shaw, Marvin E. *Group Dynamics: The Psychology of Small Group Behavior,* 2nd ed. New York: McGraw-Hill (1976).

Chapter 3

All
About
the Exercises

A FEW WORDS ABOUT THE EXERCISES

And now that you're ready to become familiar with the humanistic strategies, here is what you'll find. Each technique in this chapter is categorized according to one of its principal humanistic aims. The categories provide a means of communicating which area of awareness is being focused on in each exercise and the results aimed for in its use. In almost every case, the exercises could be included under several of the classifications because of overlap with each other. The categories of awareness are:

1. Relating to Others
2. Discovering Myself
3. My Strengths
4. My Self-Image
5. Expressing My Feelings
6. My Memories
7. Sharing Myself
8. My Values
9. The Arts and Me
10. Me and My Fantasies

As each exercise is presented, the following information is given:

1. The affective purposes
2. The linguistic purposes
3. The level(s) of the language class with which the activity can be used
4. The suggested size of groups to use in carrying out the exercise
5. Materials needed

6. Procedures for conducting the exercise
7. Variations to the exercise (in some cases)
8. Comments that may be helpful to know about (where appropriate)

Here are some things for you to be aware of relating to the above information.

Linguistic Purposes

Since this book is intended for teachers of any foreign or second language, the linguistic purposes of each exercise can at best be general and are therefore by no means exhaustive. As a creative individual, you, the teacher, will discover ways to make the exercises suit additional vocabulary and structures that you wish your students to practice in the target language you instruct.

Levels of Language

Do not take literally the level(s) of language for which the exercises can be used. Because a level, such as "beginning," is not mentioned does not obviate its use. It may be that, with proper structuring on your part, you can modify the expectations and perhaps find ways of including the exercise. An exercise not listed for advanced levels can be used profitably by increasing the expectations made of students. The term "beginning level" is used to refer to what is typical of the first year of junior or senior high school the first college semester of the language; "intermediate" to the second year or semester; and "advanced" to the third year or semester or beyond. It should be noted that many of the exercises have been successfully used in the elementary and middle school grades as well.

Where it is stated that an exercise can be used for all levels, you will have to take appropriate measures for implementing it within a given level. Of course, more structure will have to be provided for beginning levels. You will probably have to give beginning students sample or key statements to complete or structures to be practiced to serve as guidelines. The vocabulary necessary may also have to be reviewed or supplemented.

For all levels, the vocabulary of feelings and emotions given in Appendix A and that of words describing positive qualities of people listed in Appendix B will be needed to carry out a number of the activities. However, the entire lists should not be given all at once since they are quite long.

Size of Groups

Most of the exercises call for placing students in small groups. An appropriate number of students per group is given in each case. For some activities, a reason for the recommended number in a group is mentioned. In other cases, you can base the group size on the length of time available for the activity. The larger the group, the more time the exercise will take.

Procedures

Many of the exercises contain suggestions on what to say when introducing the theme of the activity. Some of the introductions may be longer or more complex than you wish. However, they are purposely written in detail to furnish thoughts about what you might say and to stimulate further ideas.

Homework

With many of the exercises, a homework assignment can be given before the activity is carried out in class. Specific suggestions are included for some of the exercises. You can decide whether your students need the added preparation prior to the exercise being done in class or whether they can handle the language spontaneously. Follow-up written assignments are given for some of the exercises, but almost every activity is conducive to a written activity afterwards. Where an assignment is not given in advance of the activity, you can request that it be carried out at its conclusion.

Time of Year

Some of the exercises are intended for certain times of the school year, when the students are new to one another or are well-acquainted. Where such information is not given, the activity can be used at any time.

Cross References

Appendix D contains a cross reference of information about the exercises to help you locate the activities according to these dimensions: linguistic purposes, level(s) of language, and time of the year to be used. Remember that with these first two headings the suggestions are not intended to be absolute.

The Rest Is Up to You

As you make use of the strategies, you will discover ways to improve them and variations for carrying them out. Your students can be extremely helpful along these lines.

The intent of this book is to draw upon your creativity and imagination as a teacher. You are free to decide where, within the materials used in your classes, given exercises can be included. With thought, you will find additional ways to use the exercises in order to fulfill your purposes.

By the same token, since this book is intended for teachers of any foreign or second language, no attempt has been made to furnish numerous examples of what the students might say in the target language. Guidelines of what can be expected are given in English to illustrate possible responses, where these might be helpful. However, in many of the exercises, especially those for the intermediate and advanced levels, the potential responses are limitless and preclude providing absolutes to hope for or anticipate. Remember that the students will be truly talking about themselves, so expect answers to be individual.

For a long time many curriculum materials have been designed to program foreign language teachers to follow a highly specific, rigid format. How often I have heard complaints from teachers because of the highly structured nature of the materials used in their schools. The techniques in this book are intended to give you some of the freedom to express your individuality that you may have been looking for.

The humanistic exercises in this chapter are intended to act as catalysts to your own individuality and creativity. It is my hope that they stimulate you to try them, to develop and improve on them, and to dream up some new ones of your own. So I encourage you to use them freely, adding your own spontaneity and imagination.

HUMANISTIC EXERCISES FOR
THE FOREIGN LANGUAGE CLASS

Relating to Others

*The more we talk, the more we know ourselves. The
more we know ourselves, the more we understand life.*

— Ellen Greenland

Meeting, becoming acquainted, and getting to know each other better are the
objectives of the exercises in this section. The first three activities help a group
make contact with others in the class, where many are still unfamiliar with their
classmates. These activities serve as invitations to speak to strangers and "break
the ice."

Several of the activities act to cultivate students getting to know each other
and relating in ways that help develop a feeling of closeness.

The last two exercises, "I See Myself in You" and "One, Two, In My Shoe,"
are helpful in cementing relations that have been established for quite some time.

In all the exercises, contact and communication with others is the focus.

EXERCISE 1. **COLORFUL NAMES**

Purposes:
> Affective—
>> To help students get acquainted
>> To encourage students to speak to a variety of others in the class
>>> whom they do not know
>> To encourage students to express their feelings through colors and
>>> shapes
>> To arouse curiosity in students about each other
> Linguistic—
>> To practice the vocabulary of colors, shapes, feelings, and giving
>>> one's name

Levels: Can be used at any level as an initial warm-up to the class. However,
if used by a firstyear class which has not as yet studied the language, the
activity should be delayed until students have at least learned expressions
dealing with names ("My name is _____," "Your name is _____")
and the vocabulary of colors and some emotions.

Size of groups: Total class rotating, speaking with one person at a time

Materials needed: A wide selection of colored construction paper, straight pins or masking tape, and a number of pairs of scissors. Signs should be made stating: "Cut out a name-tag for yourself in a color and shape that represents you in some way. Write your name on the paper, and pin the name-tag on." A record with pleasant, relaxing music should be played during this exercise.

Procedures: As the students enter your classroom, have the construction paper spread out on tables, with scissors and straight pins or masking tape available. Have the signs with the directions of what to do clearly visible. Have a name-tag you have already made for yourself pinned on you to help the students see what you want them to do. As students enter your classroom, you can greet them at the door and also tell them to make name-tags for themselves.

A nice added touch is to have happy, relaxing music playing in the background to set a tone of pleasantness as students are creating their name-tags. You may wish to add to the signs posted a note saying that they should be seated once their name-tags are completed.

If this is the first class meeting, you may have a number of things to communicate before starting with this activity.

Then announce to the students:

"We are now going to meet one another. I am going to play some music. You will get up and walk around and look at the name-tags and focus on the people as they pass by. When I stop the music, get a partner and greet the person. Tell him your name. Then each of you ask why the other chose the color he did for his name-tag and why he cut out that shape.

"A sample of your conversation might be:

> 'Hi, I'm Keith.'
> 'Hi, I'm Carol. Why did you choose blue, Keith?'
> 'Blue means calmness and peace. I feel relaxed today. Why did you choose bright pink, Carol?'
> 'Bright pink means excitement and warmth to me. That's how I feel on the first day of school when I see my friends. What does your diamond shape mean, Keith?'
> 'A diamond is bright and is worth a lot. Why is your shape like an arrow, Carol?'
> 'An arrow can go far. I am ambitious.'

"Each time the music is played, walk around and look at the name-tags of others. When the music stops, talk with a new partner."

See that the students pair off with only one person at a time. If a group gets together, not everyone will have a chance to speak. Allow the students the opportunity to have about five or six partners. Then get the attention of the total class and ask questions based on the colors and shapes of some of the students' name-tags. Anyone who remembers can offer the information to the class. Examples of these questions are: "What does the abstract shape mean to Paul?" and "Why did Wendy choose green?" Select a variety of colors and shapes to ask about. You also can review what some of the students said to the total class immediately after the response or after all of the questioning of students ends: "What does green mean to Wendy?" and "Why is Paul's shape abstract?"

EXERCISE 2.   **IDENTITY CARDS**[1]

Purposes:
   Affective—
      To warm-up a new group of students
      To facilitate students' getting acquainted more easily
      To get students to speak to others they do not know
   Linguistic—
      To practice speaking in the first and second person singular
      To practice asking and answering questions

Levels: Intermediate and advanced; beginning students would have to carry out the activity in the native language if they have no knowledge of the target language.

Size of groups: Total class

Materials needed: Five- by eight-inch cards, straight pins or masking tape for everyone in the class, a record with pleasant background music, and a record player.

Procedures: This exercise is intended for one of the first few days that a new class meets. The idea is to get students to break the ice and speak to others in the class through a structured experience.

See that each person receives a five- by eight-inch card and a straight pin or a piece of masking tape. The students are to fill out the cards with the information you give them and pin them on. The information will give them the basis for conversing with other classmates. A number of different questions can be answered on the card. Some typical suggestions will be given here. The writing must be large enough for passers-by to read.

In the middle of the card the student's first name should be printed in letters about an inch and a quarter to an inch and a half high. The four corners of the card can have answers to different questions, in letters about a half inch high, such as the following diagram shows:

```
┌─────────────────────────────────────────────────────────────┐
│                                                               │
│  Three adjectives that              Something you do          │
│  describe you                       well                      │
│                                                               │
│                        NAME                                   │
│                                                               │
│  Someone you would                  A place you'd like        │
│  like to spend a day with           to be right now           │
│                                                               │
└─────────────────────────────────────────────────────────────┘
```

Instructions are given to fill out the card with the information desired, making letters large enough to be read by others. The students then pin or tape the cards on. Announce to students that they will circulate as the music is played and read the name cards of those they pass. When the music stops, each person should take a partner he does not know and speak with that person about the items on his card. When the music starts, the students circulate until it stops for a round with a new partner. Give students a chance to speak with about six partners.

The interchanges can be handled in a variety of ways:

1. Each person questions the other and receives a response about the items on the card: "Whom would you like to spend a day with?" or "What is something you do well?"

2. Each person mentions what is on his partner's card and adds his own response to the statement: "Gina, you can sew well and I can play the guitar well."

3. More advanced students can comment or raise questions about what is on the cards: "Why would you like to spend a day with Franklin Roosevelt?" "How did you learn to scuba dive so well?"

Several other ideas for what to ask students to put on their cards are:

1. Your favorite song
2. Your favorite television show
3. Your favorite group
4. What you would like to be if you weren't a student
5. Your favorite doodle (what you sketch unconsciously while talking)
6. Your favorite dessert
7. A country you would like to visit
8. The most significant year of your life
9. A person who had a significant influence on your life

The students should continue to wear these cards all period or even for the next few class meetings as an aid to learning each other's names. This activity is fun and gives students several specific things to talk about. The music plus hearing everyone talking at once gives a feeling of being at a party. The combination helps to break the ice.

You can follow this activity by asking students to recall the items on different people's cards: "Where would Don like to be right now?" "What does Janet do well?" "What is one word that describes Nina?" "Whom would Steve like to spend a day with?"

At the end of this exercise, while the students are still standing, you can ask them to form into groups for the next activity.

EXERCISE 3. **LOTS IN COMMON**

Purposes:
> Affective—
>> To encourage students to note ways in which they are like others in the group, to find out what they have in common with one another
>> To warm-up the group and develop a spirit of fun
> Linguistic—
>> To practice using categories of related vocabulary and to ask and answer questions related to this vocabulary

Levels: All levels

Size of groups: Total class

Procedures: The teacher can orient the class by mentioning the fact that people have a great deal in common they do not realize. The idea of the activity they are going to take part in is to find out and take note of a few of the many things the students in the class have in common. The teacher could introduce the activity by saying something along these lines:

"We all have lots in common with others but we don't always know it or realize it. Let's explore this together. I'm going to call out some categories of things. You are to find everyone in this group with the same thing in common with you. Sometimes you'll have to use your eyes to discover the commonality, but each time call out the thing you're looking for."

The teacher should then call out, one at a time, a number of categories appropriate for that class in terms of vocabulary already learned. For example, the teacher can tell the group, "Find everyone in the class who has the same color eyes as you." The students are to circulate, calling out the color of their eyes, and form a group with all others in the class having eyes of the same color. The teacher then acknowledges each group by asking, "What color eyes does this group have?" The total group usually will respond enthusiastically in chorus.

You can vary the questioning of groups by asking, "Where is the group with blue eyes?" Follow their response with, "Does that group have brown eyes?" This will evoke a choral response of, "No, that group has blue eyes."

Or you can ask the blue-eyed group, "Do you have brown eyes?" And they will respond, "No, we have blue eyes."

The teacher then calls out another category, such as, "Find all the people who have the same color hair as you." When the groups form, the teacher can tell the students to discuss with a partner how they feel about having the color hair that they do.

Here are a few suggestions for other categories to use:

"Find everyone in the class who is similar to you in height: short, medium, or tall."

"Find everyone wearing shoes of the same color as you."

After one or two examples, you can pose the category in the form of a question:

"What is your favorite pet?"
"What is your favorite season?"
"What is your favorite color?"
"Who has the same horoscope sign as you?"

Once the students are in groups, for *some* of the categories, have them discuss with a partner in the group an appropriate question based on the situation they have in common; for example, "Why is this your favorite pet, season, or color?" If they are in the groups by horoscope signs, ask them to find anyone who has the same birthday. Always ask the groups to identify themselves chorally before the total group first.

Comments: This activity is a good one for breaking the ice with new classes, since the students circulate and get to contact many others in the class. It can create excitement and laughter and is a way of helping shy students to speak up. The initial quietness of a group is dispelled, since having students call out the categories as they seek each other definitely breaks the silence. The possibilities for categories are unlimited. Just leaf through your instructional materials for ideas.

EXERCISE 4.   **ONE-WORD DIALOGS²**

Purposes:
    Affective—
             To communicate at a feeling level about the here-and-now
             To check out how our messages are received when we communicate
             To encourage using the imagination
    Linguistic—
             To show that we can communicate even with a limited vocabulary

Level: All levels

Size of groups: Four

Procedures: Tell the class that even if we only know a few words, we still can communicate. If we were to go to a foreign country with only a limited knowledge of the language, we still could get many of our thoughts across.

Announce that in their groups of four, two of them will hold a conversation. The one rule they must follow is that they will take turns talking, but each person can only use one word to communicate what is on his mind each time it is his turn. The other two will write down the dialog that follows, with each writing the "conversation" of one of the two students.

After about two minutes, call time and have the other couple read back the dialog. As each "line" of dialog is read back, the person who received the message will state what he thought the intended meaning was. The person who sent the message will tell whether that is what he actually meant.

Ask to have two or three dialogs that the groups thought were interesting read before the class. Then exchange roles and the second couple will hold a one-word conversation, while the first will write it down and repeat the previous format.

Variation: For advanced levels during the second round, you can state that a rule is that no one can ask questions. This is much harder, though, and more challenging for them to understand the communication taking place.

Comments: You can ask what kinds of things they tended to talk about in the dialog. Usually it will be concerned with the two of them and will be about things they are feeling right now.

EXERCISE 5.   **SEARCH FOR SOMEONE WHO . . .**[3]

Purposes:
    Affective—
        To warm-up the group
        To get students to mingle with many other students and want to talk
            with them
        To learn more about others in the class
        For fun and excitement
    Linguistic—
        To practice conversing in a variety of tenses which students have
            studied, such as the present, past, present perfect, future, etc.
        To practice the interrogative form
        To respond to questions in the affirmative and the negative

Levels: All levels

Size of groups: Total class, rotating a number of times, speaking with one person at a time

Materials needed: A handout containing statements that students will use to form questions and answers for interviewing each other

Procedures: Pass the dittoed handout to everyone. Give the following introduction and instructions to the class. (Be certain that the directions are clearly understood by all before the exercise starts.)

"There are many things about us that others, even if they know us, are not aware of. To find out some of these things, we're going to interview each other by asking the questions on the paper I just gave you.

"The idea is to see who can get the most questions answered on this interview sheet. (Set a time limit.) You will have seven minutes. Speak to only one person at a time. Ask each person a specific question, such as 'Do you go to bed after midnight?' The person either will answer, 'Yes, I go to bed after midnight' or 'No, I don't go to bed after midnight.'

"You can continue interviewing one person until you receive an answer of 'yes' to a question. Then write the person's name on the line beside the question and move on to another person. Do not accept a one-word answer of 'yes' or 'no.' Everyone must respond in a full sentence, since we are practicing the use of different tenses we have learned.

"Use a person's name only once and find only one person for each question on the sheet. Remember you only can talk to one person at a time. If you hear someone answer 'yes' to a question for someone else, you cannot use that person's name unless you interview the person yourself. At the end of the seven minutes, we will see who has the most questions answered."

When the time is up, ask how many had all of the questions answered. (Often no one gets them all completed, which is fine since such students would then stop asking others the questions.) If there were fourteen questions on the sheet, next ask how many had thirteen answered, twelve, etc., until you determine who had the most. Recognize these students by name, saying, "Anthony and Barbara had the most questions answered."

The next phase will be of interest to the class and will permit additional practice in the structures. Ask students to raise their hands in response to this question, "Which was the hardest question for you to find an answer for, one you did not get answered?" (Many will want to be called on for this.) Have the person answer in a complete interrogative sentence, for example, "Who has owned a turtle?" Then ask, "Who found someone who has owned a turtle?" Call on two or three people who raise their hands to respond in a complete sentence, "Randy has owned a turtle."

After this information has been given to the class, you can ask, "Who has owned a turtle?" and either call on individuals or the total class to answer. You also can ask individuals, "Have you owned a turtle?" If a student (Nancy) replies in the negative, ask "Has Nancy owned a turtle?" which will afford some practice in the negative.

Do not overdo practicing after each question is answered, but keep a lively pace. The students will be interested in hearing answers to the questions they could not get answered and will glow when they have the answer to such a question. Do not spend a long time on this phase of the exercise. Let the activity end while interest is still high. A suggested time for the second phase is about seven minutes but no longer than fifteen.

Here are some sample statements which can be used on such a questionnaire. Fourteen to twenty questions can be used for an exercise. Make up your own examples, using the vocabulary and structures you want students to practice. Mix this with ideas that are timely and appropriate for your class and add some humor and imagination.

SEARCH FOR SOMEONE WHO . . .

1. likes to garden. _____
2. owns a bicycle. _____
3. plays the piano. _____
4. has two brothers and a sister. _____
5. wears a size 7 shoe. _____
6. goes to bed after midnight. _____
7. loves chocolate. _____
8. does not watch television. _____
9. jogs. _____
10. has eaten frogs' legs. _____
11. likes spinach. _____
12. talks to plants. _____
13. would like to be a disc jockey. _____
14. was born on Wednesday. _____
15. can name three South American countries. _____
16. has visited Rome. _____
17. has owned a turtle. _____
18. has gone scuba diving. _____
19. saw a scary movie last week. _____
20. will visit a relative next month. _____
21. is trying to break a habit. _____
22. would like to save more money. _____
23. went skiing during the past year. _____
24. will celebrate his (her) birthday next month. _____
25. would go to the moon if invited by an astronaut. _____

EXERCISE 6.   **A TOUCHING EXPERIENCE**[4]

Purposes:
    Affective—
        To energize the class at times when students may be tired and less
           alert
        To encourage being observant of others
        To encourage creativity in responses
        For fun
    Linguistic—
        To practice the vocabulary of colors, parts of the body, articles of
           clothing, and accessories that people wear
        To afford practice in speaking spontaneously
        To practice giving and comprehending directions

Levels: Beginning but can be used at all levels

Size of groups: About six (five to eight can be used)

Procedures: Divide the class into groups and have each group stand up and form
a circle. The students should have nothing in their hands. Explain that they have
learned a number of colors, parts of the body, articles of clothing, and accessories and are going to practice using this vocabulary.

State something like this:

"I'll call out an item. Everyone in your small group must touch that item
on someone else in the group while repeating all together the name of it as you
touch it." Demonstrate this with one group as the others watch. Then call
out other items, one at a time, for all groups to carry out. Here are a few
examples:

"Touch a left hand."	"Touch white."
"Touch a watch."	"Touch a shirt."
"Touch a thumb."	"Touch glasses carefully."
"Touch a ring."	"Touch green."

Be certain that the class remembers to repeat "left hand," "a watch," "a thumb,"
etc., after each command.

After you have named four or five items for the class, give the responsibility for saying the commands to the students in their individual groups. Tell the class:

"Now you will think up things to touch in your group. Whenever someone
in your group calls out an item, everyone in the group will touch it on someone
else and name it at the same time. Remember, you can use colors, parts of the
body, articles of clothing, jewelry, or designs you see in fabric, such as flowers
or stripes."

Comments: You can allow this activity to continue for five to seven minutes.
It will put the students in a lively, awakened, spirited mood. They will want to
participate by creating commands for the others to carry out. Part of the fun
is in thinking of less obvious commands, for example:

"Touch a dimple."	"Touch curly hair."	"Touch a fingernail."
"Touch long hair."	"Touch a button."	"Touch an arm with your elbow."

It is also reinforcing to have others notice what you, in particular, are wearing;
"Touch a plaid shirt," or "Touch flowers on a sleeve."

Intermediate classes can add the kinds of fabric students are wearing, that
is, cotton, nylon, wool. The color of hair can be included as well: "Touch blonde
hair." Colors, clothing, and fabric can be combined in the commands: "Touch
a green blouse," "Touch a yellow sweater," "Touch a red velvet ribbon."

Rather than chorally responding with only the name of the item being
touched, students can be asked to say, "I am touching" plus the item. The pace
is not as lively this way, but it affords practice in the present progressive.

For any cultural groups or classes where touching someone else would
cause a concern, you can vary this activity by saying "Point to" or "Show me,"
instead of "Touch."

As a general rule the "touching" in this exercise is viewed as fun and harm-
less and part of showing knowledge of the target language.

EXERCISE 7.   **INTERVIEW WITH YOU**[5]

Purposes:
> Affective—
>> To give each student an opportunity to learn more about how one of
>> his classmates thinks and feels
>> To draw pairs of students closer together
> Linguistic—
>> To practice the first person in different tenses
>> To answer questions spontaneously

Levels: All levels

Size of groups: Dyads

Materials needed: A set of questions or sentence stubs on dittos

Procedures: Introduce the activity in this way:
> "Today we are going to get to know someone in the class a lot better than
we do now. We will do this through questions. Each of you will have a partner to
interview. I will give you a set of questions to ask each other. You will both
answer all the questions.

"Each person in the pair will have a number, either one or two. For the first round, number one will ask the question and number two will answer. Then number two will ask the same question and number one will answer. For question two, reverse who answers the question first and second. For each new question, rotate this order.

"Now pair off with someone you have not had much opportunity as yet to get to know very well. I will then pass out the questions and you can begin."

The initial questions on the sheet should be of a less personal nature, gradually building up to more personal ones later. When the interviews are completed, the students are to tell their partners in what ways they feel they know each other better. As a total class, the students can discuss their reactions to the activity. They also can talk about how to get to know people better than they do.

Create questions that are appropriate for the levels of your classes. Here are some suggestions. These are in the form of incomplete statements, called "sentence stems" or "sentence stubs." Either compose questions based on these sentence stubs or have each person just complete the statement as it is given here.

1. I am a person who _____
2. I am happiest when _____
3. I would like to be _____
4. One thing I can do well is _____
5. A friend can count on me to _____
6. I like people who _____
7. I'm proud of myself when _____
8. In ten years I _____
9. One thing I like about myself is _____
10. I like to daydream about _____
11. The person I admire most is _____
12. My favorite pastime is _____
13. It's really fun to _____
14. If I were given a lot of money to spend, I'd _____
15. Right now I feel _____
16. One of my strongest points is _____
17. I can see that one of your strong points is _____
18. One way I would enjoy spending time with you is _____
19. What I like best about you is _____
20. If I could have one wish come true, I'd ask for _____

You can ask students to suggest other statements to complete. Be certain to maintain a positive focus in all of them, and include statements which involve talking about one's partner, such as items 17 and 18 above.

EXERCISE 8. **FORTUNE COOKIES**

Purposes:
   Affective—
         To encourage students to wish good things for their classmates
         To try to project what would make others in the class happy
         To provide fun, mystery, and a bit of excitement
   Linguistic—
         To practice writing verbs in the future or the subjunctive

Levels: All levels

Size of groups: About six

Procedures: Students are placed in groups and told to make fortunes for the persons to their right, something they think would make them happy. Each fortune is written on a slip of paper. One at a time the fortune is passed to the person for whom it is intended and is read aloud by him. The student must make a comment or react after reading it, and the others can discuss the fortune, if they wish, before going on to the next one. Some fortunes from each group can be read in front of the class.

Variations:
      1. In groups of four, have each student write a fortune for the other three people. The slips of paper are folded and placed in front of the person whose fortune it is. Have three rounds of turns, with each person reading one of his fortunes at a time.
      2. Have each person include a fortune for himself. Each student reads all four of his fortunes at once. The group guesses which one was written by the person himself.
      3. Have each student write a wish for students in any of the above formats. In this case the subjunctive mood will be practiced in some languages.
      4. Fortunes can be collected and read in front of the class rather than in groups.

Comments:
      This activity should be done after students know one another fairly well so the students can predict more accurately what would make specific classmates happy. Be sure they make up some fortunes for you, too.

EXERCISE 9. **I SEE MYSELF IN YOU**

Purposes:
      Affective—

To encourage students to notice commonalities between themselves
and their classmates

To promote students feeling closer bonds with each other

Linguistic—

To practice the first person plural

Levels: All levels

Size of groups: Total class or groups, if desired

Materials needed: Dittos containing the names of everyone in the class; completion of the assignment by the members of the class

Procedures: This activity should be used later in the school year after the students know each other quite well. Tell the class:

"When we meet someone new, we usually look for something we have in common. Sometimes we try to find a mutual acquaintance or pastime. But the conversation keeps going till some common base is found. And then we feel we've made a connection with each other and can communicate.

"In this class we have had a great deal of contact with each other. By now we should be able to find something positive that we have in common with everyone here. I'm going to pass out these handouts, which have the names of everyone in our class. I want you to write beside each person's name something positive you two have in common, in other words, how you are alike in your thinking, feeling, ideas, beliefs, values, behavior, personality, or appearance.

"Between each name there are a few lines for you to write your responses and sign your name. Bring the completed dittos to class on (give due date) Wednesday, as we will be telling one another what we feel we have in common.

"The second part of the assignment is to decide which three people in the class are most like you and in what ways. There is a separate ditto on which to write their names and list all the ways you are alike. As you fill out the first part of the assignment, you will probably discover who these people are."

Here is a sample of what the dittoed handouts contain:

MEMBERS OF OUR CLASS   HOW WE ARE ALIKE

Amy _____

_____

_____

Bill _____

_____

_____

Carl
_____

_____

_____

etc.

THE THREE PEOPLE MOST LIKE ME   HOW WE ARE ALIKE

1. _____   _____

                                           _____

                                           _____

2. _____   _____

                                           _____

                                           _____

3. _____   _____

                                           _____

                                           _____

There are several ways to carry out this activity. One is to have the students walk around the room and stop a moment to talk to each person in the class. At that time, the pairs of students exchange how they believe they are like one another. (The dittoed handout can be referred to.) When the students speak to one of the people they feel resembles them the most, they can inform him of this.

If you wish to have a longer exchange between individuals and those they feel resemble them the most, ask students to turn in ahead of time a slip of paper with their names and the three people listed below. You will have to figure out a way to pair off or group students for this phase of the activity. There may be an opportunity to speak with only one of the three on the list. The number of times a person is chosen will affect how you group the class. Some people may not be among the three on anyone's list. Point out that this is not a popularity contest. It merely means you see more parts of yourself in those you have named.

At the conclusion of the activity, you can have the students cut out the names and remarks on their dittos and pass them to the person to whom they refer. The three people seen to most resemble others will also receive this additional information in writing.

As a total group, ask students what they discovered from this exercise. Be certain that your name is included on the class list, too.

EXERCISE 10.   **ONE, TWO, IN MY SHOE**[6]

Purposes:

Affective—

> To communicate positive feelings to everyone in the class
>
> To provide a great deal of positive feedback for everyone in the class
>
> To allow good feelings which may not have been expressed as yet to be exchanged among students
>
> To create warmth and close ties among the students in the class

Linguistic—

> To practice writing in the first and third persons
>
> To read silently and orally messages containing adjectives describing positive qualities

Levels: All levels

Size of groups: Total class *or* groups of six to eight

Materials needed: Dittoed handouts with the names of everyone in the class; slips of paper on which the students have carried out the assignment which will be given by the teacher

Procedures: This is a good closing activity right before a holiday vacation late in the school year or at one of the last meetings of the year. The class members should be well acquainted with each other for this activity to be carried out with the greatest success.

Give the class at least a week to carry out this assignment. Pass out the dittoed sheets containing the names of everyone in the class, including your name as well. Give a brief introduction to the activity, followed by announcing the assignment:

"As we have shared many of our thoughts and feelings and experiences through the year, we have come to know more about ourselves and each other. We probably have discovered many things that we like about each other that we weren't aware of before. Even though we have exchanged a number of positive feelings we have for others in the class, many are still not expressed.

"During the next week, we are going to write a note to each person in the class. In each note tell the person some of the positive things you like about him. Do this in a few sentences. You will probably want to know who has sent you each note you receive. However, you can decide whether or not you want to sign the notes you send.

"Use the class list and check off each name as you write a note to the person. Write the person's name on the outside of the slip of paper on which the note is written. Then fold the paper a couple of times so that the note is small but you can see the person's name on it.

"A week from today, bring to class one of your shoes, not the pair you're wearing. We will place the shoe on our desk with our name beside our shoe. We will then pass the notes to one another by walking around the room and placing the note in the person's shoe. The shoe will be our mailbox.

"Each night write a few notes so you do not have to do them all at once. You can give more thought to the messages when you have more time to do them. If you need help in how to say something, ask me during the week."

Remind the students during the week (or you can allow two weeks) to write the notes and to bring in their shoe and a name card to place beside it.

This activity should be the closing exercise of the class period. Allow enough time for the slips to be passed out. Tell the students to wait until everyone has passed out all of the messages. Then direct the students to go to their seats and read their messages. Do not let the students return to their seats until all of the slips are distributed or they will know who left them certain notes which may not be signed. Tell the students to put aside in a pile the notes that they especially like or are surprised by.

When everyone has finished, you can either have each person share with the total class one of the most meaningful or delightful messages received or this can be done in small groups in which several such notes are read by each person. This activity leaves people feeling especially warm and close to one another.

NOTES

1. This is a popular warm-up activity with a number of variations to it. The exercise is commonly used at workshops, where I was first introduced to it and have experienced it many times since. Original author unknown.

2. Thanks to Hannah B. Weiner and James M. Sacks from whom I learned this technique, which they developed as a warm-up strategy.

3. This exercise is an elaboration of a strategy developed by Leland W. Howe and Mary Martha Howe.

4. The idea for this exercise is adapted from a game known as "Touch Blue." Origin unknown.

5. The use of an interview for getting acquainted is a well-known humanistic technique.

6. I experienced this exercise at a workshop. Original author unknown.

Discovering Myself

The greatest discovery is finding yourself.

–Gertrude Moskowitz

We are all curious to learn more about ourselves—to discover what we aren't already aware of—to know ourselves better. The popularity of horoscopes and handwriting analysis attest to the desire to find out more about the complexities that make us the unique individuals we are.

The exercises in this section possess intrigue and appeal. Most are humorous and fun to participate in. The learner is led unwittingly into gaining insights into himself by means of association and other amusing avenues. These activities could be labeled exercises in awareness or identity. The student is put in touch with some answers to the ever-present questions: "Who am I?" and "What am I like?"

EXERCISE 11. PARTS OF SPEECH LIKE ME[1]

Purposes:
> Affective—
>> To have students think introspectively and spontaneously about themselves
>
> Linguistic—
>> To review a variety of parts of speech: nouns, verbs, adjectives, and adverbs

Levels: All levels

Size of groups: Three to four

Procedures: Ask students to write down any three nouns that come to their minds that they really like. Follow this by asking them to write down three adjectives that they feel good about. Allow some time. Next request that they write down three verbs which pop into their minds that they like. And last, ask for three adverbs that appeal to them. Give them a moment to carry out the task after each set of directions.

Then instruct the students to take the list of nouns and to take turns sharing how the nouns they wrote are in some way like them. They should then move on to the adjectives and tell how these words are like them. On to the verbs and have them share how these are like the ways they do some things. With the adverbs, the students should tell what they have in common with each one.

As the groups finish with each part of speech, get a few examples on the floor for everyone to hear before going on to the next part of speech in groups. It is interesting to note similarities in choices of words in the class. For example, a number of students might select the word "love" for a verb. Be certain that the students understand how to apply the words to themselves. If "candy" was one student's noun, he should not say "I like candy a lot," but "I am sweet like candy" to show what he has in common with it.

Explain to the class that they each chose the words they liked for specific reasons relating to themselves. Therefore, this is a way to find out more about themselves.

This exercise can be humorous and is an intriguing way to review different parts of speech.

EXERCISE 12.   **THE SHAPE I'M IN**

Purposes:
    Affective—
        To encourage students to think introspectively
        To learn about oneself by association
        To note how identical symbols evoke different responses in people
    Linguistic—
        To practice the vocabulary of shapes
        To practice the vocabulary which relates to describing shapes
        To practice the use of adjectives

Levels: All levels

Size of groups: About six

Procedures: Announce to the students that they are going to find out some things about themselves by making a choice from a number of shapes. Tell them that upon seeing the shapes they should quickly decide which one they like best. Then reveal the shapes on an overhead projector or on the blackboard. All of the shapes should be seen at the same time. If they are on the blackboard, have them already drawn and covered by a screen or map, which you pull up to reveal them.

As they view the figures, remind them to decide which one appeals to them most. The shapes are a triangle, a circle, a square, a hexagon, and a zigzag line. They should be about the same size and can be depicted like this:

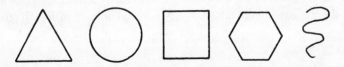

Ask the students to draw on a slip of paper the one that they like best. Then in groups of six, each student should relate to the figure he has chosen by telling how he sees himself in it:

"I like the hexagon best. I am like a hexagon because I am neat and orderly and I have many interesting sides to me. I am well-balanced. I am also different. There are not many hexagons in the world."

When the groups are finished, have the students get up and mill around the room holding the sketch of the figure they chose in front of them for others to see. The students are to stop and ask a number of others how the figure they chose is like them. After they have the opportunity to speak with about six students, tell the students to form a group with all others who chose the same figure they did. It may be necessary to limit the number in the most popular groups. During this round, the students will get a chance to hear how others chose the same symbol as they, but for similar or different reasons. Have a couple of students from each group tell the total class why they chose their symbols.

This activity illustrates how many different perceptions can be seen in the identical thing. At the same time, the students learn more about themselves by means of association.

EXERCISE 13. **CLOCK LINE-UP[2]**

Purposes:

    Affective—

        As a warm-up to facilitate getting acquainted

        To introduce movement when the class has been sedentary

    Linguistic—

        To practice telling time

        To practice the numbers one to twelve

Levels: Beginning to intermediate

Size of groups: Total class

Procedures: This is a simple exercise which can be used to get students out of their seats and acquainted with each other. However, it can be used at any time to energize the group for a change of pace.

Announce the following to the class:

"Imagine that there is a huge clock on the floor here with the numbers from one to twelve around it. (Walk around as you point out the parts of the face of the clock.) This is where the three is, where the six is, where the nine is, and where the twelve is. In between are the other numbers.

"I want you to think of the time on the clock that means the most to you. (Allow a minute for the class to decide.) Now get up out of your seats and place yourself on the spot representing that number or hour on the clock."

Once everyone is placed around the dial of the imaginary clock, tell the class to discuss with those standing on the same number what is significant to them about that time. If only one person is on a number, he should speak with those closest to him. Then in the total class, ask someone who is standing where the number one is on the clock, "Why is one o'clock important to you?" When this person finishes responding, he calls on someone standing where the number two would be and asks, "Why is two o'clock important to you?" and so on around the clock. If the class has learned the past tense, the question asked could be, "Why did you choose one o'clock?"

After one round of numbers is completed, the students can skip around and ask anyone at all why he likes or chose that specific time. A review can be held at the end of the exercise in which you, and later the students, ask questions such as: "Why does Chuck like three o'clock?" or "Who likes six o'clock because he is eating his favorite meal then?" This is a light exercise, and it can be fun to hear the variety of reasons different times on the clock were chosen as important to people.

EXERCISE 14. **SECRET MESSAGE**[3]

Purposes:
  Affective—
    To encourage creative thinking
    To become aware of the fact that we have the answers to our own
        problems and know what is right for us
  Linguistic—
    To practice word order patterns
    To practice commands (a number of examples will be in this form)

Levels: All levels

Size of groups: Five to six

Procedures: To use this exercise, it is helpful for the target language and the native language to have the same letters of the alphabet, except for ESL. Or the students can use the alphabet of the target language and their equivalent names in that language, too. If nothing else works, they will have to begin with their name in their native language.

Tell the students that each of us really knows the answer to his own problems. We just have to tap our own resources to find them. As a homework assignment, tell students to spell their first name *in reverse.* If their name is long, they can use a nickname. They are to construct a sentence, or two if their name is quite long, using each letter in their name as the beginning of each consecutive word. All of the words together will form a secret message that they are giving themselves which is true and wise and should help guide them.

Be sure to show them a couple of examples on the board. Use your own first name to illustrate. I'll use my nickname and given name to point out what I mean:

Y D U R T

(*Y*ou *d*eserve *u*nderstanding, *r*esponsibility, *t*rust.)

The meaning for me is that I am capable and deserve to be listened to and believed in.

E D U R T R E G

(*E*very *d*ay *u*se *r*eason, *t*enderness, *r*eality, *e*mpathy, *g*oodness.)

This message clearly tells me how I should direct my life: both rationally and with warmth.

Here is an example in Spanish from a student:

N E L E H

(*N*o *e*mpie*ces* (a) *l*lorar *e*specialmente *h*oy.)
(Don't begin to cry, especially today.)

The meaning for the student was that she should not get depressed but should perk up and see the bright side of things.

If the students should not be able to write the message in the target language, let them do it in English if this is the native language, and discuss the meaning they see in it in the foreign language.

Tell students as they develop their secret message to concentrate on each letter until the message comes. They then will have to interpret the meaning of it once they complete the statement. Request that they bring it to class next day, and mention that they will share the message and the meaning. Suggest that they can do more than one or use their given name for one and their nickname for another if they wish.

In class they will share their messages in groups. Then ask for some to be given to the total class.

This exercise is intended to tap the inner wisdom each person has about himself.

EXERCISE 15.   **HANDY-TALK[4]**

Purposes:
   Affective—
      To reveal to students that there are two sides to all of us

To help students gain some introspection into themselves
To promote creativity, greater self-knowledge, and fun
Linguistic—
To create original dialogs in the language

Levels: All levels; beginning level with a half year of the language

Size of groups: Approximately five

Procedures: Announce to the students that they have studied a number of dialogs since they've been learning a language, but now they're going to create their own. Tell them they'll need a piece of paper and a pen or pencil. Ask them to follow your instructions just as you give them.

Tell them that the original dialog they are going to create will take place between their right hand and their left hand. Ask everyone to put his pencil or pen in his right hand and to write one sentence that his right hand might actually want to say if it could talk to the left hand—not a superficial dialog, but a meaningful one. Allow time for this.

Now tell everyone to switch the pen to the left hand, skip a line, and write a one-sentence answer that the left hand really would want to reply with to the right hand. (Prepare for laughter as all the "righties" in the class judiciously scribble with the left hand. They'll take longer to write when using the hand they are unaccustomed to writing with.)

Then instruct the class to follow this procedure, switching the pen back and forth between hands, until they have a six-line dialog with three statements from each hand.

When the dialog is finished, ask them to read it over to themselves to determine what hidden meaning is in it for them. Break the class into groups of five and ask them to read their dialogs to each other and to share the meaning or insights they found, if they wish to (remember the right to pass).

Ask for volunteers who are willing to share theirs with the total class. Some students may suggest others to read theirs in cases where the dialogs are especially humorous. Process and summarize the activity. Don't forget to share yours with the class, too. You could go first.

Here are examples of two dialogs, one in French and one in Spanish, which were written when this exercise was used. They are translated into English as well, in the event that these languages are not familiar to you. Both dialogs begin with the right hand addressing the left hand. In the French version, the letter "D" is used to indicate that the right hand (*la main droite*) is speaking and "G" to show that the left hand (*la main gauche*) is responding. In the Spanish version, "D" is used for the right hand (*la mano derecha*) and "I" for the left hand (*la mano izquierda*).

French Handy Talk

D: Allons! Tu peux le faire, malgré que tu n'en aies pas l'habitude.

R: Come on! You can do it, even though you're not used to it.

G: Tu es folle! Je suis trop faible!

L: You're crazy! I'm too weak!

D: C'est une question de fortitude.

R: It's a question of perseverence.

G: Ce n'est pas la question. Je me sentirais ridicule!

L: That's not the question. I'd feel foolish.

D: L'impossible est souvent ce qu'on n'a pas encore essayé.

R: The impossible is often what you haven't tried yet.

G: (Elle le fait) Que je suis contente! Rien n'est impossible!

L: (The hand does it) I'm so happy! Nothing is impossible!

(The hidden message found in this dialog: My attitude can defeat me or bring me success. Nothing is impossible if I put my mind to it and really try.)

Spanish Handy Talk

D: ¿Por qué siempre descansas tanto?

R: Why do you always rest so much?

I: Porque no me necesitan.

L: Because I'm not needed.

D: Tienes que practicar porque algún día tendrás que trabajar.

R: You have to practice because some day you'll have to work.

I: A mí no me importa.

L: That's not important to me.

D: ¡Eres imposible!

R: You're impossible!

I: Es verdad. Por eso no trabajo.

L: That's true. That's why I don't work.

(Hidden message: I'm not working up to my capacity.)

EXERCISE 16.   **FIRE-WATER**[5]

Purposes:

    Affective—

        To use imagination and spontaneity

        To gain introspection into some of one's qualities through association

Linguistic—
> To provide practice in speaking in the first person
> To practice the use of adjectives

Levels: Intermediate to advanced

Size of groups: Dyads (if there is an uneven number, join the activity)

Procedures: Ask the students in each pair to number off so one is number one and the other is two. Tell all of the "ones" to imagine that they are actually fire and that they can talk. Instruct them to talk about their positive qualities in the first person while their partner just listens. Suggest they listen closely, as what they say about themselves as fire may actually be true of them.

After a few minutes, tell all the "twos" to imagine that they are water and to do the same thing. Here are a few examples: "I am fire. I am warm and bright and have a lot of energy." "I am water. I am calm and clear and am good for people." When finished, ask each couple to discuss what things they felt were really true about themselves that they said when they imagined they were fire or water.

Regroup students into groups of four or five. Group the students so that only those who were fire are together and those who were water are with each other. Ask each group to discuss how similar and different their responses were. Have the groups feed their results into the total class. Process and summarize what was learned.

Variations: Almost any objects can be used for this exercise. A follow-up to the exercise is to give out a list of objects and have the students in each group give a one-sentence statement as to how they are like each item; for example, "In what way(s) are you like a song, a bird, a painting, a television set?" After each round in groups, get a few on the floor. Include yourself in some rounds, and be sure to process the activity.

Comments: Students may mention things they ordinarily would not if it weren't for the personification, because this makes it acceptable and fun to see the parallels. Using the symbols of fire and water helps unlock thoughts not necessarily revealed to oneself before.

EXERCISE 17. **SUPPOSE YOU WEREN'T YOU**[6]

Purposes:
Affective—
> To be introspective about oneself while calling on the imagination

Linguistic—
> To afford practice in the conditional and the subjunctive

To practice different categories of vocabulary

Levels: All levels

Size of groups: Five to six

Procedures: Tell the students that in this exercise they will be using their imagination. Introduce the activity by stating something like this:

"Today we're going to imagine that we could become different things or objects and still have some of our own qualities. I'm going to name a category. You decide what you would be in that category, what would fit you and your personality and why.

"Here's an example: If you were a color, what color would you be? I would answer this way: 'If I were a color, I'd be yellow because it's warm and bright and full of energy.' "

Ask students to write down their choices for each category. Then tell the students to complete in their groups the statement just given, "If I were a color, I would be . . . ," with each taking a turn and telling *why* the particular color was chosen. Have a few examples given for the total class and be certain that everyone listens when someone shares with the total class. Some students will want to continue their own discussion, but point out the importance of everyone paying attention when the total group is addressed.

Give a series of other categories, one at a time, based upon vocabulary pertinent to your own class. Here are some examples:

If you were a season of the year, which season would you be? Why?
If you were a day of the week, which day would you be? Why?
If you were a country, which country would you be? Why?
If you were a musical instrument, which instrument would you be? Why?
If you were an article of clothing, which article would you be? Why?
If you were a piece of fruit, which fruit would you be? Why?
If you were a dessert, which dessert would you be? Why?
If you were a number, which number would you be? Why?
If you were a month of the year, which month would you be? Why?
If you were a TV show, which show would you be? Why?
If you were a shoe, what kind of a shoe would you be? Why?
If you were a feeling, which feeling would you be? Why?

Be certain after each round in groups to have a few given for the total class to hear before going on to the next category.

Ask students to look over their choices and to notice whether there are any similarities or patterns among them. Have these shared with the whole class.

EXERCISE 18.   **MONEY TALKS**[7]

Purposes:
   Affective—
         To facilitate students thinking introspectively about themselves by
               means of association
         To share the association with others in the class
         To observe how identical objects evoke different responses and
               perceptions in people
   Linguistic—
         To practice the first and/or the third person in the present tense
         To practice the use of adjectives

Levels: All levels

Size of groups: About six

Materials needed: Each student should be prepared to have a penny, a nickel, a
dime, and a quarter. In countries where the money system is different, have each
student bring in four specific coins which differ in size, shape, color (if possible),
and value. All students should bring in the same coins.

Procedures: Announce in advance that students should bring to class a penny, a
nickel, a dime, and a quarter for a specific class meeting. This assignment in itself
will arouse curiosity in the students.
   Divide the class into groups of six. You can initiate the exercise in the
following way:
   "There are many ways we can learn about ourselves. Today we're going to
discover some qualities about ourselves and others in the class in an unusual way.
   "Take out the four coins you were to bring to class today and line them up
in front of you. (Each student will need a place to put the coins where everyone
in the group can see them. The arm of a chair, a table that all can sit around, or a
notebook placed on the lap can serve this purpose.)
   "Listen to all of the directions first. Look at the front and the back of each
coin very carefully. Examine everything on each coin. Read what is written on
the coins and study the pictures on them. As you do this, decide which coin is
most like you and why. In other words, which coin fits your character more or
things you identify with yourself?
   "When you decide, push that coin forward so the group can see it. When
everyone in your group has made a decision, take turns telling why you chose the
coin you did. Listen carefully to what each person says, as we will continue the
activity later based on what was said in your group."
   Allow time for the students to carry out this phase of the exercise. Then
tell the students to ask someone in their group for a quality the person expressed

which he saw in the coin and himself. For example, "Roger, give me some of your uniqueness." "Linda, I'd like some of your smallness." "Beth, may I have some of your love of freedom?" (You can decide whether there is a particular structure you want students to practice during this part of the exercise.)

At this point ask a few students to share with the total class why they selected the coin that they did. See that students who chose each of the four coins participate. You can do this by asking, "How many of you chose the penny?" and then call on a couple to tell why they chose that coin. Continue this for all four coins. It is interesting to see how many chose a particular coin and to hear how different the reasons for the same choice can be.

If there is time, continue the activity in this way: "In making your choice of a coin, you probably narrowed your selection to two coins before deciding. Which coin was your second choice, and how is that coin like you?"

You can ask for a show of hands to see which coins were chosen the most and the least. Several of the responses can be given in front of the class again. Based upon the results of this exercise, you can ask a number of questions, such as:

"Which coin did most people select for their first choice?"
"Which coin was selected the least?"
"Why does Jessica feel that she is like a nickel?"
"Who said he was like a quarter because he has a lot of 'cents' (sense)?"
"Why was the color of the penny important to Marianne?"

Conclude the exercise by stating:

"We can learn more about ourselves by using association. In this case, we all looked at something familiar to us and related it to ourselves. We also can find out some things that are important to us in this way." You can end by asking students what they learned about themselves in this exercise. This can be given as a homework assignment to be turned in, if you wish.

EXERCISE 19.   **THE ASSOCIATION GAME**[8]

Purposes:
Affective—
To develop insights into how we tend to choose our friends
To discover commonalities we share with those we are close to
Linguistic—
To practice the use of adjectives

Levels: All levels

Size of groups: About three

Materials needed: The written homework assignment completed by each student

Procedures: Ask students to carry out this assignment and bring it to class on a certain day. Turn a sheet of paper horizontally and across the top write the names of two of your close friends of the same sex, two close friends of the opposite sex, your mother, your dad, yourself, and two people in this class you feel particularly close to. (This last one you, the teacher, can determine whether or not to include; their actual names can be omitted, if desired.) Below each name in a column, write as many adjectives as you can in the foreign language to describe what each person is like.

To carry out this exercise, put the students into groups of three, as there are quite a few ideas to be discussed by each. Ask them to discuss these questions (either place them on the board or on a ditto):

1. Go over your list of people you are close to and note whether you used similar adjectives to describe them. If so, what are these qualities that they have in common?

2. Who is most like you?

3. Is there anyone on the list not like you and the others?

4. Are there more similarities or differences between your male and female friends? In what ways are you similar to your friends?

5. Are you similar to one of your parents, both, or neither?

6. How similar are you to the two students you feel especially close to in this class?

7. What is the strongest and most important quality that your associates have in common?

Have a discussion in the total class based on several of these questions and what students learned from this exercise. A good conclusion to the discussion is having each person state before the entire group what is the most important quality his associates have in common.

You can ask students to write about what they learned from this exercise and what they and their close associates are like.

EXERCISE 20.   **POSITIVE POP-UP**

Purposes:
    Affective—
           To determine outstanding characteristics of oneself
           To explore one's self-image

Linguistic—
> To practice the vocabulary of adjectives

Levels: All levels

Size of groups: Dyads

Procedures: Tell the students that they are going to explore some of the important characteristics they see in themselves and in others. Ask everyone to close his eyes. You can give a few relaxation suggestions as you do before a fantasy to get the class settled down. (see "Conducting Fantasies," page 178.)

Then ask the students to think about themselves and their positive qualities and characteristics. Tell them to relax and just let the words indicating these qualities pop into their minds by themselves. Allow several minutes to go by.

Then have the students open their eyes and write down eight of these words, each on a different slip of paper. Next have the students arrange the words in the order of importance to them, with the qualities that are most satisfying or valuable ranking the highest. The slips of paper can be easily shuffled to rank order them.

Now see that each person has a partner. Ask the students to focus on each other for a few minutes and then write down on slips of paper eight positive qualities they see in their partners and rank order these. Have the pairs of students share the lists of qualities they see in themselves and the order in which these are valued and why. A spontaneous or structured dialog can take place between them. Questions that can be asked are:

1. What are the qualities on your list?
2. Which quality gives you the most satisfaction?
3. Why did you rank it first?
4. Which quality did you rank second in importance?
5. What is an experience you recall in which you made use of one of your top three qualities?

After a while the partners should tell each other which positive qualities they see in each other and how these were ranked. The students can ask each other questions such as:

1. What do you see as my most valuable quality?
2. When have you seen it in me?
3. Which qualities do you see in me that are not on my list?

The students can compare their own lists of qualities with those their partners give them. They will probably wish to question each other as to when some of the qualities were perceived.

As a total group ask:

1. To what extent are the qualities you came up with similar to or different from the ones seen by your partner?

2. Were you surprised by any of the qualities your partner perceives in you?

3. Which quality seen in you by your partner means the most to you? Why?

4. Combine your list and the one given to you by your partner. Which are the top eight qualities on your list now?

As a follow-up, have the students write about several experiences they can recall in which they made use of the qualities on their own lists and the ones on the lists given to them by their partners. Ask for their reactions to the qualities perceived in them by their partners.

EXERCISE 21.　　　　　　**EXTRA! EXTRA!**[9]

Purposes:

　　Affective—

　　　　To tap the imagination of students

　　　　To help students gain some introspection into themselves in a creative
　　　　　　way

　　Linguistic—

　　　　To develop unique material of a personal nature that students will
　　　　　　want to write and talk about

Levels: Advanced

Size of groups: About five

Procedures: Ask the students to close their eyes and to get comfortable. Say several things to help them relax. (Refer to "Conducting Fantasies," page 178.) Then give the following instructions:

"Visualize the front page of a newspaper from the present, past, or future, in which a *very good* piece of news has been written up. Look at the front page and focus on the headline until you can read what it says. (Pause to allow some time here.) . . . Remember this is a very welcome piece of news from the present, past, or future. (They may need reminding of the facts.)

"Now change this same headline so that you omit a word or a couple of words in it and replace these words with *your first name.* The headline will be similar, only your first name is now in it . . . Visualize this new headline . . . Begin to read the subheadlines related to the story that has your name in the headline . . . Begin to read the story written about you that's on the front page . . . (Give a longer amount of time here.) And now turn to the editorial page and read the glowing reaction written there about you related to this headline story . . . "

After a sufficient time, ask the students to open their eyes and in small groups to share anything they may want to, based upon their story and the message they received from it. Or ask them to write their headline and the story they visualized and then share what they want with the group.

Comments: This activity should be used after a good deal of trust has been built in the group so that students will feel free to share. Some may only want to share the headlines with the meaning behind them, since these may point out areas in which they want to change. However, the fact that the news is positive will make the result a happy, rather than threatening, one. This is a good activity in which *you* are the first one to share.

The most important part of getting this activity off to the right start is to say emphatically in the opening sentence that this is a "*good* piece of news." Otherwise, almost everyone will conjure up a *bad* piece of news, which will be an interference to try to change once this comes to mind. The activity can enhance introspection in the direction that students want to go to grow and to improve.

Here is an example of how the positive focus helps so much. My own headline, "World War II Ends," could be quite depressing when changed to "Trudy Ends." Because this is supposed to be a *good* piece of news, I can focus on what parts of me I want to get rid of and will feel good about as a result.

NOTES

1. I came across an exercise at one time which triggered off the idea for this technique. The present exercise is an embellishment of the kernel idea of that activity, but I regret I am unable to locate the original exercise in order to acknowledge the source.

2. This technique is an expansion of an activity experienced at a workshop. Author unknown.

3. This exercise was originally developed by Daniel Malamud.

4. Credit for this strategy is due to Daniel Malamud.

5. I learned of this strategy at a Gestalt workshop conducted by Marvin Lifschitz.

6. I learned of this exercise at a workshop given by Stefano Morel.

7. This technique is an expansion of one in an extensive collection edited by J. William Pfeiffer and John E. Jones (*A Handbook of Structured Experiences for Human Relations Training.* La Jolla, Calif.: University Associates [1974]).

8. This technique was adapted from one by Daniel Malamud.

9. This exercise is a slight modification of one by Daniel Malamud.

My Strengths

Nothing is so strong as gentleness, and
nothing is so gentle as real strength.

—The Reverend Ralph W. Sockman

Although we all have many strengths, we often fail to recognize a number of them. Frequently we are more aware of our weaknesses than our strengths. In addition, we are programmed to keep our strong points to ourselves or others will see us as immodest.

In building self-confidence and a strong self-image, individuals must be aware of their strengths, get feedback as to what positive qualities are seen in them, and be able to acknowledge their attributes.

The exercises in this section enable students to tell others the strengths they see in them and allow students the opportunity of stating some of their own strong points. These exercises generally facilitate students' feeling closer to each other as they hear assets they didn't realize others saw in them.

EXERCISE 22.   **SOMEONE I JUST MET**[1]

Purposes:
> Affective—
>> To encourage students to verbalize positive thoughts about their classmates
>> To receive positive feedback
>> To reveal positive areas to students that may be unknown to them
> Linguistic—
>> To practice the use of adjectives of positive qualities
>> To practice speaking in the third person

Levels: Intermediate and advanced

Size of groups: Three

Procedures: This exercise is intended for the first day or one of the first days the class meets. It is to warm-up the class and get students acquainted and feeling at ease.

Ask the students to form into groups of three, with people they do not know yet. Tell them:

"You are going to get to know each other by talking about unusual things rather than the typical things exchanged with new acquaintances. As the three of you talk, tell each other two things you wouldn't normally share about yourself when you first meet someone. Try to get to know each other quite well."

Allow about five minutes for the groups to get acquainted. Then go into part two of the exercise:

"Now I want you to imagine you are talking to your best friend about the two people you just met. Tell your friend some of the positive things you thought about the two classmates you just spoke to.

"I might say something like this: 'Norma, I just met two very unusual people. Jody Newman is energetic, very sincere, and open. I liked her right away. Bob Marshall has a good sense of humor, is a good listener, and has a very warm smile. He's easy to get to know.'

"At first this may seem a little odd, to talk about a person when he's actually there. But you'll be finding out some positive impressions you made on others and it will get easier as you go along. Try to listen and enjoy what you hear."

Comments: The students will like hearing pleasant things said about them, even though there may be a little embarrassment mixed in with it. As the year goes on and they continue to exchange positive thoughts and feelings related to themselves and each other, the embarrassment is replaced by anticipation.

EXERCISE 23.   **IMAGES**[2]

Purposes:

> Affective—
>> To call on the imagination
>> To provide students with an unusual form of positive feedback
> Linguistic—
>> To practice the use of nouns and adjectives describing positive
>> qualities

Levels: Intermediate to advanced (beginning classes would have to do this activity in English)

Size of groups: Dyads followed by the total class

Procedures: This activity is intended to be used during the first or one of the first class meetings. It is to warm-up the class and help students become interested in knowing one another.

The students should be previously paired off with a partner they have just finished speaking with during another warm-up activity. (See Exercise 40, "I've Got a Feeling," for how to integrate this activity with others.) Each person should be with someone he has not known previously. If there is an odd number of students in the class, join in this activity yourself. During the previous activity the students will gain some impressions of their partners.

Instruct the class as follows:

"Whenever we meet someone new and speak to him awhile, we have some impressions of what the person is like. You now have a few ideas about what the person you've just spoken to is like.

"You are going to introduce your partner to the class, but in a different way from usual. Think about the person and what you feel you know about him. Then decide what image you see that reflects your impressions of your partner. To introduce your partner, tell us the person's name, the image that reminds you of him, and why. I might say that Fred reminds me of a teddy bear because he is warm and friendly and comfortable to be with; or when I think of Bonnie, I see a girl in the Swiss Alps carrying a pail of milk and singing, because Bonnie is wholesome and natural.

"Take a moment now to think of the impressions you have of your partner and see what image comes to your mind."

Where possible, the students should be sitting in a circle so everyone can see each other during the introductions. Your assistance may be needed to furnish the vocabulary some students will require in stating the images they saw. This experience provides some humor, laughter, and lightheartedness at times. It is amusing and also amazing to note the different images people come up with and the reasons for them. This activity provides a pleasant way to become acquainted.

*　　*　　*　　*　　*

THE DYADIC BELT FORMATION

A novel formation that is fun and involving is the dyadic belt. Since everyone in the group is actually paired off with one person at a time, the communication is in dyads, from which the name of the formation comes. While in a dyadic belt, participants will change partners frequently by rotating in a systematic fashion.

The following exercise, "I Like You Because . . . ," and Exercise 42, "Without Words We Speak," call for the use of this formation. Therefore, an explanation of it is given here for your convenience.

Instruct the class to form two circles, with the same number inside the circle as outside. Each person in the inner circle should be in front of someone in the outer circle. The students in the inner circle should turn and face those in the outer circle, as illustrated in the following sketch:

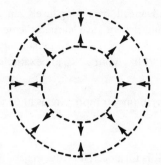

Instructions are given to the class as to the type of communication they will have with their first partner. After a minute or two, a signal is given to move to the next partner. Have the students rotate to quite a few partners in the circle. Flicking the lights on and off will help signal when it's time to change.

There are several ways that students can move to change partners. Use only one of these at any given time:

1. Ask those in the inner circle only to move to their right so as to face the next person in the outer circle each time a change of partners is desired.

2. Ask those in the outer circle only to move to their right so as to face the next person in the inner circle each time a change of partners is desired.

3. Ask those in the inner circle to move to their right for one round and those in the outer circle to move to their right for the next round, rotating this way for each round.

Exercises calling for a dyadic belt either have participants involved in one type of exchange with a constant rotation of partners or a new set of instructions given with each change of partners.

*   *   *   *   *

EXERCISE 24.   **I LIKE YOU BECAUSE . . .**

Purposes:
    Affective—
        To have students give and receive positive feedback
        To look for the good in others
    Linguistic—
        To practice adjectives describing positive qualities

Levels: Intermediate or advanced; beginning levels can use this if a basic structure is provided to complete and if they have learned the necessary vocabulary, that is, parts of the body, descriptive adjectives, and personality traits. The structures "I like you because . . . " or "I like your . . . " are examples of structures which can be used.

Size of groups: Total class in one or more circles in dyadic belt formation

Procedures: A dyadic belt is formed. The students are told that there are many positive qualities about others that we are aware of but often do not take the time to express. Tell the students that today they will have the opportunity to let each other know what some of these positive thoughts and feelings are. Instruct the students to tell the partner they are facing some positive things they like or feel about each other. After about a minute, have the students move to a new partner and continue the process until each student speaks with a number of different students.

Comments: Depending on how well the students know each other and the level of language known, determine whether to shorten or lengthen a bit the amount of time each pair of students has to exchange positive thoughts. It is better to keep the class moving than to allot so much time that the students run out of what to say.

This activity can be done when the students know each other only slightly and repeated again as they know each other better. In introducing the activity in the former case, make a statement to the effect that even though we do not know each other very well, we can still find many things in everyone here that we like. In fact, by letting others know the positive things we think and feel about them, we can get to know them better.

Explain the procedures as stated earlier for carrying out the activity. Once again expect reluctance to go on to another partner. The good feelings exchanged cause students to want to say more and hear more. This activity can provide a great deal of warm feeling and enthusiasm in students and much positive reinforcement for all. It can be a good beginning activity and a good end-of-the-year one as well.

If you are not participating in this activity yourself (an even number is required) and your group is sizable, a microphone set on PA (public address) on the tape recorder is useful for this exercise; you will have to be heard while everyone in the class is talking simultaneously as you announce to move on to a new partner. Or you can flick the lights on and off as a signal to change partners.

EXERCISE 25.   **THE WONDERS OF YOU**[3]

Purposes:
>   Affective—
>>   To give and receive positive feedback

To get students to think carefully about outstanding positive traits in each other

Linguistic—

To practice the use of adjectives (especially in the variation of this exercise)

Levels: All levels

Size of groups: Six to eight

Procedures: Start the activity by telling students: "We are going to do an exercise which will sound simple to do but which requires some thought. Look at each person in your group one at a time and decide what is the most outstanding positive quality you feel this person has. You will probably think of more than one, but choose the most important one.

"Write down each person's name and the quality you pick. Include yourself also and state what is an outstanding characteristic or trait of yours. This is not bragging as we are all aware that we have many strengths, and it's all right to admit what they are."

Allow time for the class to carry out the assignment, and then add these instructions:

"In your groups focus on one person at a time. Everyone should tell the quality to the person by starting with his name, such as 'Rich, you are always such a good sport' or 'Renee, I admire you for never talking against anyone.' After the group finishes a round, the person who received the feedback shares what it is he sees as a very special quality about himself. (It will be easier to do this last rather than first.)

"The person sitting to the right of the one receiving the feedback will write down in the foreign language what each individual is saying. When everyone in the whole group has been the focus person, give the paper with the feedback on it to the one to whom it belongs to look over and to keep."

The students can discuss in their small groups and in the total class how they felt about the things they heard. A good question to pose is: "Did any of the outstanding qualities people see in you surprise you?" (Advanced level students can ask for explanations as to when others noticed certain qualities in them.)

End the activity by mentioning: "Often we don't recognize in ourselves positive qualities that we possess. This activity was to give you some insights into what strong points others see in you and to note whether you are aware of them as well. It was meant to open your eyes to see yourself more clearly, as you really are."

Variations:

1. Tell the class to use adjectives in their statements to people, such as "Michele, you are extremely generous" or "Nick, you are always so patient." You can make use of the vocabulary list in Appendix B for this exercise.

2. Ask the students to list a number of positive qualities of others in their group, indicating the most outstanding one as well. Students will list for themselves only their most outstanding characteristic.

EXERCISE 26.   **ME POWER**[4]

Purposes:
   Affective—
        To instill in students that it is acceptable and desirable to acknowledge their own strengths
        To help break through the embarrassed, modest feelings students have about publicly admitting or hearing their strong points
        To hear the good qualities of others in the class
   Linguistic—
        To provide practice in free composition in which a number of superlative adjectives will be used

Levels: Intermediate and advanced

Size of groups: Approximately five

Procedures: Introduce the topic by saying something of this nature: "We've all done many good things and had a number of successes and accomplishments in our lives. We also have many positive qualities about us, some of which others may not know. We usually are afraid or embarrassed to share these things in our lives with others because they may think we're conceited or bragging. We're going to have a chance to share some of our strengths and accomplishments in a situation where such things about people are made known."

Then give this assignment to the class. Ask the students to imagine that they are going to give a speech before a large group of people. When people give speeches, an introduction is given about them beforehand in which many very complimentary things are said. State that the person who is to introduce you doesn't know you at all. He contacts you and says, "I'd like to tell the audience about a number of your accomplishments but, of course, I don't know you. Would you be good enough to write an introduction for me that will point out your major successes and accomplishments and a number of your best qualities? I'd really appreciate it. No one will know I've asked for your help."

Ask the students to write the introduction of themselves for this person. Suggest that they don't have to be modest but should point out all of the terrific things about themselves and be honest. Tell them to use their name in the introduction.

Be certain to tell the students that they will be working in groups and someone in the group will read their introductions to the others. Collect, correct, and return the papers. Divide the class into groups and have the students hand their introductions to another member in the group. Tell the students to notice how it feels to hear their own introductions given and to hear the introductions of the others in the group. Mention to the students that since everything they have written is true, they should try to feel comfortable when their introductions are read.

Each introduction is then read in the small groups. Tell the students to discuss their feelings about doing this in the small groups and then in the total group. Have yours read also and discuss your feelings with the class.

A number will say they felt embarrassed when their introductions were read but that they really liked hearing the introductions of the others in the group. This is a paradox which can be explored further in the processing phase.

Comments: Here are a few comments students have made in the feedback about this exercise:

"I enjoyed this exercise although I felt somewhat self-conscious."

"I didn't feel comfortable at all when someone read my introduction though I felt great when it was accepted by the others in the group."

"I felt torn between wanting to feel good about myself and the hang-up of being modest."

"I loved listening to everyone else's introduction, and I learned some interesting facts about people in our group."

A discussion can follow about how we can learn to accept and be gracious about our positive qualities without feeling uncomfortable, apologetic, and embarrassed when others tell us about them. As other exercises are experienced in which positive feedback is given and received, the students are able to take these things in stride better and learn to enjoy, accept, and look forward to such exchanges.

EXERCISE 27.   **TIMID? NOT I!**[5]

Purposes:
   Affective—
      To focus on one's capacity to act with strength under stress
   Linguistic—
      To practice the past tense(s)
      To practice asking questions
      To practice free conversation and composition

Levels: Intermediate to advanced

Size of groups: About four to five

Procedures: Begin the topic by stating:

"There are occasions in our lives when it is difficult to stand up for ourselves or for others or for some cause. The circumstances are such that it is hard to put aside feeling timid and to risk what will happen. Yet we all have taken a positive, powerful stand in such situations because we knew it was right, though not easy to do.

"Think of a time in which you overcame feeling timid. You acted with strength, and the situation turned out well. We will share these experiences with each other."

Have the class write about the event at home before discussing it in class. If the group is more advanced, allow a few minutes in class for thinking of a situation to relate spontaneously. Divide the class into groups of four or five to talk about their episodes. The group members can ask questions and make comments as the stories are related. The groups can recommend some people to tell their experiences for all to hear.

Ask the students:

1. How did you feel as you listened to these stories?
2. Did your group tend to laugh while hearing these situations? If so, why?
3. In what kinds of situations did members of your group overcome feeling timid?
4. When is it wise to put aside feelings of timidness and to act strongly?
5. What helped you to act strongly even though it was difficult in your situation?

The students can write about their experiences and turn them in after the discussion. They also can include questions 4 and 5 listed above. Or you can ask them to list other instances in which they overcame feeling timid, describing each situation in a few sentences.

EXERCISE 28. **ALLEMANDE RIGHT[6]**

Purposes:

Affective—

To give positive reinforcement to everyone in the class
To leave a warm feeling in everyone in the class

Linguistic—

To practice the second person singular in the present tense
To practice adjectives describing positive qualities

Levels: All levels

Size of groups: Total class

Procedures: This activity is appropriate after students are well acquainted with each other. It is a good activity to use before a holiday vacation, at the close of the period on a Friday, or at the end of the last class meeting for the year.

The class members form a circle and either hold hands or put their arms around each other's waist, if they have reached that level of closeness. The circle should be a tight, close one.

Tell the students, one at a time, to speak to the person to their right so everyone can hear them and to start the sentence they will say with the word "You . . . " When everyone has had a turn, reverse and address the person to the left, and start by using the person's name. Be certain to join the circle yourself.

Comments: This activity encourages students to say something positive about the classmates to their right and left without even requesting that they do so. A feeling of warmth and closeness generates from this exercise, which makes it a good choice for closure.

EXERCISE 29.   **EGO TRIP**[7]

Purposes:
> Affective—
>> To get positive feedback about one's strengths from those who recognize them
>> To help students realize the vast number of strengths they have
>> To build confidence and good feelings in students about themselves
> Linguistic—
>> To practice the first person singular of the present tense
>> To practice the use of adjectives describing positive qualities

Levels: All levels, but the discussion phase will have to be structured for the beginning level

Size of groups: Three

Materials needed: Dittoed handouts for students to have others complete

Procedures: Hand out four copies of a ditto to each student. Allow about two weeks to complete the assignment. The ditto should contain the foreign language, level, and your name (the teacher's) on it so it will be seen by outsiders as an official homework assignment. The nature of the assignment is unusual, and students may feel some embarrassment in carrying it out otherwise.

Announce to the class:

"We all have many, many strengths, but we don't know what all of them are. For our next activity, we are going to learn more about our strengths from those who know them best.

"Each of you will receive four copies of a ditto to give to people you are very close to and friendly with. Include members of your family, if you wish. Tell these people that this is a homework assignment for your foreign language class, that we are trying to learn more about ourselves. Explain that you have been asked to have this form answered by people you are close friends with. Tell the people the date you must have the form back, and arrange to see them to pick it up and go over it with them. Bring the completed forms to class on (give date due)."

The ditto is very simple, but its purpose is to make the assignment official and to make it easier for the students to approach others to complete it. Here is a sample of what to put on the ditto:

Mr. Bender (your name as teacher)
Spanish 2

Assignment: Give these forms to four people whom you are close to and friendly with and who know you well. You can include family members, too. Ask each person to fill out this form for you. Since we are trying to find out more about our strengths, the responses you get will be very helpful to you. This sheet will not be collected by the teacher. It will be yours to use in our discussion. When you collect each person's response, read it in his presence and discuss it with him.

To the person filling out this form: Please write a number of the qualities and characteristics that you see are the strengths of the person who gave you this form to fill out. You can address the person directly in your written response, since he or she will be reading it. Please discuss it with the person when you return the form. Thank you for your help. Use the back of the page if more space is needed.

Student's name _____

Name of person filling out form _____

THESE ARE YOUR STRENGTHS

(Leave the remainder of the paper blank)

On the day the assignment is due, put the students into groups of three. You can tell them to talk about the following questions and ask them one at a time. Or you can put the questions on a ditto where they can be referred to:

1. What similarities were there in what people said about you?
2. Were there surprises in what people said to you?
3. Did you feel anything different about the person after you discussed the form than you did before?
4. In your group, talk in the first person and tell the others, "These are my strengths," and finish by adding what was said about you.

As a total class, have the students tell the thing they like best which was said about them. They also can add what was said that surprised them the most. If there is time, ask how they felt about this experience.

In a written follow-up activity, have the students write about what they learned from this experience. You can also have them include any of the questions discussed in small groups or in the total class.

Comments: This activity can make students feel very happy and elevated in spirits. It is an excellent ego builder and facilitates students' feeling good about themselves. Since friends and family do not exchange all of the many good things they see in each other, this activity makes it acceptable to ask for this information and to let it help students see themselves in very positive ways.

Remind students a couple of times to give out and collect the forms and when to bring them to class.

This activity should be reserved for when the students are well acquainted and accustomed to stating positive qualities they have.

EXERCISE 30.   **HOW STRONG I AM**[8]

Purposes:
    Affective—
        To have students assess their own strengths and share these
        To have students give each other positive feedback
    Linguistic—
        To practice the first person singular in the present tense
        To practice the second person singular in the present tense
        To practice the use of adjectives describing positive qualities

Levels: All levels

Size of groups: About six

Procedures: Introduce this awareness exercise as follows:

"We all have many strengths. Some of them we are aware of. Other people may see strengths in us that we do not realize we have.

"Take a piece of paper and write down the names of everyone in your group. Below the names, write two of the strengths you see in each one in your group. Then write your own name and list as many of your strengths as you can think of. You will have (length of time) five minutes to write down a number of your strengths and two strengths for each person in your group. You will be sharing what you write later."

After the class finishes this phase of the exercise, continue:

"You now will focus on one person at a time. The person will begin by telling all of the strengths he has written about himself and others he can think of. Then the others in the group will share what strengths they see in the focus person while the student to his right writes them down. When everyone is finished, give the list of strengths to the owner of them to keep."

When the activity is done, ask students to discuss in their small groups and/or the total group:

1. Did anyone say something that surprised you?
2. Which strength that someone else sees in you meant the most to you?
3. To what extent was your list of strengths similar to or different from the one others in your group find in you?
4. What reactions do you have to this activity?
5. What did you learn from this exercise?

Conclude the activity by discussing at least one or two of the above questions in the total group. This exercise should be used once the students are well enough acquainted to know a number of strengths of their fellow classmates.

NOTES

1. I learned of this exercise at a workshop given by Tete and Joan Tetens and Mike Gordon.

2. Elaine Goldman used this activity at a workshop in which I participated.

3. Variation 2 of this exercise is an adaptation of those usually referred to as Strength Bombardment. The originator of that technique is Herbert A. Otto.

4. I learned of this idea at a workshop conducted by Jerry Gillies.

5. The central theme for this exercise was developed from an idea of Keith Miller.

6. Activities in which everyone receives positive feedback are commonly used in humanistic classes and workshops at the close of a day or to end a session.

7. Herbert A. Otto developed the idea behind this strategy.

8. Thanks to Herbert A. Otto, the originator of the idea for this activity.

My Self-Image

I love myself when I am myself.

– Hugh Prather

The exercises in this section are closely related to those in the previous section on "My Strengths," which actually deals with building the self-image through acknowledging one's strengths.

The activities which follow focus on such things as appreciating one's physical appearance, age, uniqueness, successes, and growth. In these strategies, the positive things in life receive attention. By learning to take pride in oneself in such areas, the self-image is enhanced.

EXERCISE 31.   **ACCENTUATE THE POSITIVE**[1]

Purposes:
    Affective—
             To encourage students to think positively and to look for the good in
                their daily lives
    Linguistic—
             To practice the past tense
             To practice superlatives

Levels: Intermediate to advanced

Size of groups: About six

Procedures: This activity is to help students focus on the positive things that happen to them and that they do for others. The exercise can be introduced by saying something similar to the following:

"Many good things happen to us all the time. In addition, we do many good deeds for others, and others do many for us that make us feel happy. Sometimes what goes wrong in our lives, however, prevents us from noticing all the good as much as we could.

"Today we're going to share some of the good events in our lives with each other. First of all, think about the good things that happened to you last week. Then, in no more than three sentences, tell your group what was the most positive thing that happened to you last week."

Start off by telling the class the most positive thing that happened to you last week in three sentences.

By limiting each person to three sentences, no one person will dominate, and each person's positive experience will receive equal weight in the eyes of the group. After the small groups finish, ask to have a few volunteers share theirs before the whole class. This experience gives an opportunity for the class to get in touch with the happiness and good news of each other. Often students will react with "ohs" and "ahs" as these positive experiences are revealed.

In the second part of the exercise, ask students to tell something that they said or did last week that made someone feel good. This should be stated in no more than three sentences. You can assure the students that they should feel good about doing something to benefit others and not feel embarrassed about mentioning it. Here again ask for a few to be told to the entire class after the small groups finish. Be certain to share something *you* did that made someone feel good also.

End by asking students to tell one good thing that happened to them today in two or three sentences. This is to encourage the students to find something positive in the present, no matter how slight it may be.

Students can ask one another questions at the end of each round of responses if time permits.

Comments: Once all parts of this activity have been completed, ask the students to discuss what they learned about themselves as a result of this exercise. Comments usually are made about how easy it is to recall the negative things that happen to us. Some may say that we have to look for the good side of life more because it is there if we don't let the negative become too dominant. This is an effective exercise in helping students think positively about what happens to them and in guiding them along the lines of being optimistic. This exercise can be repeated at intervals to encourage developing a positive outlook.

EXERCISE 32. **SUCCESS STORY**[2]

Purposes:
> Affective—
>> To get students to think about the success experiences they have had in their lives
>> To give students the opportunity to share and appreciate their own success and that of others
> Linguistic—
>> To practice the past tense(s)
>> To practice the vocabulary of adjectives

Levels: Intermediate to advanced

Size of groups: About six

Materials needed: An object brought in by each student in keeping with the assignment

Procedures: Initiate the assignment by saying something similar to this:

"We all have had experiences in which we were successful. Sometimes we have been the winner in a situation in which there was competition, such as an athletic contest or a spelling bee. Other times we may have succeeded in doing something that is important only to us. For years a friend of mind kept his study extremely messy, much to his dismay. When he finally straightened it up, this was an accomplishment for him.

"I want you to think over the times you have been successful where it has meant a lot to you. Think of your earliest years and on up to the present. Write a list of fifteen occasions when you can recall meeting with success. Write some down for different ages.

"Then select one that is particularly important to you to share with the class. If you have anything to show us that is connected with that success experience, bring it to class. It may be an object, a snapshot taken at the time, or something you recall having with you or wearing then. In other words, see whether you have a souvenir of your success to bring to class to show. Bring your list of successes with you as well."

On the day of the activity, put the students into groups of six. One at a time, each student should tell his success story and show the evidence he may still have of that occasion. Divide the time up so that each student has about three minutes, two to tell his story and one for questions and comments by the group members. Give a signal, perhaps flicking the lights once, to let students know they should finish that person's turn in the next thirty seconds. Then announce that it is time for the next person's turn. Keeping track of the time this way allows the groups to finish together, and everyone receives equal time to be focused on. If some groups have an additional member, redistribute the division of time and go to those groups to let them know when to rotate.

When this phase of the activity is over, tell the students to share which categories the successes on their lists come under, that is, athletic events, achieving in school subjects, relationships with others, money. They also can tell each other in a few sentences about three other successes on their lists, each at a different age.

In the total group, the students can share with the class their most important success, doing so in one sentence. In this way, everyone will be heard, as the class will be curious to know what others had to say, and the time taken will be minimal. You can ask what reactions the students had to doing this exercise.

To summarize, you can mention that often we do not realize just how successful we are. We tend to give greater attention to what we think are our failures. However, by continually recognizing our personal achievements, we can build added confidence in ourselves and feel that we will continue to succeed more and more.

You may wish to have a follow-up activity in which the students write something based on their lists of successes. Or they can write in advance or after the activity their most important success story.

Comments: Encourage bringing in concrete things related to the success story to be shared, as these items will add greatly to the interest of the activity.

EXERCISE 33.   **AGELESS**

Purposes:
    Affective—
        To get students to think positively about their age
        To get students to think positively about being other ages
    Linguistic—
        To practice the present tense
        To practice the past tense(s)
        To practice the future tense

Levels: All levels

Size of groups: About six

Procedures: Introduce the topic of age:
    "Today we're going to discuss a topic which many people are dissatisfied with, but we're going to find the *good* side of it. The topic is age.
    "It seems when we are young we want to be older, and when we get older we wish we were younger. Often people are self-conscious about their age. When asked how old they are, they may add or subtract a few years or even joke about it to avoid answering the question.
    "The truth is we should be proud of our age and be happy to be whatever age we are at any point in our lives. The exercise we'll do today will help us along these lines.
    "I'm going to give you some questions to answer in your groups. After each person has a turn, we'll go on to the next question."
    Give the questions one at a time and after each round have some responses given before the total group:

    1. What do you like about being your present age?
    2. What did you like about being younger?
    3. What will you like about being five years older? Ten years older? Twenty years older?
    4. What will you like about being elderly?
    5. What do you think the ideal age is? Why?
    6. How can you make whatever age you are the ideal age to be?
    7. How can you help others who do not feel good about their age feel better?

You can end the activity by stating that at all ages of life there are countless things to look forward to. We have many aspects of ourselves to be proud of, and our age is one of them.

EXERCISE 34.   I LIKE YOU—YOU'RE DIFFERENT[3]

Purposes:
>   Affective—
>>   To encourage students to feel proud of their differences rather than feeling the need to be conformists
>>   To encourage an open attitude toward others and their differences
>   Linguistic—
>>   To practice the present tense
>>   To practice the present perfect
>>   To practice the past tense(s)

Levels: All levels

Size of groups: Total class

Materials needed: A card filled out and turned in by every student

Procedures: Before giving the assignment, introduce the activity as follows:

"Very often we feel it's important to be like other people, and we worry if we feel that we're different. At times it's fine to be like others, but it's also important to accept and be proud of our differences. There are many ways that we're like each other in this class, but there are also things about us that are not true of anyone else in this class.

"For tomorrow write down on a card three things you feel good about that make you different from everyone else in the class. That is, they are not true of anyone else here."

Give three examples from your own life to show what you mean. Be imaginative and humorous, if possible, to set the example for others to do so.

Tell the students to write their names on the cards turned in and not to tell anyone what they wrote. Announce that you will collect the cards and read them aloud, and that they will guess the identity of the people.

Before starting the activity the next time, reiterate the positive aspects of being different. Then read each card aloud, asking for guesses as to who each one is. Based on all the names guessed per card, have the class vote on whose card it is. Then announce who the correct person is. If the right person is not among those named, after the vote tell them this and have the guessing continue until the correct person is given. Include a card for yourself also, and don't make your differences so obvious that they will know it is you.

When all cards have been read and the identities guessed, ask questions to get the students to recall the information on them: "Who remembers something different about someone in the class?" The students then can make statements such as: "Barbara lived in Chile" or "Bob won an art contest."

After a number of these statements have been made, have the students ask questions of the class based on the cards:

"Who has climbed Mt. Everest?"
"Who is the oldest of seven children?"
"Who can eat more ice cream than anyone in the class?"

Ask the students how they felt about this activity and what they learned from doing it. You can conclude the discussion by summarizing:

"Sometimes we feel uneasy because we believe we're different. Other times we feel discouraged when we think there's not much that sets us off as being different from others. Often people are interested in us *because* of our differences. We've just learned a number of new and interesting things about those in our class that makes us want to know even more about them. It was fun sharing our differences, hearing others impressed by them, and now we probably can think of many more ways in which we are different and are proud of it."

For a follow-up activity, the students could write a list of positive ways they can think of now in which they are different from the rest of the class and include these in a composition.

EXERCISE 35.   I'M ATTRACTIVE, YOU'RE ATTRACTIVE[4]

Purposes:
  Affective—
    To give students the opportunity to verbalize before others something they like about themselves, since customarily we are supposed to keep this to ourselves
    To encourage students to really look at their peers and focus on seeing the beauty of others
  Linguistic—
    To give practice in using the expression "I like"
    To practice the vocabulary of parts of the body

Levels: All levels

Size of groups: Six to eight (so students get more feedback)

Procedures: Introduce the class to this activity by presenting some of these ideas:

"Often we do not tend to see ourselves as others do. We are particularly critical of our appearance and usually find many faults with it. We are very hard on ourselves. One reason we continue to feel this way is that people often keep the nice things they think about us to themselves and don't tell us." You can ask, "How many of you recall thinking some complimentary things about someone that you didn't tell the person?" Every hand, including yours, should go up in response to that question.

Then continue along these lines: "Today we're going to share some things we don't often share. We all like some things about our physical appearance and often want to change others. What I'd like you to do is to think of something about your physical appearance that you especially like—not your clothing, but your appearance. In a few minutes we will tell one another what that is." (Allow a moment for thinking.)

"You're also going to take a few minutes now to look at each member in your group, noticing one thing that you really like about the physical appearance of each person. When you decide what it is, write it down, including the person's name. It might be that you like one person's hair, another person's eyes, and someone else's slim waistline or smile, and so forth. As you make your list, don't forget to include yourself and what you like about your appearance. Since we're not accustomed to saying these things about ourselves and others, it might feel a little embarrassing at first, but that soon will pass when you see how nice it feels to hear these things said."

Give the class a few minutes to carry out these instructions. Then tell them that each group will focus on one person at a time. Everyone will tell that person what it is he particularly likes about the student's physical appearance. When the group finishes, the person who received the feedback will share what it is *he* likes about himself. (It is easier to do this last rather than first.)

Instruct the student to the right of the person receiving the feedback to write down in the target language what each individual is saying. After everyone has had a turn, then the papers are given to the individual who received the feedback to review and to keep.

In their small groups the students then can discuss what feelings they have as a result of the exercise. In the total group, comments then can be made on how this exercise felt to them. Ask a few specific questions to guide the discussion, such as "Did anyone say something that surprised you?" Based upon student comments, summarize the purposes of the exercise and the feelings related to it.

Comments: Here are some sample comments made by students who experienced this exercise:

"At first, I felt embarrassed, but by the end, I was pleased."

"I was surprised that two people admired my figure, especially since I don't think it's so good."

"It was interesting that most people liked my smile but no one has ever told me that before."

"I was able to pay close attention to what others looked like."

"Wow! Was it ever flattering!"

"This made me have some warm feelings for others in the group."

This is an exercise that students will not want to rush through. They may want more time than you believe it will take, since it is so highly involving and personally reinforcing.

There is a linguistic and an affective purpose for having the student to the right of the focus person write down what is said: (1) to practice writing the language, and (2) to give a record to the person of the positive things mentioned, since it will be difficult to recall all of it and the students will want to remember what was said.

EXERCISE 36. **IS THAT ME?**[5]

Purposes:

> Affective—
>> To have students receive positive comments about their physical appearance
>> To allow students to see how unduly hard on themselves people can be about their own physical appearance
>> To promote more positive thinking about one's physical appearance
>
> Linguistic—
>> To practice the vocabulary of parts of the body, principally the face
>> To practice using adjectives and the expressions "I like" and "I don't like "

Levels: All levels

Size of groups: Six to eight

Materials needed: A camera and enough colored film to take a picture of everyone in the class; if pictures are taken indoors, a flash attachment will be needed.

Procedures: Set up an expedient way to take a snapshot of everyone in the class. The pictures should be close-ups, so that the face of each student is what is photographed and it can be clearly seen. Find out whether photography is a hobby of any students in your class. If so, have such students take the pictures. If not, you can take them or have some students who say they usually take good pictures assist you or do it entirely.

You may wish to use a Polaroid camera. An advantage of a Polaroid is that you can see immediately whether you have taken a clear picture and, if not, can take another right away. A disadvantage is that it is often hard to get the correct time exposure for the proper coloring for Polaroid pictures. You can waste a lot of film retaking pictures, unless those taking them are experienced in using a Polaroid.

Inform the class that you are going to take a snapshot of everyone in the group. Arrange a time to carry out this activity, and decide whether to do it indoors or out. If a Polaroid camera is used, tell those taking the pictures to look at each shot as it is ready to see whether it is in focus and the person's eyes are open. Should this not be the case, the picture should be retaken. Another very important factor is that if a Polaroid is used, the pictures should *not* be shown to anyone before they are used in the exercise or the entire impact will be lost.

Divide the class into groups of six to eight. Select who is to be in the group ahead of time so that you have the snapshots of those in each group separated from the others. Each picture should have the person's name on the back and be placed face down in a pile. You can place the snapshots in an envelope also so they can be removed one at a time with the side with the name being face up.

Introduce the activity by saying something similar to this:

"When we see a picture of ourself, we usually have a strong reaction to it. Either we like or don't like the way we look in it. We now are going to see the pictures that were taken of us in class. This is what we will do:

"One picture will be pulled from the envelope so that only the name of the person can be seen. That person will receive the picture and will turn it over, look at it, and react out loud as to how he feels about it. He also can state whether he thinks it looks like him. Everyone else in the group will remain silent, observe the person's face as he first sees his picture, and listen to what is said. The picture then will be passed around the circle and one at a time each person will state his reaction to the snapshot and to the owner's comments. Whether or not you like the pictures of others that you comment on will not matter, for if you do not think the picture is a good one, you actually are saying, 'You look better to me than you do in the picture.' Someone pick a picture, hand it to the owner, and begin."

When this phase is done, discuss these questions in groups and with the total class:

"How many of you liked your snapshot?"
"How many found that others liked your snapshot better than you did?"
"What did you learn from this activity?"
"Do we accept our own physical appearance as much as we accept the physical appearance of others?"

Comments: Suspense and interest are inherent in this activity as each person waits to examine his own picture. The nonverbal and spontaneous reactions of each person as he first sees himself are especially fun to observe. Expect laughter and such comments as, "Oh, no!" Some students may learn that what they find objectionable in their picture is liked by others in their group.

EXERCISE 37. **SEE HOW I'VE GROWN**[6]

Purposes:
> Affective—
>> To have students assess their growth
>> To make students more conscious of how they have changed for the better
> Linguistic—
>> To practice the present and past tense(s)
>> To ask and answer questions

Levels: Intermediate to advanced

Size of groups: About four to five

Materials needed: The assignment completed by the class

Procedures: This activity should be used later in the school year after the class has participated in a number of humanistic exercises together. The students will be more likely to find ways they have changed by then, some of which will be because of the exercises experienced. The openness needed for this activity will be more developed by then as well.

Tell the students that we constantly try to improve ourselves so as to be fuller human beings. As we develop, we find ways to change to help our growth. Ask the students to think of a number of ways they have changed for the better. These can be ways they feel or behave in general or in specific situations.

Ask the students to write a number of ways they have changed, stating what they were like before, compared to now. Request that they be as specific as possible. Furnish a few examples related to yourself to clarify the assignment:

"I used to be concerned when my room wasn't neat. Now I'm more relaxed about it, and I put a few things away at a time."

"I used to feel that I had to wear clothes which looked very professional. Now I enjoy wearing clothes that are quite casual."

"I used to keep my feelings and my problems to myself more. Now I talk to people about what is bothering me."

"I used to feel that I had to work constantly. Now I take time out for leisure and recreation."

When the students bring in the assignment, put them into groups of four or five. You can provide the students with some appropriate structures for conversing about the ways in which they have grown. Here are a few suggestions for questions to guide their discussion:

1. What is one way you have changed?
2. What did you do before?
3. What do you do now?
4. What helped you to change in this way?
5. When did you make this change?
6. Is there any direction or pattern your changes seem to show?

The students in the group should ask one person some of these questions. After that person talks about one of the ways he has changed, the next person gets a turn while the others ask him questions. Continue in this fashion until everyone has had a number of turns. Then each student should try to answer the last question, finding a direction of growth that his changes suggest he is heading toward. This can be shared with the total class as a conclusion to the exercise.

To follow up the activity, the students can write about how they have changed and what has helped them to do so. They can add what insights they have gained about themselves from carrying out this exercise. As the members of the groups hear how the others have changed, they will recall other ways in which they themselves have grown. Ways they want to continue to grow and change can conclude the written composition.

EXERCISE 38.   **PRICELESS GIFTS**[7]

Purposes:
    Affective—
            To encourage introspective thinking about another member of the
                class
            To develop further closeness and sharing in the class
            To promote creativity, humor, and warmth
    Linguistic—
            To have students write a personal message which they wish to
                communicate to another member of the class

Levels: All levels

Size of groups: Total class

Procedures: This activity is most appropriate at the Christmas-Chanukah season or during the last week or day of school.

　　Place the name of every person in the class on a separate slip of paper and fold it. Be certain that no one's name is overlooked. Include your name as well. About two weeks before the date you will carry this out in class, have each student pick a slip with someone else's name on it. No one should have his own name. See that anyone who is absent that day receives a slip upon returning to class.

　　Instruct the students not to reveal whose name they picked. Tell them to make a gift which they will give to the person whose name they picked. The gift should fit the person and his particular personality and represent some things they know about the individual. They are not to buy a gift for the occasion but may spend up to a dollar if they need some materials or items to prepare the gift. Invite their originality.

　　Ask the students to wrap the present, put the person's name on it, write on a card a message which is appropriate for the person, and sign the card with their name. Tell the students to see you if they need some help in how to say what they want to on the card in the foreign language. Let the class know when the gifts are to be exchanged. Remind the class several times about the gifts, and ask them to write a reminder to themselves the day before so no one forgets to bring in the gift. If you have storage space which can be locked, have the students bring in the gifts several days in advance to avoid this and to prevent someone not receiving a gift because a person is absent the day of the exchange.

　　Have the gifts in a central place from which they are distributed. Each person should open his and read the message. Then have each individual, one at a time, read his message aloud and show his gift to the class. This activity can create a very warm, glowing, close feeling in the class and is a fitting way to end before winter or summer vacation. The activity is also fun.

EXERCISE 39.　　**FIRST AND LAST IMPRESSIONS**[8]

Purposes:
> Affective—
>> To provide positive feedback to class members
>> To illustrate how getting to know people based on a positive focus
>>> can enhance one's perceptions of others
> Linguistic—
>> To practice the past tense(s)
>> To practice the use of adjectives

Levels: Intermediate to advanced

Size of groups: About six to eight so that more feedback is received per person

Procedures: It would be helpful to have this activity follow another one and to keep the students in the same groups. Tell the class:

"We all know that first impressions count. We have had first impressions of everyone in this class. But we also have been able to get to know each other in our class a lot better than usually happens in school. So, many of our impressions may have changed from the first time we met. This may be true even if you have known some of the students for quite a while outside of our class.

"We are now going to find out how impressions of us have changed as the students in the class got to know us better. In your groups, focus on one person at a time. Each group member will tell that person how his first impressions have changed since they first met. After everyone speaks to one person, move on to another person in the group until everyone has had a turn to be the focus."

Comments: This exercise may concern the students at first as they might fear hearing negative things about themselves. If the class is cohesive and a warm spirit of oneness has developed in the group, the impressions of people, whether initially favorable or not, should be more positive now. Although the exercise feels somewhat threatening, it has proved to be very valuable and an eye opener to students. They often hear exceptionally favorable feedback about themselves that they otherwise would be unaware of.

You may wish to qualify the instructions in this way: "How have your present impressions grown more favorable than your first impressions of each other?" This would point out that everyone should present positive feedback, which is what the students seem to give anyway. By the end of the year, they are quite accustomed to dealing positively with each other. This activity should be presented at the close of the school year.

NOTES

1. Sharing positive events in one's life is frequently used in many humanistic programs and in Re-evaluation Counseling.

2. A number of group facilitators refer to the idea of success in their exercises. Herbert A. Otto was one of the originators of this type of exercise.

3. This exercise is an expansion of one I have heard of. Original author unknown.

4. Thanks to Harold Lyon, Jr., who originated the idea for this strategy.

5. This exercise is an adaptation of one developed by Elizabeth Flynn and John LaFaso.

6. The kernel idea for this exercise was experienced at a workshop. Origin unknown.

7. Many thanks to Daniel Malamud for the idea for this activity.

8. The basic idea behind this exercise was found in an unpublished mimeograph which contained no title or author.

Expressing My Feelings

Your feelings are your true strength.
Be in touch with them.

— Gertrude Moskowitz

In many societies, people are taught to keep their feelings to themselves. This becomes so much a part of such individuals that they find it difficult to express their feelings when they actually want to or when asked what they are. Constantly keeping our feelings to ourselves is inhibiting rather than freeing, for we continually experience numerous feelings at any given moment.

The main purpose of the exercises in this grouping is to put students in touch with their feelings and to express them verbally and nonverbally. Some of the activities invite the students to share positive feelings they have for others in the class, for even such good feelings as these are seldom expressed.

EXERCISE 40. **I'VE GOT A FEELING**[1]

Purposes:
    Affective—
        To point out how easily feelings can be changed for the better
        To help warm up and relax the group
    Linguistic—
        To practice speaking in the present tense
        To practice the vocabulary of feelings

Levels: All levels, but beginning classes could not carry this out in the target language as an opening activity at the start of the year

Size of groups: Total class

Procedures: This activity can be done to start off the first class held during the new school year. If not done then, it can be used during the first week of school. It can be used at any other time as well but is even more effective prior to students knowing each other, the teacher, or the way the class will be conducted.

It is helpful to have the class seated in a circle or in a way that everyone can see each other. If used to start a class when students are not yet acquainted, give the following instructions:

"At any given moment, we have a number of feelings going on in us. Think about how you're feeling right now, not hungry or tired, but emotions going on in you. Decide on the most important one for you right now and be frank. We then will go around the class, and as a way of introducing ourselves, we'll give our names and tell how we're feeling. It will sound like this: 'I'm Tina and I feel worried,' or 'I'm Hank and I feel excited.' Take a moment to think over your feelings now . . . (Pause) . . . Who will begin?" (If the students do not possess the vocabulary to express their feelings, you can give them each a selection of words from Appendix A on a dittoed handout to act as a guide.)

Include yourself in the exercise. You may wish to start it off and have it continue around the circle. Expect some timidity if this is the beginning of the year and the students do not know you or each other, especially if they have not yet experienced a variety of humanistic activities.

Follow this by a warm-up exercise, preferably in dyads, so that the students keep the same seating in a circle. Have them pair off with someone they do not know or know only slightly. Tell the students to get acquainted with each other. They can be told to share two things about themselves with their partners that they ordinarily wouldn't share this early in an acquaintanceship. (Refer to Exercise 22, "Someone I Just Met.") Then have everyone introduce his partner to the class and tell one positive feeling he now has about his partner. Or have the students pair off to get acquainted and introduce one another as is done in Exercise 23, "Images."

After the introductions are over, ask the students to take another turn and complete this statement: "I'm ____(name)____ and I feel _____ ." There should be a number of changes in the feelings in the second round. Whatever the feelings were the first time, they should be more positive the second time.

You can conclude by asking the class what seemed to cause the change in feelings. End by summarizing what was said and adding:

"In only fifteen minutes, many of us changed how we felt in this class. Most people feel better now. How we relate to others affects how we feel. When we share the positive thoughts we have about one another, it relaxes us and brings out good feelings.

"This is an example of how we will be bringing out the positive side of everyone in our class as we learn (name of the foreign language) this year. The purpose will be to help you feel better about yourself and your classmates, and it will make learning the language more fun, easier, and more relevant to you."

EXERCISE 41. **FEEL WHEEL**[2]

Purposes:
    Affective—
        To encourage students to begin to identify their feelings
        To demonstrate how our feelings can change by the kinds of interaction we have with others

Linguistic—
   To practice the vocabulary of feelings
   To practice "because" statements

Levels: All levels, but the beginning level will, of course, be more limited in what can be said in the target language in the exercise

Size of groups: About five or six

Materials needed: Dittos of a circle divided into four quadrants as shown in this sketch:

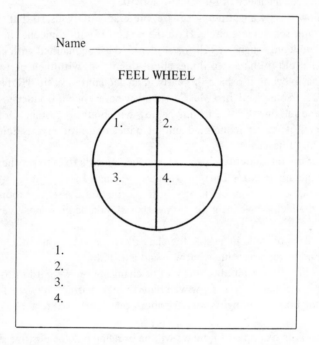

Each student will need two copies of the ditto.

Procedures: This activity is good to use when you want to demonstrate that feelings can change for the better through the humanistic exercises students have just experienced in your class. It can be used the first time your students participate in awareness activities. If you select some highly motivating and involving activities which foster some sharing and some fun, most students should find a change in their feelings from the beginning to the end of the class period.

   As students enter your classroom, instruct them to take two copies of the "Feel Wheel" handout. Tell them to write their names on each and to put a number one on one sheet and a two on the other. Before you say or do anything in your class, instruct the students to write down on Feel Wheel No. 1 four emotions they are feeling right now—one in each part of the circle. Mention not to include being hungry or thirsty or cold but actual emotions. Tell them to write below the Feel Wheel one sentence for each emotion, explaining why they are feeling each of these. Beginning classes may not be able to write the reasons they feel as they do in the target language. You can decide whether to skip that phase or whether to allow the native language to be used. When this is done, tell the class to put the paper aside till later.

Follow this by presenting several humanistic exercises for students to experience. Then ask the students to take Feel Wheel No. 2 and write in the spokes of the wheel four emotions they are now experiencing, with a sentence explaining why they feel each. If the students are in groups from the previous exercise, they can remain with the same group. Otherwise have them get into groups of five or six.

Tell the students to compare the feelings in Feel Wheel No. 1 and Feel Wheel No. 2 and to note any similarities and differences between them. Ask the students to share the feelings they recorded in the two Feel Wheels with the members of their group and to note whether there are any similarities in the group. After they have had the opportunity to do this, ask for a representative from some of the groups to tell the total class what commonalities were found in that group.

If the humanistic activities the students experienced were successful, most students should have much more satisfying emotions in the second Feel Wheel, even if those recorded were positive to begin with. Trusting that this will be the case, ask the students what caused them to feel better the second time. You may hear such things as: "We got to know each other better," "I learned some things about myself that I feel good about," "What we did was different from what we do in school," "We had fun."

Comments: This exercise can be used more than once with a class. If saving time is a concern, do not have the students write the reasons why they felt each emotion and/or have the discussion in groups of three at the end.

Expect some students to have difficulty figuring out how they are feeling. This exercise provides a good experience for students to start giving this some thought. Most people have a rather small vocabulary of words of emotion, even in their native language. The vocabulary of feeling words is provided in Appendix A to encourage clarifying, recognizing, and talking more explicitly about one's feelings.

EXERCISE 42. **WITHOUT WORDS WE SPEAK**[3]

Purposes:

Affective—

To get students acquainted through the use of nonverbal as well as verbal communication

Linguistic—
To converse using vocabulary about feelings and perceptions

Levels: Intermediate to advanced

Size of groups: Total class in one or more circles in dyadic belt formation

Procedures: Instruct the class to get into dyadic belt formation. If your class is large, two dyadic belts can be formed. This activity is best done when students do not know each other at all, to help get the group better acquainted. A number of different directions will be given to be carried out in pairs. After each direction is given and followed, the group will be instructed to move to another partner, as is done in the dyadic belt formation (see page 78), for the next direction.

Below are examples of directions to be given for each set of partners. Each number indicates that it is a new round with a new partner in the dyadic belt. The students should be told that they will get acquainted with one another in some ways that are a little different from the ways they usually meet classmates. Mention that they will enjoy the experience. If there is an uneven number in the class, join the circle yourself.

1. Look at your partner and *without talking,* see if you can get a feeling for what the person is like. Do not think about yourself now, but focus on the other person. (Remind the students to remain quiet and not talk at this time. Allow about 30–45 seconds to pass before the next direction.) Now share something positive you felt about this person. (Allow about a minute for this exchange.)

2. Move on to the next person. Repeat the same two phases, looking at the person to get a feeling of what he/she is like and sharing something positive you felt related to this student.

3. Move on to the next person and share how you are feeling right now.

4. Move on to the next partner, and this time try to get the feeling of what the person is like in a different way. Take the hands of this person, and without talking, see if this helps you to get a feeling of what the person is like. (Let 30–45 seconds pass.) Tell this person what positive feelings you have about him/her.

5. Repeat this with the fifth partner.

6. Tell person number six how you're feeling right now.

7. Look at your next partner and without speaking, think about what it takes to make that person happy. (Allow 30–45 seconds.) Now share what you thought.

8. Give person number eight a nonverbal message to show something that is fun for you. Then guess what your partner was trying to tell you.

9. Give your next partner a nonverbal message to show how you're feeling right now.

You can have additional activities if you want the students to make more contacts with others in the class. End by asking students to tell the total class what were some of the things they experienced during this exercise.

Comments: This exercise can be quite lively. Try to keep the students from talking when they are supposed to be silent so as to focus on the feelings they are to get in touch with. Expect to have to coax the students to move on to the next partner on occasions. This will take the form of your asking them to move on several times before they actually part.

EXERCISE 43.   **SAY IT WITH YOUR HANDS⁴**

Purposes:
Affective—
To explore how feelings can be communicated nonverbally
For fun
Linguistic—
To practice the vocabulary of feelings

Levels: All levels

Size of groups: Dyads

Procedures: This activity can be used at any time, but it is good as a warm-up when the class is just getting acquainted. It also can be useful as a light exercise dealing with feelings.

Tell the students that we show our feelings in different ways. Our eyes, the expressions on our faces, our posture, our gestures all reveal how we feel.

Ask the students to close their eyes as they are going to try to express some feelings by means of their hands. Each student should have a partner. As you mention a particular feeling, each person will take the hands of his partner in a way that communicates that feeling. Request that there be no talking and that they keep their eyes closed.

Then one at a time tell the students to express a number of contrasting feelings to each other by means of their hands. Here are some suggestions:

timidity	anger
dominance	playfulness
friendliness	tenderness

Then have the students open their eyes and discuss with their partners:

1. Which feeling was the easiest to communicate and why?
2. Which feeling was the hardest to communicate and why?
3. How did it feel to communicate this way?
4. Think of two other feelings and close your eyes again to communicate them.
5. Think of two more feelings and communicate these with your eyes open. Were there any differences between expressing your feelings with your eyes open and closed?

If you wish to continue the exercise, ask the students to suggest some feelings to do. You also can ask which of the feelings the class as a whole found the easiest and the hardest to express and why.

EXERCISE 44.   **TALKING PICTURES**[5]

Purposes:
> Affective—
>> To help students identify with the feelings of others
>> To encourage empathy for others
>> To stimulate the imagination
> Linguistic—
>> To motivate students to write something original

Levels: All levels

Size of groups: About five

Materials needed: Enticing pictures which bring out feelings in the viewer. The pictures should have some story inherent in them, but the story should not be an obvious one so that students will interpret the pictures in a variety of ways. The pictures should be large. Dittoed handouts with guiding questions should be distributed.

Procedures: Either ask students to collect and bring in as many pictures as they can find that bring out a good deal of feeling when one looks at them or, if you have a good collection of such pictures, use yours.

Divide the students into groups. Have them select one of the pictures that was brought in by their group that they all like, one that seems to have an emotional, but not obvious, story to it. Ask the students to place the picture where each one in the group can see it.

Ask them to focus on one person in the picture and notice everything they can about this person: clothes, gestures, facial expressions, colors. Tell them to imagine that they are that person. They can all agree to be the same person or not.

Direct the students to write as though they were the person in the picture. Give them each some questions on a dittoed handout to guide their thinking. A series of eight to ten open-ended questions, such as those listed below, can be used for each person to complete and compare.

> One thing I really want is . . .
> Sometimes I wonder . . .
> I wish that . . .
> A person who means a lot to me is . . .
> I feel proud when . . .
> I get angry when . . .

The questions should be geared to the level of the students and can make use of particular structures.

The groups discuss what kinds of feelings the picture brings out in them. They can write a story related to the picture through the eyes of one of the people in it and share the story with the total class.

When everyone is finished, each group's picture is placed where all can see it and a sample story or set of incomplete sentences about each one is then read for all to hear.

EXERCISE 45.   **NAMES PEOPLE PLAY**[6]

Purposes:
    Affective—
        To enable students to develop greater sensitivity into a rarely discussed
            area that all of us experience as we interact each day of our lives
    Linguistic—
        To practice the vocabulary of feelings and structures related to giving
            one's name, for example, "My name is . . . " and "I used to be
            called . . . "

Levels: Intermediate to advanced

Size of groups: Three to six, depending on the amount of time available

Procedures: Inform the students that they are going to discuss a topic about which they probably have many feelings. You could introduce the topic in this way:

"All of us were given a first name when we were born. We had no choice in this name. Yet this name represents us, stands for us, identifies us. When people say this name, we respond to it.

"Think of your first name and any nicknames you ever have been called. Discuss in your group how you feel about your first name and any nicknames you have been given during your life."

Start out by sharing your feelings about your own first name and any nicknames that you were given at any time. After the small groups have discussed the topic, ask for a few volunteers to share their feelings about their given names and nicknames before the total class.

In the second phase of this activity, tell the students to imagine that they can select any first name they want for themselves, but they *cannot* keep their present name. Ask them to decide what they would call themselves and why. Let the class know what name you would select and why, to start off the activity. Have a few shared before the total class once the small groups finish their exchange. Conclude by asking what they learned about themselves or others regarding names and nicknames.

Comments: Students find this a personally interesting topic to discuss. If they are sufficiently able to express themselves in the target language, they may wish to spend more time discussing this topic than you project it will take. If you wish to shorten the time spent on the activity, keep the groups smaller. You can ask students to write about this topic before it is discussed to help prepare them for their participation. As a follow-up activity, students can be asked to write what they learned about themselves and others related to the names people are called.

EXERCISE 46.   **SENSE APPEAL**

Purposes:
> Affective—
>> To become more conscious of appealing elements in the environment
>> To take note of what is pleasing to one's senses and to share that pleasure
> Linguistic—
>> To practice the verbs hear, see, taste, smell, feel, and touch, which relate to the five senses
>> To practice the vocabulary of feelings and nouns

Levels: All levels, with vocabulary help for the beginning level

Size of groups: About five

Materials needed: Completion of the assignment by students who will bring in a variety of objects

Procedures: Build up to the assignment first:
"There are many things in the environment that are very pleasing to us. Sometimes we are not consciously aware of what these elements are. In some way

they appeal to at least one of our senses. (You can ask the students what the five senses are.)

"We are going to explore our senses and think about the many things that please each of them. At home tonight write a list of things that please your senses. Make a column for each of the senses and below it write as many things as you can think of which you especially appreciate with that sense. On my list under 'smell' I would have such things as lilacs, fresh grass, cologne, gasoline. Make your lists as long as possible.

"Then for each of the senses, select something that you especially like that you can actually bring to class. Bring the five items to class in a bag so that no one can see them. For the item to be tasted, you may have to supply some eating or drinking utensils.

"You will be put into groups of five to share some of the favorite elements that appeal to your senses. Except for the one which you like to see, you will close your eyes when the items are presented to your group in order to try to guess what they are. If eating utensils are needed for your 'taste' item, prepare to serve four people. We will be discussing how each of the items you bring in makes you feel, also."

When the assignment is due, have the students in the groups take turns with one sense at a time. If "smell" is the first sense to be worked with, one at a time a student gives the others in the group the opportunity to smell the item he brought in. After the students have smelled the item with their eyes closed, they will guess what it was by saying, "I smell _____" (or the past or present progressive tenses can be used). After each person has taken a guess, the one who brought it in will say what it is and how it makes him feel or what mood it puts him in. For example: "That smell is a peony." The group will then ask, "How does the smell of a peony make you feel?" The person who brought in the item will reply, "When I smell a peony, I feel heavenly" or "I feel alive and exstatic when I smell a peony."

When everyone has had a turn in the groups to sample all of the items brought in, have them talk about the other things on their lists that were not brought in. Are there things mentioned by others that pleased them too that they didn't think of? Did some people have identical items on their lists?

In the total group ask:

"Was it difficult to focus on your senses?"
"How can we develop and appreciate our senses more?"
"Which sense did you enjoy using the most?"

As a closing activity, form a dyadic belt. Those on the inside circle should hold the items they brought in to be smelled and touched. Those on the outside circle are to keep their eyes closed. The inner circle group rotates around the circle and presents the objects brought in for smelling and touching to each member of the outside circle. The latter will smell and touch the items and guess what they are.

As a follow-up activity, the students can write how they felt about the experiences they just had in class. They can also write of the different things which appeal to their various senses.

EXERCISE 47. **FEELING MIME**

Purposes:
  Affective—
      To assess how one is presently feeling
      To draw attention to how others feel by comparison
      For fun
  Linguistic—
      To practice the vocabulary of feelings
      To practice asking and answering questions and responding in the
        negative
      To practice the first, second, and third persons singular in the present
        and past tenses
      To practice the subjunctive mood, if so desired

Levels: All levels

Size of groups: Eight to twelve or can be done as a total class if there are no more than twenty in the group

Procedures: The students are seated in a circle so everyone in the group can see each other. One student starts by turning to the person to his right and asking, "How do you feel right now?" This person responds by nonverbally acting out the emotion he presently feels. The others in the group try to guess by asking appropriate questions: "Do you feel anxious?" "Do you feel angry?" "Do you feel excited?" The focus person responds in the negative, "No, I don't feel anxious," etc., until someone in the group guesses correctly. He then responds with the emotion he feels and acts it out again while saying it: "I feel excited right now."

The student to the left of the one who initially asked "How do you feel right now?" says the following to the person on his right as he acts it out: "Jim feels excited right now. How do you feel right now, Dolores?" The pattern continues in this way with each person summarizing and acting out how everyone who has responded so far feels: "Jim feels excited" (acts it out), "Dolores feels silly" (acts it out), "Tim feels relaxed," (acts it out), etc. As the students take turns, the procedure is as follows: B asks A the question. Then C asks B, and D asks C, and so forth.

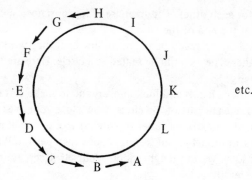

etc.

This means that the later a student takes his turn, the more feelings he will act out and accredit to the owners of them. As the number of students whose feelings are to be remembered gets longer, the exercise becomes more humorous. The way different students imitate the feelings also adds enjoyment to the activity.

Other tenses can be practiced in this exercise as well. For example, after everyone has had a turn, the teacher and/or students in each group can ask, "How did Chuck say he felt?" A member of the group would respond, "Chuck said that he felt worried." An alternate type of question that could be asked is: "Jan, how did you say Chuck felt?" Jan would reply, "I said that Chuck felt worried." Whenever the given emotion is mentioned, it must be acted out in pantomime as it was by the person who originally demonstrated the feeling.

EXERCISE 48.   **MEDITATION ON US**

Purposes:
> Affective—
>> To help build close ties among students in a conscious way
>> To encourage students to think positively about themselves and
>>> others in the class
> Linguistic—
>> To practice the vocabulary of feelings

Levels: All levels

Size of groups: About six

Procedures: This activity is intended to be used as a closure after students have worked with these exercises quite a while and feel close to each other. It is especially effective after a more serious activity in which students share personally meaningful memories or feelings or in which students have expressed very positive feelings they have for each other. This exercise is appropriate as a closing activity before vacation or at the end of the year.

The students should already be in groups in which they worked on one or two exercises together. They should be seated in a circle. Here are the instructions to give for this activity:

"Take each other's hands and look at everyone to make certain that you know who is sitting in each part of the circle. Now close your eyes and don't talk. With your eyes closed, think of each person in your group, one at a time, and experience some warm thoughts and feelings about each person. When you have done this, think of some warm thoughts about yourself. Keep your eyes closed until I tell you to open them."

Be certain that no one talks. If anyone does, in a whisper quietly say, "No talking."

To allow enough time, verbalize to yourself this experience with the members of a given group or, better yet, join a group. When students have had enough time to complete the activity, in a calm, soft voice, give this set of instructions:

"With your eyes closed, think of how you felt doing this exercise and how you are feeling right now. (Allow a minute to pass.) Now open your eyes and share these feelings."

After about three or four minutes, ask to have a few students share their feelings before the total group.

EXERCISE 49.   **I ENJOYED, I ENJOYED**[7]

Purposes:
>   Affective—
>>   To give students the opportunity to express warm thoughts and feelings
>>   To bring out positive thoughts which might not otherwise get expressed
>   Linguistic—
>>   To practice the past tense(s)
>>   To practice the first and third person singular

Levels: All levels

Size of groups: Total class

Procedures: This exercise is intended as a closing activity after the students know each other well and after they have experienced awareness activities for quite a while. It is fitting before a holiday vacation or during the last week or the last day that school is in session.

If possible, have the class seated in a circle so everyone can be seen by all. An alternative is to have the students stand in a circle and hold hands. Here is a way to introduce the activity:

"There are many good feelings and thoughts that we have, but they don't necessarily get expressed. We are now going to have the chance to share these with the class.

"The question I'd like you to answer is, 'Did anyone in our class say or do something that you especially liked, enjoyed, or appreciated during our (name of the target language) class?' Take a moment to think about it and then we'll each have a turn to tell the class who the person is and what it was that we enjoyed or appreciated."

Be certain to participate in this activity yourself. This exercise is conducive to bringing out glowing feelings and even some laughter.

EXERCISE 50. **THE LAST GOOD-BYE**[8]

Purposes:
> Affective—
>> To encourage students to exchange positive thoughts and feelings as yet unexpressed
>> To provide warmth at a time when good feelings mixed with some sadness may be felt by students
> Linguistic—
>> To practice the first person singular
>> To practice the second person singular
>> To practice the vocabulary of feelings and adjectives describing positive qualities

Levels: All levels

Size of groups: Total class

Procedures: This exercise is intended for the last class meeting of the year. It is a sentimental one and can be used as the last activity of the last day of class.

The students should be standing up in a circle and holding hands. Ask them to do the following:

"Close your eyes. Picture that our (name of the foreign language) class has ended for the year. The last time we are meeting is over with now. The bell has just rung, signaling you to leave the class. You pick up your belongings and leave the classroom. You walk down the hall farther and farther away from our class. It is time for you to leave the school building and go home.

"As you open the door and go outside, you begin to feel incomplete. As you continue on your way home, you realize that there are certain things you regret not having said to people in the class. There are some good feelings and thoughts you have not had the chance to express. What would you like to say to some of your classmates? . . . (Pause) . . . Open your eyes now and here is your opportunity. Say the things you'd really like to say now to as many people as you can."

The students will walk around talking to each other, and the class ends as a party does when everyone is saying good-bye. You should circulate to as many different people in the class as you can also. This ending to the class provides an informal air and it will feel less like school and more like a group of people you are close to and now have to leave.

NOTES

1. The idea of introducing yourself by stating your feelings is an activity used by many group facilitators. The original author is unknown. This technique is an embellishment of that idea.

2. Also known as the "Here-and-Now Wheel," this technique is quite a popular one. I was initially introduced to the Feel Wheel at a workshop. Original author unknown.

3. I was introduced to this activity by Elaine Goldman.

4. I first learned of this exercise from Ilana Rubenfeld.

5. This activity is an expansion of one I learned from the work of Robert and Isabel Hawley.

6. The germ of the idea for this activity came from a conversation with Don Miller many years ago.

7. I learned of this technique from Daniel Malamud.

8. I encountered the kernel idea for this strategy in a collection edited by J. William Pfeiffer and John E. Jones (*A Handbook of Structured Experiences for Human Relations Training.* La Jolla, Calif.: University Associates [1973]).

My Memories

Memories light the corners of my mind.
Misty water-color memories of the way we were.

— Alan and Marilyn Bergman

Although some of the other exercises encourage students to share events from the past, those in "My Memories" tend to be lighter in nature. They are therefore conducive to being used earlier in the year when the students are getting acquainted. In these activities the students are generally asked to recall pleasant, humorous, or favorite memories of theirs as a means of getting to know what classmates were like in the past.

EXERCISE 51.   **NAME GAME**[1]

Purposes:
        Affective—
                To note the significance people's names have for others
                To facilitate learning the names of members of the class
        Linguistic—
                To practice "because" statements
                To practice expressions in giving names of people

Levels: Intermediate to advanced; the beginning level would have to carry out the activity in the native language since this exercise is intended for the first or second lesson of the school year.

Size of groups: Five to six

Procedures: This activity would come after one or more exercises in which the names of students were used. This could take the form of exercises in which introductions were given or where name-tags have been worn (see Exercise 1, "Colorful Names"; Exercise 23, "Images"; Exercise 40, "I've Got a Feeling," etc.). If the students are wearing name-tags, at this point ask them to remove them temporarily and put them face down.

Next tell the students to write down as many first names as they can remember of people they did not know before. Allow a couple of minutes for this. Then tell the students to notice the first three names they wrote down.

Now ask the students to think about those three names and whether they have special significance to them. Do they identify with those names in some way? Why did they recall those names first?

The class members are divided into groups of five or six to share the significance of the first three names on their lists. Each group then can report to the total class some of the reasons the first three names were recalled.

A discussion can follow along these lines:

1. How well do you usually remember people's names?
2. What kinds of feelings and associations tend to help us remember names?

If the students are beginners, this lesson can be used to introduce an elementary lesson in telling one's own name and that of other class members.

EXERCISE 52.   **HAIR! HAIR!**[2]

Purposes:
    Affective—
        To become aware of the emotions students have had through the
            years about a part of their appearance often considered very
            important to them
        To share interesting, humorous, and touching personal stories on a
            somewhat unusual topic
    Linguistic—
        To practice writing and speaking in the past tense(s)
        To practice the vocabulary of colors and length of hair

Levels: All levels, with sample structures given for the beginning level to complete

Size of groups: About four

Materials needed: Each student will have to complete the written assignment to be given and bring it to class.

Procedures: Here is a suggested way to introduce the assignment to the class:

"For our next activity, we're going to write and talk about a topic that most of us have a lot of feelings about. There are probably many stories we each have concerning this topic, yet it is very unusual to think about and discuss in class. The topic deals with what feelings, emotions, and memories we have related to our hair. Just how important is our hair to us?

"We've all heard that a woman's hair is her crowning glory. Throughout history it has been a sacrifice for a woman to have to cut and sell her hair.

"Samson lost his power when Delilah cut his hair. In the military service, new recruits get their heads shaved for cleanliness but also to give them a feeling of being subservient—to give them a poorer image of themselves. In recent years some parents and adults have objected to long hair on males.

"Often our hair influences how we feel or how we think we look. It can affect our personality. We complain that our hair is a mess, or that we can't do anything with it. And how angry we are at the barber or beautician who cuts our hair too short or not the way we wanted it.

"So for all of us there are probably times when we have had different feelings about our hair and some stories of what happened to us."

You can then tell some story connected with your hair. Here is an example: "When I was growing up my hair was very fine. My mother couldn't manage it so she kept it very short. I wanted to have long hair very badly, but her instructions to the barber were: 'Cut it so the tips of her ears are showing.' How I hated that! When I became old enough to take care of my own hair, I kept it very long, and I still do. Twice a year the beautician gets a treat and takes an inch off. And my own daughters always had long hair and they still keep it long."

Then continue: "Think about all the memories you have of your hair and write (give the length of the assignment) about a page on the stories, past and present, and the feelings you had about your hair. We will be reading them to each other in groups and discussing them. Start in the past and go up to the present in your stories. Bring in any snapshots you have showing your hair at the times you are telling us about."

The day the assignment is due, divide the students into groups and have them read their stories to the group and show the pictures of themselves they brought in. As the stories are read, the group members can ask questions or make comments.

When each person has had a turn, have the group discuss these questions and then process them before the total class:

What does your story say about the meaning your hair has to you?
What did your group discover about how others feel about their hair?

Answer these questions yourself before the total class.

You can correct the compositions before they are read in the groups rather than afterwards, if you prefer.

EXERCISE 53.   **CHILDHOOD FAVORITES**

Purposes:

Affective—

　　　To recall pleasant childhood memories
　　　To exchange these memories with others

Linguistic—
    To practice nouns and possessive adjectives
    To practice asking and answering questions
    To practice the past tense(s)

Levels: All levels

Size of groups: Triads

Materials needed: Dittos with questions to be asked and answered

Procedures: Begin the activity by talking about childhood memories:

"We all have a number of childhood memories that made us happy in some way. As we get older, we tend not to think about them very much. Yet to do so helps us relive the good feelings we had at the time.

"Today we're going to recall some of our favorite things from childhood. You each will have a handout listing some categories. In your groups take one category at a time. The first person will ask the second person a question, such as 'What was your favorite candy?' After the second person answers, he asks the third person the same question. The third person then will ask the question of the first person. It now will be time to start a new round of questions. You do not have to go in the same order for each round.

"In some cases, your answers will be brief. For other questions, they will be longer. You can ask one another additional questions or add comments, if you wish. You will find as each person answers that other memories will come back to you. When you finish all of the questions on the handout, add some of your own categories to the list and take some extra turns using them."

Pass out the dittos. Here are some possible categories that can be used:

WHEN YOU WERE A CHILD, WHAT (OR WHO) WAS YOUR FAVORITE:

1. Toy?
2. Candy?
3. Food?
4. Play activity?
5. Book or story?
6. Place to go?
7. Song?
8. Outfit?
9. TV program? Radio program?
10. Hobby?
11. Friend? Why?
12. Grownup (other than family)? Why?
13. Teacher? Why?

14. Relative (not a parent or guardian)? Why?
15. Memory of snow?
16. Memory at a beach or pool?
17. Thing to do that was scary?
18. Birthday? Why?
19. Comic strip?
20. Ride at the amusement park?

When the exercise is completed, ask the students what their reactions to this experience were and what they learned from it. Ask what other categories the groups thought of. The groups may wish to have a few more rounds based on the categories their classmates thought of.

EXERCISE 54.   **FAMILY ALBUM**

Purposes:
    Affective—
        To share a type of remembrance that is not customarily done in school
        To permit classmates to see some of the important others in the lives of their peers
    Linguistic—
        To practice description in the past
        To practice the vocabulary of members of the family, giving the age of people, feelings, and adjectives describing positive qualities

Levels: All levels

Size of groups: Six to eight

Materials needed: A picture of each student in the class as a young child

Procedures: Ask each student to bring in a snapshot of himself as a child. Tell them that other members of the family also should be in the picture and that they should have a pleasant feeling or memory connected with the snapshot. Instruct the students to bring the snapshot in an envelope and *not* to show the picture to anyone in the class. There will be a natural tendency for students to want to see each other's pictures, and you may have to announce this again the day the pictures are brought in. The suspense and interest will be lessened if students see each other's snapshots before the exercise is carried out.

Divide the class into groups of six to eight. You can introduce the activity in this way:

"It's fun and fascinating to look at pictures from the past of ourselves and our families. Usually we don't share this pleasure with our friends or acquaintances.

Perhaps we never realized this would be interesting, just as we like to look at each other's picture in the school yearbook.

"Today we're going to share some of our past with each other through the snapshots you have brought in. One at a time open an envelope and pass one picture around your group. Each person will take a quick look at the picture. While the snapshot is being passed around, the person whose picture it is will tell us about it and why it is so special. As the snapshot gets passed around a second time, each person will comment on his reactions to the picture and what things he notices or feels. A good statement to use is 'You look like you were . . . ' Questions can also be asked about the snapshot."

As the groups finish, have them discuss how they felt about seeing the pictures of others and how it felt to have others respond to theirs. If time permits, you can have the students in each group count off to form new groups and continue in the same way, or they can walk around the class and ask to see each other's snapshots and ask questions about them.

Variations: The pictures can be passed around in the small groups one at a time while each student guesses whose picture it is. Then the pictures are shown a second time as the owner claims his picture and tells about it and the group comments on it. If you have the students guess the identity of the person in the snapshot, see that the males and females are fairly evenly distributed among all groups.

Comments: This activity enables students to see their classmates in a somewhat different light. They also get a look at some family members who helped influence the lives of their peers.

In a few instances, a student will not have access to pictures from his childhood. Such circumstances can arise if a person evacuated his country during a crisis or if there was a fire in one's home, or if one's parents have all the baby pictures and the parents live out of town. In such cases, request that a picture be brought in from some past time, even if it is not during early childhood; that is, whatever pictures the person has access to. The snapshot still should have a pleasant memory and be with at least one or more members of the family, if possible.

More structure can be provided for beginning levels in talking about their pictures by suggesting sentences to complete:

> This is me. I was _____ years old. That is my (brother). He was _____ years old.
> I had (curly, blonde) hair.
> This picture was taken (at the beach).
> I was wearing (a green bathing suit).
> I like this picture because (we had so much fun swimming together).

EXERCISE 55.   **FUNNIEST THING**[3]

Purposes:
    Affective—
        To give importance to the role of humor in our lives
        To encourage students to look at the humor in their lives
    Linguistic—
        To write a personal episode so it will communicate effectively to
            others in the class

Levels: Advanced

Size of groups: Five to six

Procedures: As an assignment, ask students to think about the many humorous things which have happened to them through the years and to write about one that they think was among the funniest. Tell them to try to communicate it so that others will appreciate the humor of the situation. Collect, correct, and return the papers.

    Divide the students into groups and have each read his episode to the others. The group members should be encouraged to ask questions and to comment on the stories.

    Ask the class to recommend stories for the total group to hear. During the processing, ask the students such questions as: "Did the humorous situations in any of the stories have anything in common?" "Did any of the stories have humor in a situation which otherwise would have been unpleasant?"

    This exercise can be preceded or followed by studying the humor of the target culture.

EXERCISE 56.   **FUN IS . . .**[4]

Purposes:
    Affective—
        To assess what one considers to be fun or enjoyable
        To determine to what extent fun is an active part of our lives
    Linguistic—
        To practice using the gerund

Levels: All levels

Size of groups: About four to five

Procedures: Bring up the topic of "fun" to the class by making some related comments about it:

"Everyone likes to have fun and to enjoy himself. There are some things that many people consider fun, such as going to the circus. That's what makes such events popular. There are also things that some of us enjoy which others do not. Some people find a game of chess very exciting, while others find it dull.

"Do we have enough fun in our lives? Can we have more fun than we do now? To find out, we are all going to complete a very simple statement with as many endings as we can think of. The statement is: 'Fun is _____.' Make a list of all the things you like to participate in or have happen that are fun for you. The longer your list is, the better. Your statements will sound like this:

Fun is . . .
1. going ice skating.
2. eating a hot fudge marshmallow sundae.
3. riding in a convertible with the top down.
4. lying in the sun when the wind blows gently.
5. being with my best friend.
6. dancing to the music of my favorite group.

On Friday bring in your list of what fun is for you. Number each item so we will know how many are on your list. Put a star in front of those you find the most fun."

When the assignment is due, place students into groups of four to five. Have the students in each group take one turn at a time stating something they consider fun. Continue for a number of rounds until everyone's list is given. Ask the students to state the things they consider the most fun at the end of their lists but to mention when they reach these. Those who have more on their lists may end up giving several by themselves if the others run out of items. Tell the students that they can add to their lists anything a classmate mentions as fun that is not on their lists but that they want to include.

When the groups finish this phase of the exercise, they should check:

1. Which activities have you engaged in *recently*? (Mark these with an "R" or the letter of the equivalent word in the target language.)

2. Which activities do you engage in *frequently*? (Mark these with an "F" or the letter of the equivalent word in the target language.)

3. Which activities do you engage in only *occasionally*? (Mark these with an "O" or the letter of the equivalent word in the target language.)

4. With what frequency do you engage in the activities you have starred as the most fun for you?

Ask the students to discuss what they discovered about themselves from this exercise. Tell them to make some resolutions for the future regarding having fun.

In the total group, have each student share the activity or situation that he considers to be the most fun. A discussion with the whole class can also follow on what students learned about themselves from this exercise. Some of the resolutions made can be shared.

As a follow-up activity, the students can submit their extended lists of what they consider to be fun with the frequency that the activities are engaged in. They can write what they learned from this exercise and what resolutions they have made for the future. As an alternative or in addition to this assignment, have the students write about one or more of the activities which they enjoy, describing occasions and events in their lives connected with those in which they had a great deal of fun.

EXERCISE 57.   **SURPRISE!**

Purposes:
> Affective—
>> To recall pleasant or humorous events in one's life
>> To share the pleasure of these events with others
> Linguistic—
>> To practice the past tense(s), as well as the past progressive and the past perfect

Levels: Intermediate to advanced

Size of groups: About six

Materials needed: Completion of the assignment by the class

Procedures: Talk to the class about the element of surprise. Perhaps in the materials you use with the class, the topic of a surprise may come up to initiate this activity. You can mention how authors try to surprise readers in their novels, stories, and plays. Television shows try to create interest through the unexpected happening.

Ask the students to think over the surprising events of their lives and to decide what has been the biggest surprise of them all. This can be a single event which surprised them or a direction in life they have taken which they never would have expected.

Give the class a few examples of surprises from your own life:

"I had an important planning meeting to attend for a big project I was involved in. The meeting was at a colleague's house. After I was there a while, suddenly a number of people came marching out of the kitchen singing 'Happy Birthday to You.' I didn't connect it with myself as my birthday was several days away. I could hardly believe that this important meeting was actually to celebrate my birthday.

"When I was graduated from college, one of my major professors tried to talk me into continuing for a master's degree. My internal reaction was, 'What would I want *that* for?' Some years later one of my friends who had a master's degree told me that her greatest ambition was to earn a doctorate. Again I thought to myself, 'What would she want *that* for?' That I went back to college to get a master's degree and a doctorate is one of the greatest surprises of my life, since at one time these degrees held absolutely no appeal for me."

The students will need some time to think before responding to this question of the greatest surprise of their lives. It is therefore probably better to give this as a written assignment in advance of the discussion.

When the students carry out the activity, divide them into groups of six to tell the surprising events of their lives. The others in the group can ask questions and comment as each person relates his story. Have the groups select the most unusual or humorous ones for the entire class to hear. As the students hear each other's stories, additional surprises in their lives may be recalled.

NOTES

1. This exercise is adapted from one by Daniel Malamud.

2. The kernel idea for this technique comes from a suggestion for an exercise made by Larry Chase.

3. The idea for this technique comes from Herbert A. Otto.

4. Although I originated this activity, I am aware that I was influenced in the design of the exercise by the work of Sidney B. Simon, Leland W. Howe, and Howard Kirschenbaum.

Sharing Myself

To really care
Means to dare
To share.

— Harvey Jackins

In a sense almost all the exercises in this book call upon the students to share things about themselves—their feelings, values, insights, memories, strengths, fantasies, etc. However, the exercises in this grouping generally promote the students' sharing many things at once about themselves.

    The students are called on to reflect more deeply about themselves and to come up with some insights they may never have thought of before. The type of sharing in these exercises is known as "self-disclosure." For the most part, this kind of sharing is more intimate and creates a bond of closeness among classmates. The aim is to have students know one another far beyond a superficial level. This is the kind of sharing that leads to caring.

EXERCISE 58.   **WHO'S WHO?**[1]

Purposes:
    Affective—
        To get students to truly notice each other, to observe and really "see"
            the members of the class
        To enable every student to receive the attention of the class
        To encourage creativity in thinking about oneself
        For fun
    Linguistic—
        To practice the first person singular
        To practice adjectives
        To practice the structure "I like to . . . "
        To practice the skills of reading, writing, and listening comprehension

Levels: All levels

Size of groups: Total class

Materials needed: The written homework assignment from each student, a magic marker, and thumbtacks or scotch tape

Procedures: Announce as homework the following assignment:

"Imagine that a friend has arranged a blind date for you with someone from out of town. It is time for you to meet this person, who is going to fly in from another city. You will meet at the airport. The person writes to you and asks, 'Since there are so many people at the airport, how will I know you?'

"Write a note to your blind date telling her or him how to recognize you. Talk about your physical appearance, your personality, things you like to do, the kind of person you are, and so forth. You can be humorous and creative as well.

"Do not write more than one page. Turn the assignment in to me and do not show it to anyone in the class. After I read your papers and make any corrections necessary, we will all read the descriptions and try to guess the identity of each one. So do not tell anyone what you have written."

After you collect and correct the papers, return them and ask the students to rewrite them. You can pass out paper to everyone so all descriptions are on identical paper. Request that students type their descriptions, if possible, or disguise their handwriting, but write or print clearly. Tell the students not to put their name on the front of the paper, but to write it lightly on the back so that it does not show through the front.

Collect these papers and number them consecutively with a large number in magic marker. Then hang them up all around the room with thumbtacks or scotch tape. Either pass out a ditto that is already numbered or ask students to number a sheet of paper. They should number their papers according to how many are in the class, so if there are twenty-five, each student should write in a list the numbers 1 to 25.

Tell the students that they are to circulate around the room and read each description. Next to the number on their sheets that corresponds to each paper read, they are to write the name of the person they think the description fits, even though they have to guess some. Have the class spread out all around the room so they do not wait in line to read each one.

When everyone is finished, the class can be seated. Ask whom they thought paper number 1 described. Listen to the variety of names volunteered and, by a show of hands ask how many agree as to whose paper it is. Send someone to read paper number 1 aloud to everyone, and then ask for the person whose paper it is to reveal his identity to the class. The suspense builds this way. When all are completed, see who had the most right. Here is an example of a letter that was written while carrying out this exercise.

Dear Stranger,

It won't be too difficult to find me. Just look for a tall, thin body with two feet that are size 8. Notice the long curly brown hair that rests on my wide shoulders.

I may look serious but I'm not. I enjoy meeting new people.

I'll be wearing blue jeans and a red and yellow sweater, earrings and lots of bracelets. I have two dimples on my left cheek and one on the right.

I will smile so you can see them. If you still can't find me, look for an impatient person biting her fingernails.

Good luck,
Your new friend

Variations:

1. In revealing who wrote each paper, have the owners stand beside their descriptions so everyone can check to see how many he had correct. Each person can now read his own aloud to the class.

2. Ask the class which descriptions were the most difficult to identify. Have the students guess to whom these belong. Then have the person identify himself, go to his paper, and read it aloud. See that in the end all papers get read aloud, if there is time.

Comments: Depending on the size of the class, you may not be able to put everyone's paper up at one time. If this is the case, put up one half or one third of the papers at a time and do the exercise several times. However, have everyone turn in the assignment at the same time.

This activity is fun and motivating. The mystery involved adds to the interest.

EXERCISE 59.   **BIRTH ORDER**[2]

Purposes:

Affective—

To gain perceptions about oneself and fellow classmates along a new dimension

To discover commonalities and new understandings among groups of students in the class to draw them closer together

Linguistic—

To practice the vocabulary of members of the family

To practice comparative and superlative adjectives and adjectives in general

To practice speaking in the first person singular and plural

To practice spontaneous conversation in small groups

Levels: Advanced

Size of groups: This depends on how the students distribute in response to a question the teacher asks in class. The groups may vary from two to six within the class.

Procedures: Ask students to answer these questions for you on a sheet of paper to be handed in:

1. How many brothers do you have?
2. How many sisters do you have?
3. Compared to your brothers and sisters, are you the younger (youngest) or the older (oldest) child in the family? (State which.)
4. If you are a middle child, make a list showing all of your brothers and sisters and where you fit in according to your age. (Give an example as seen below.)
   (1) brother (oldest)
   (2) brother
   (3) ME
   (4) sister
   (5) brother (youngest)
5. State here if you are an only child.

When you have this information from everyone, divide the students into groups according to their birth order or other commonalities. These are samples of such groups:

Oldest child   Middle child in a small family
Youngest child   Middle child in a large family
Only child

Notice whether there are other commonalities such as youngest child (female) with all male siblings. Try to keep the groups from being excessively large by finding a subdivision of commonalities for larger groups. In a class where nine students are the oldest child, here might be a way to subdivide them:

Oldest of three to five children
Older of two children

If one person is alone, find a way to combine him with the group closest to him.

This exercise begins by placing students in their birth order groups and explaining how each group was determined. Tell the class:

"Many things influence our personality, feelings, and attitudes. One of these is the order in which we were born in a family of children. This is called our birth order.

"You are now in a group according to your birth order in your family. Try to find out what things you have in common with the others in your group. Talk about such things as your feelings, experiences, attitudes, values, personality, and how you handle certain situations and how these may be due to your common birth order. See what similarities you can find in these areas in your group. For example, you can look at your feelings about independence, competition, responsibility, desire for attention, etc., and how these relate to your birth position. In other words, what did your birth order mean to you and what effect did it have on you?

"Write down the similarities your group discovers, and you will then report your findings to the total class. You can share some things about yourself and ask others in your group whether they feel or behave similarly to you as a way to find what things your group has in common."

Allow about ten to fifteen minutes for the class to work on this in groups, while you circulate to each group. Then ask all of the groups to report their findings to the total class to see what similarities and differences there are. As the reports are given, ask questions of the class to determine whether they are hearing the key ideas coming from each group.

As a follow-up activity, the students can write about how they feel their birth order has affected them as individuals and what they learned about birth order as it seems to influence other positions of birth.

If you believe your students need more preparation in order to discuss the topic initially in groups, give an assignment to write a few paragraphs on how they believe their birth order has affected their feelings, attitudes, behavior, personality, and values. Tell them in which birth order group they belong before the assignment is carried out. Then place them in groups to discuss and find commonalities. They will have a point of departure this way.

EXERCISE 60. **WHAT MADE ME ME**[3]

Purposes:

Affective—

To develop a deeper level of closeness among students

To encourage students to discover and reflect on experiences in their lives which have strongly influenced them

Linguistic—

To practice free composition

To provide an opportunity for giving a spontaneous monologue of some duration by each individual

To practice the past tense(s)

Levels: Advanced

Size of groups: About five to six

Materials needed: Completion of the assignment by the class

Procedures: The class should be given a written assignment before this activity is carried out. It can be introduced in this way:

"Throughout our lives certain experiences occur which have a strong influence on us. Many people believe that the negative things that happen to us affect us the most. However, it is the positive experiences that are the most influential to our growth as human beings.

"For our next assignment, I want you to think back from your earliest childhood memories all the way to the present. Try to figure out which positive experiences in your life significantly influenced your personality and your growth in positive ways. Which were the most responsible for your being the person you are today and the way you think, feel, and act?

"Write about as many of these as you can recall. Include what effect each experience had on you. It's true that negative experiences can affect us in positive ways, but only write about positive experiences that did so. We will be sharing these experiences in groups on (give due date of assignment)."

On the day the assignment is due, place students into groups of about six, but no more. Divide the time to be spent evenly among the students. Each can have about four minutes of time (but a minimum of three). Keep accurate track of the time.

Give the students these directions:

"You are now going to share with the others in your group the positive experiences which most influenced your growth and personality. One at a time, you will have your turn. The rest of the group will just listen. No one will comment or ask questions. You will have everyone's attention.

"You will each have four minutes. I will flick the lights once to signal you when you have thirty seconds left. At the end of four minutes, I will announce that it is the next person's turn. If anyone finishes before his time is up, the group can then comment or ask questions of the person in the remaining time. Otherwise, there will be no discussion. As you relate your experiences, start with early childhood and continue till your most recent years."

If some groups have one person more than the others, either have a group with fewer students, upon finishing, join one with more students to hear the additional person's experiences, or have the extra people share their experiences with the total class. In small groups and/or the total group, the students can discuss their feelings about the exercise.

Variation: Ask students to write and then speak about the happiest moments in their lives and what these meant to them.

Comments: The purpose of not allowing students to speak while someone relates his experiences is to give equal time to everyone. Otherwise those in the group can get the topic away from the focus person, who may then not get a chance to reveal his experiences to the others. Giving a limited amount of time to each person encourages getting to the point and omitting what is less important.

This activity can build a much deeper level of feeling among the students. They will hear very fascinating and warming disclosures from their classmates and come to understand them better as a result.

EXERCISE 61. **HIGHLIGHTS OF MY LIFE**[4]

Purposes:
>Affective—
>>To have students reflect on their lives to determine what the best experiences have been
>>To appreciate one's life even more
>>To share with others experiences that have given much pleasure and/or pride
>Linguistic—
>>To practice the past tense(s)
>>To practice asking and answering questions
>>To practice the skill of writing

Levels: Intermediate to advanced

Size of groups: About three to four

Materials needed: Dittoed handouts with squares on them

Procedures: Introduce the assignment as follows:

"During our lives we experience a number of events which give us great happiness or pride. However, we rarely think about all of them at once. Sometimes we may feel that nothing good happens to us. At such times it helps to recall how lucky we have been.

"I'm going to ask you to think about your life from your earliest memories up to the present. Recall as many unusually good times in your life as you can. Try to think of ones for all different ages.

"As you recall each highlight of your life, fill in a square on the dittos you have by writing how old you were, giving the occasion a title, and drawing a sketch to represent it. You will each have two pages or eight squares to fill in. Number the squares and fill them in with your earliest happy events first followed chronologically by the later ones. End with one that happened recently. The sketches do not have to be works of art. Stick figures will do.

"We will use the drawings to help tell others in the class the story of each of our happy events. Be prepared to talk about them."

When the assignment is due, divide the class into groups of three or four. Since each person has a number of stories to be told, keep the groups small. The sharing can be done with each person revealing one event from his earliest years first. In the next round an occasion which occurred a little later can be related, etc.

Or the students can look at each other's sketches and ask about those which strike their curiosity for each round. The drawings will enhance the interest of the activity. There may not be time for the students to talk about each of the special events of their lives. Those listening can ask questions.

The class can be asked to write about each event either as a means of preparing for the activity or as a follow-up to it. Conclude the exercise by asking students to express their reactions to the experience and what they learned from it.

Comments: You can ask students to write down a list of the highlights they think of in chronological order, including their approximate age at the time. Then tell them to select eight of the most special events to sketch on the dittos. In this way they will have an opportunity to come up with more events and to place a priority on them. In giving the assignment, mention a couple of highlights from your earlier years as examples of what you mean.

EXERCISE 62. **SOMEONE SPECIAL**[5]

Purposes:
> Affective—
>> To reflect over one's life to trace those who have had an impact on it
>> To appreciate those who have been a positive force in one's life
> Linguistic—
>> To practice the past tense(s)
>> To practice the use of adjectives describing positive qualities
>> To practice the skill of writing

Levels: All levels

Size of groups: About five

Materials needed: The assignment completed by the class

Procedures: Discuss with the class how throughout our lives we are influenced by others. Sometimes the influence is positive and other times it is negative. However, in everyone's life there are some individuals who have had a strong impact on us. Our direction of life changed because of them. The influence might be a way of thinking, acting, or doing something in a different way. It could be a change of attitude, belief, or plans that occurred.

Ask the students to think of all the people who greatly influenced their lives in a positive way from their earliest years to the present. Then have them decide who had the greatest influence of all. Ask the students to write a description of what this person was like and how he or she changed the course of their lives. Tell the students to be prepared to share this experience with others in the group they will be in. If they have a snapshot or some tangible remembrance of this person, request that this be brought in as well.

When the assignment is due, put the students into groups of about five. One at a time, the group members should tell the story of the most influential person in their lives and share any pictures or relics brought in with the others. You can provide questions to guide the composition and the discussion, such as:

1. How old were you when you met this person?
2. What was this person like?
3. Do you still see this person?
4. How did this person influence you?
5. How would your life be different if you had not met this person?
6. Have you ever tried to have the same kind of influence on the lives of others that this person had on you? If so, under what circumstances?

In the total class, a number of students can tell who their influential person is and how their life is different as a result of this contact. Reactions to the exercise and/or a discussion of what was learned from it can follow.

Comments: When giving the assignment, make it clear that the person chosen as the most influential should have done *positive* things which in turn brought about a positive influence. Otherwise some students will come up with people who did very negative things to them, which they combated by going in the opposite direction.

This exercise can be a warm experience as it often brings back feelings of appreciation, caring, and closeness.

EXERCISE 63. SECRET AUTOBIOGRAPHY[6]

Purposes:
  Affective—
      To have students share a number of important things about themselves that others may not know as yet
      To arouse the curiosity of students in one another
  Linguistic—
      To practice writing in the past tense(s)
      To afford practice in listening comprehension
      To practice the vocabulary of giving one's age

Levels: Intermediate to advanced; latter part of beginning level

Size of groups: Total class

Procedures: Students will have to complete the written assignment to carry out the activity. Here is how you can announce it:

"Famous people often have books written by others about their lives. This type of book is called a biography. Sometimes they write the books themselves. In this case, it's called an autobiography.

"Everyone here is an important person. I want you to imagine that you have been asked to write your autobiography. However, as you write it, you decide to add some mystery to it by not coming out and telling who you are.

"For Monday (give date assignment is due), write (give length) a one-page secret autobiography of yourself. Write the highlights of your life starting from your birth. All of the autobiographies will be read aloud to the class to see if we can figure out the identity of each one. When you finish your autobiography, add one big hint at the end to help us. At first we will try to guess who you are without the hint. If no one guesses correctly, your big clue will be read to the class. In writing your autobiography, use the facts of your life, but you can add humor and creativity in your style of writing, just as authors do."

You may decide to ask for only a few paragraphs to be written. Depending on the length of the assignment and the number in the class, you may want to spread the activity across two to three days for reading the secret autobiographies to the students.

After several are read and the identity of the persons are revealed, ask the class some recall questions. As you continue the process, have the students make up questions to ask the class, based on information gathered from the secret autobiographies. Be certain to write one for yourself and don't make it obviously point to you. It's fun when the class has difficulty identifying yours in the group.

Variation: This activity can be conducted in the same style as Exercise 58, "Who's Who?", where the papers are posted around the room and everyone reads them all and writes down which person he thinks each paper belongs to. In this case, limit the amount of writing to about two paragraphs or it will take too long to read them all.

EXERCISE 64.   STEP RIGHT UP AND SEE ME[7]

Purposes:

> Affective—
>> To help students gain more introspection into themselves by noting their wants, needs, likes, interests, and what is important to them in the present and from the past
>> To enable students to feel much closer to their classmates by visually seeing and hearing about their wants, needs, likes, interests, and what is important to them in the present and from the past
>
> Linguistic—
>> To encourage students to learn the vocabulary of objects (nouns) that are personally relevant to them and to members of the class
>> To practice using possessive adjectives

To practice speaking in the present and past tense(s)
To practice the use of "I like" and "I don't like"
To encourage students to ask and answer spontaneous questions of
each other

Levels: Intermediate to advanced; beginning level with much assistance and structure and toward the latter part of the year

Size of groups: About three to five

Materials needed: An exhibit which each student has brought in to be set up; tables lined up against the walls of the room for displaying the exhibits; a ditto explaining the assignment

Procedures: Give the students several weeks to carry out this assignment. Announce to the class what they are to do:

A booth at the self-fair displaying favorite interests, memories, and events

"During the next three weeks I'd like you to think about many things related to yourself. For example: What do you like to do? What are your true interests?

What things are or used to be important to you? What are your favorite events and memories? What are your favorite activities and belongings?

"As you think about these questions, collect objects and pictures that represent your answers to them. In a few weeks in our class we are going to have a fair or carnival with booths. Each of you will set up a booth to exhibit what you have collected. The display will represent you. It will be all about you.

"We will all see each other's displays and ask questions about them. Include your objects wherever you can. When this is not possible, use pictures. You can include snapshots and photographs, too. Each item in your exhibit should be labeled in writing in the foreign language. Give me a list of the words that you need to know that we haven't studied yet. I will help you with these words. Each exhibit will be placed on a table, and you also will be able to use the wall behind it to hang up or prop items. (Give students a *written copy* of all these instructions to refer to in preparing their exhibits.)

"What we will be doing is letting others in the class get to know us much better, and also getting to know ourselves and our classmates better, too.

"Start looking at your belongings and thinking about these questions now and collect some things right along. Do not wait until the last minute to gather your collection. Try to have about (give an appropriate number) ten to fifteen items in your exhibit." (Otherwise some students bring in only a few items and others a carload, which will make the former feel uncomfortable.)

It would be helpful for you to set up an exhibit of items representing you or at least mention some examples of what would be in yours to give the students a clearer idea of what you mean. [In my own exhibit I would have (1) a piece of antique jewelry, (2) a foreign object of art and a painting of a mother and child, and (3) a theater program, as examples of what I'm very fond of, what I collect, and my favorite pastime. Since I love to find bargains when I shop, I would include the best bargain I've ever found. I am a saver of things and would bring an outfit I still have which is now twenty-eight years old or a book I bought at age nine. I liked to embroider as a child and would bring in a sampler in cross-stitch that I sewed when seven years old.]

Depending on how many are in the class, decide on a realistic number of students to have bring in their exhibits at one time. If there are thirty-six in a class, you could ask twelve students to bring in their exhibits on one day. Have all the displays set up ahead of time on tables around the room. Then have six students whose exhibits are dispersed in different parts of the room "open their booths" at the fair. Divide the remaining students into six groups of five. These groups will each go to a different booth, where the "exhibitor" will answer questions that are asked about the items on display. Allow two or three minutes for the groups to converse with the exhibitors and then signal each group to move on to the next open exhibit. Continue the process until all six booths have been seen by each group. (If there are twenty-four in the class, put the remaining students into groups of three to circulate to each booth.)

Then have the next six exhibitors open their booths and those who just closed theirs join the groups which an exhibitor just left. Continue the same procedure as before. You can turn the lights on and off as a signal to move on to the next booth or use a microphone set on PA on a tape recorder to amplify your voice, since there will be talking in all parts of the room.

Watch the time closely and keep the students moving, as they will linger longer at some booths. Supply intermediate levels with suggestions of what they can ask: "What does this ___(item)___ mean to you?" "Is this a picture of you as a child?" "Did you make this dress?" "Why did you bring this ___(item)___?" "Where did you get this ___(item)___?" "Does this theater program mean you like to act or go to the theater?"

On another day have a different group of students bring in their exhibits and set up the same procedures. Spread them out in time to maintain interest in the activity.

Encourage the students to use the vocabulary of words on display as they interact with the exhibitor. A list of the new words which will appear in the booths should be given out to students in advance of seeing those particular displays. In this way, they can become familiar with any new vocabulary to be used.

Comments: Although two to three minutes may sound very brief, it can be sufficient for most levels to find questions to ask about each display. The groups may not hear about every item in a booth, but they will realize that they must ask questions concerning those which interest them the most. You can state that each person in a group must ask at least two questions of each exhibitor.

The exhibitor will get practice in responding to a variety of questions by the time all of the groups visit his booth, and those circulating will be able to ask a number of questions.

When the fair ends each time, ask the students what they learned about the exhibitors, focusing on each, one at a time. "What did you learn about Dan?" or "What do you remember about Lee?" are typical questions that can be posed. Be certain to ask what students discovered or thought about in preparing their own display.

As a follow-up activity, have students write what they learned about themselves and others in the class from the exhibits.

This activity can create a great deal of interest and excitement in the class. Do not extend the activity over many class periods or these feelings may diminish. Two to four class meetings are sufficient and these can be a week apart. Depending on the number in your class and the length of a class period, decide on how many exhibits to have brought in at a time.

EXERCISE 65.   **MYSTERIOUS ME**[8]

Purposes:
    Affective—
            To observe what tangibles about us reveal insights into us
            To call on the imagination

Linguistic—
To practice the third person singular
To practice the use of adjectives and nouns
To write a narrative about oneself

Levels: All levels

Size of groups: About six

Procedures: As you give the assignment, tell the class:

"There are many clues around us that reveal what we are like. Imagine tha
you are a famous person but have kept your life a mystery to the public.

"A top reporter for a well-known newspaper gets an idea of how to
discover what you are really like in order to write your unknown story. The
reporter breaks into your house one day when no one is home and goes to your
bedroom. He searches through your drawers and in your closets and looks at
everything in sight. Based upon the condition of your room and what he finds
there, the reporter feels confident that he can write a revealing story about the
real you.

"List all of the things the reporter will find that give clues as to the kind of
person you are. Then write the story about yourself as the reporter would, based
upon the evidence found in your room."

When the papers are due, have them read to the class and the identity of
each guessed. In this case, tell the students to write a fictitious name rather than
their own in the body of the paper.

As an alternative, the students can all write on identical paper, still using a
fictitious name instead of their own. Put the students into groups of six and have
them place their papers in a pile face down. Everyone picks a paper to read aloud
and the others guess the identity of the mystery person. Even if a person picks his
own paper to read, it won't matter. The items the reporter finds are read first,
followed by the write-up. Ask each group to select one story to be read to the
total class.

The students can then discuss in small groups and as a total class:

1. What did you learn about yourself and others from this exercise?
2. Why was the identity of some easier and others harder to guess?

EXERCISE 66. **AND IT JUST HAPPENED**

Purposes:
Affective—
To assess what of significance is presently occurring in one's life

Linguistic—
> To practice the past tense(s)
> To ask and answer questions

Levels: Intermediate to advanced

Size of groups: About five or six

Materials needed: Completion of the assignment by members of the class

Procedures: Start the next topic off by stating:

"We've been thinking a lot about our past in the exercises we have done in class. We have talked about influences, memories, experiences, and people from our past.

"In our next activity, we're going to look at the most recent events in our lives. Although many good things happened to us as we were growing up, they continue all of our lives. I want you to think of some of the very worthwhile experiences which have occurred to you recently. Then decide what is the most significant one you have had recently—something of great importance that happened to you."

The students can be asked to write about the event at home for later discussion in class. If the class is more advanced, the discussion can follow your introduction of the topic after allowing a couple of minutes to decide what the significant event is. Have the students ask questions of each other or make comments as each story is revealed.

To conclude, have each student summarize his recent important event in one or two sentences for the entire class to hear. By considering the time per student, all can get a turn to communicate the essence of the experience this way.

The significant event can be written up before or after the discussion takes place.

EXERCISE 67. **MEMORIES OF US**[9]

Purposes:
Affective—
> To recall pleasant and sentimental events students have experienced together
> To leave warm feelings in closing

Linguistic—
> To practice the past tense(s)

Levels: All levels

Size of groups: Total class

Procedures: This activity is meant for the end of the school year and can be included as one of several closing activities done in a series. It is also fitting before a holiday vacation once students know each other quite well, have experienced a number of humanistic activities together, and there is a feeling of closeness in the group.

The students should be seated or standing in a circle so everyone can see the entire class. In the latter case, the students should join hands. Depending on the level of the class, decide whether to ask the students to prepare for this exercise in advance or to do it spontaneously. Start the activity by saying:

"We have spent the last (amount of time) eight months getting to know each other very well. As a result, a number of pleasant things have happened to us here.

"I'd like each of you to think of the best thing that happened to you in this class or some experience you found meaningful and will still remember in the future. Everyone will have a turn at completing either of these statements: 'The best thing that happened to me in this class was _____' or 'In the future I will remember when_____.' Take a minute to think of a fond memory you are taking with you and then we will share these memories."

Comments: This activity serves to bring out warm feelings in the members of the class. Some of the memories brought up will also have significance to others in the group, who will enjoy having them recalled.

NOTES

1. This activity is an adaptation of an exercise found in the work of Elizabeth Flynn and John LaFaso.

2. Daniel Malamud is the originator of this strategy.

3. This activity has some commonalities with one by Herbert A. Otto and one by Daniel Malamud.

4. Several group facilitators have used a strategy similar to this one. Herbert A. Otto seems to be the originator of the basic idea. This exercise is a modification of the customary way it is carried out.

5. I cannot attribute the kernel idea for this exercise to anyone, but referring to someone who has influenced one's life has been used by various group facilitators.

6. Writing about oneself is commonly done when using awareness techniques. Larry Chase suggests the use of a "secret" autobiography.

7. The idea for this strategy comes from the work of Harold Lyon, Jr.

8. This technique is an adaptation of an exercise found in the work of Robert and Isabel Hawley.

9. This exercise is based on an idea from an unpublished mimeograph in which no title or author was given. I would appreciate knowing the source.

My Values

He does not believe that does not live according to his belief.

— Thomas Fuller

If you ask students, "What do you value in life?" you may very well encounter silence. Many people of all ages are not consciously aware of what they believe in.

The following exercises are intended to help students discover some of their values: what is important to them, what they believe in, what they feel sentimental about, and what they want from life.

EXERCISE 68.   **CHERISHED OBJECT**[1]

Purposes:
   Affective—
      To develop a deeper level of closeness among students
      To encourage students to think about and decide what is precious and
         meaningful to them
      To enable students to see each other in a more intimate light
   Linguistic—
      To practice the past tense(s)
      To practice the structure "It is important to me because . . . "
      To practice asking and answering questions
      To practice the skill of writing

Levels: Intermediate to advanced; beginning groups could do this exercise if provided with simple open-ended statements to complete.

Size of groups: About six to eight

Materials needed: A "cherished object" from each student

Procedures: Tell the class to look over all their belongings at home and to decide, out of everything they have, what is the most significant and personally meaning-ful object they own. Ask them to think of why the item is so valuable to them. You can request that they write the answer to this question and bring the object and what they have written to class.

Place the students in groups of six to eight. Have one person at a time in each group show the precious object to the others and share the significance of the item with them. The object, if not too delicate, can be passed around for each to see. Members of the group ask questions or comment about the object.

As each group finishes, a display can be made of the objects with the paragraph each person wrote beside it. (You may want the paragraph turned in ahead of time so you can make corrections and have the students recopy their papers to assure accuracy.)

The class will be interested in seeing the objects others have brought in and reading what is said about them.

Variation: When the groups are finished and a display of the items is set up, have half the groups stand near their displays while the other groups are each asked to look at the displays of another group. The onlookers can read the descriptions and/or ask people in the group to tell them about some of the objects displayed.

The groups can rotate so they have an opportunity to see what one or more groups brought in and also to tell others outside their group about their cherished objects.

Comments: If there is insufficient time to carry out the activity so fully, the objects can just be shared with the original group. The class will be curious to know about what others brought in though. One way to take less time is to ask for one or two students from each group to tell the entire class about their objects and to hold them up. The groups can be asked to volunteer these people themselves. They will tend to select those which were the most unique or sentimental or touching.

In concluding, ask the class members to discuss in groups and/or as a total class what they learned about themselves and others from this experience. This can also be assigned to be done at home in writing as a follow-up to the exercise.

This activity can be carried out at any time of the year. However, it is a good strategy for getting students to feel closer to each other, and is therefore especially helpful early in the year for this purpose.

EXERCISE 69. **FAMOUS FIGURES**[2]

Purposes:
  Affective—
      To become aware of hidden aspects and aspirations of students
      To bring into focus parts of what makes up the students' ideal self-
          image
  Linguistic—
      To practice the vocabulary of words that describe positive qualities of
          people

Levels: All levels

Size of groups: Three to five

Procedures: Tell students to imagine that they could be any famous person, male or female, from any walk of life, past or present, from any country. Ask them to decide whom they would want to be. Tell them to write down the names of three to five people they would choose. Allow some time for thinking or else give this as a homework assignment. Ask them to include at least one person of the opposite sex.

Next ask them to rank order their choices from the person they would want to be first, second, etc. In groups have the students share what qualities about these people made them select each one and why they ranked them as they did. Ask them to notice whether these people have any qualities in common.

After going over this in groups, ask for a few volunteers to share their comments before the whole class and share yours as well. Have the students share their first choice with the total group. Then ask them to name the person of the opposite sex that they chose. The students should state the names of these people and the qualities that caused them to be chosen. Carry out a review afterwards by asking questions such as: "Who said he would like to be Robert Redford?" and "Why would Pat like to be Cleopatra?"

A discussion on what they learned about themselves from this exercise follows. An assignment to write about this can be given as well.

EXERCISE 70.   **FIREMAN, SAVE MY . . .**[3]

Purposes:
> Affective—
>> To encourage students to think about what they really cherish and
>>> place a high value on
> Linguistic—
>> To converse freely in the language
>> To stress the conditional tense

Levels: Midway through the first year and all other levels; beginning students can be given sentences to complete in carrying out the exercise

Size of groups: Approximately five

Procedures: Ask the students to close their eyes and imagine the following scene:
> You have been away all day and are returning home. As you arrive at your house or apartment, you find it is on fire. Luckily, all members of your family and your pets are safe. But almost everything else is destroyed.

A fireman then calls down to you, "I can save just one thing that's in your house for you. Tell me what you want." Think about all the belongings in your house and decide what is the *one thing* you would ask to have saved.

After the students have time to think about this (or you could have them reflect on it as a homework assignment), ask them to share this in their groups. They should tell what item they would want to have saved and why. When everyone has had a turn, ask the students to decide what value this shows they place a strong emphasis on. Tell the students to be specific. For example, if someone would save a photograph album, he should not say that his value is being sentimental, but that he places a strong emphasis on his family. Have the class discuss these values in small groups and as a whole, and summarize the kinds of values they come up with.

EXERCISE 71.   **WHAT MAKES YOU ANGRY?**

Purposes:
  Affective—
      To help understand the basis for much of one's anger
      To help crystallize one's values through a process of reasoning
      To become more introspective about anger
      To note commonalities in what makes people angry
  Linguistic—
      To write and speak on a topic about which people have strong feelings

Levels: Advanced

Size of groups: Four to five

Procedures: As homework, request that students make a list of the things which really make them angry and bring it to class. In groups, have them go over their lists.

Tell them that our beliefs and convictions and values are often at the heart of what makes us angry. Often when we get angry, we feel guilty about it. Yet something we have strong convictions about has been violated.

Instruct the students to study their own lists and to write out what values they find beneath each of the things that makes them angry. Have them write down a list of these values. This can be done in class or as a homework assignment. When completed, the students should discuss what values they discovered they have with the same group in which they discussed what makes them angry.

Comments: This can be an enlightening experience. It is easy to think of things which make us angry, but if we are asked what are some of our most important values, that is a much more difficult question to respond to. This exercise gives a means for getting at some of our important values and helps to better understand the guilt-inducing feeling of anger. Students enjoy sharing their lists of what makes them and others angry. They find drawing out their values from this list a fascinating approach to understanding their anger and becoming aware of their values.

EXERCISE 72. **GLORIOUS GARMENT**

Purposes:
> Affective—
>> To examine what students value
>> To encourage thinking sentimentally
>> To share these sentiments and to discover what others cherish
> Linguistic—
>> To practice the vocabulary of articles of clothing
>> To practice the use of adjectives

Levels: All levels

Size of groups: Can be done as a total class or in groups of about six

Materials needed: An article of clothing brought in by each student

Procedures: Announce the assignment, which must be completed before this exercise can be carried out:

"Throughout our lives we have worn many different articles of clothing. Often we have feelings about the clothes we wear. Some clothes are really comfortable and make us feel more relaxed or at ease or outgoing. What we wear can affect how we feel and how we feel about ourselves.

"In some cases we grow attached to an article of clothing. It has sentimental value for us. It's this kind of clothing that we're going to give attention to in our next activity. I'd like you to go home and look through your clothes closets and dresser drawers, and ask yourself what single piece of clothing has meant the most to you. It may be something you have saved for a number of years and don't even wear any more.

"After you carefully select your favorite article of clothing or the one with the most sentimental value, write (give the length) several paragraphs about it. Include the following:

1. Describe the article of clothing.
2. Why has it meant so much to you?
3. What do you associate with it?
4. Is there any story or event you connect with it?
5. How did you or do you feel when wearing it?

"On the day that we carry out the activity, bring in your article of clothing. Make a card with large letters on it to label what the article is, such as 'My baby boots,' 'My comfortable old shoes,' 'My favorite belt.' The card will be placed on or beside your article in our display. We then will hear the stories and ask questions about the clothing you brought in."

Remind students the day before the assignment is due to bring in their "gorgeous garment." Arrange an attractive display and gather the class around the exhibit. Have the students raise questions about items of interest to them. Seeing the articles on display will arouse curiosity. The students will not know to whom the items belong, and this adds to the intrigue.

A student might ask, "Whose striped sneaks are these?" When the owner declares, "They're mine," other class members inquire about the information included in the written paragraphs: "Describe your sneaks for us," "Why do these sneaks mean so much to you?" etc. Other questions can be spontaneously added: "How old are these sneaks?" "Do you still wear them?" "Does your mother like them?"

In answering the questions, try not to have the students read their paragraphs but respond spontaneously. By having written the answers to some of these questions, they should be more able to respond orally.

Variation: Instead of a display for the total class, divide into groups of six to eight. Each group can have its own display and carry out the activity the same way. The groups volunteer two of their members to share the story of their piece of clothing with the total class, which will ask questions of each person in the same way.

Other variations of this exercise are to have students bring in (1) their oldest article of clothing or (2) their most humorous one. The tone of the activity would then change from being sentimental to being more entertaining.

Comments: If you wish to have a display for the entire class, consider how many students you have. You may have to have one half or one third of the class bring in their wares at a time so that everyone has an opportunity to share his story with the others.

EXERCISE 73. THE GIFT I'VE ALWAYS WANTED[4]

Purposes:
 Affective—
  To have students assess what they value and aspire to
  To have students become aware of what their peers value and aspire
   to
 Linguistic—
  To practice writing simple sentences
  To practice listening comprehension

Levels: All levels; advanced levels can upgrade the expectations of the exercise.

Size of groups: Total class

Materials needed: Completion of the assignment by the class

Procedures: Students must first be given the assignment:
"At different times in our life we are given gifts. Sometimes the gifts are just what we want, other times not.
"Imagine that it is your birthday or Chanukah or Christmas and you are to receive a special gift. You are told that you can decide what the gift will be and whatever you choose will be yours. The gift can be an actual object or some quality.
"Out of everything you can possibly have in your gift box, decide what you will ask for. Write it on a slip of paper (or a five- by eight-inch card). You do not have to sign your name to the card, but I will collect it from you as you come into the classroom tomorrow. Complete this statement on your card: 'The one gift I want more than anything is _____ .' I will be reading everyone's answers in the class. We will not know whose responses they are. The gift must be something just for *you*, though, and not for your family or mankind.
"As you think of all the things you might want and select one, be aware of what this says that you value."
The day the assignment is due, collect the cards at the door as the students enter to assure that you receive one from each person. You may wish to read the cards by yourself before reading them to the class to note any themes or categories of similarities among them.
As you read the cards to the class, tell the students to note which three gifts, other than their own, they would most like to receive if they could.
As a total class, ask the students to note what similarities they found in the choices of the gifts people wanted. What categories did the wishes encompass (love, health, money, occupation, etc.)?
Divide the students into groups to discuss the three gifts they would most like for themselves from those chosen by members of the class, and why. If the students wish, they can share in their groups what their own choice of a gift was and why it is important to them. After hearing what others wanted as their gifts, the students can discuss whether they changed their minds as to the one gift they would like the most.

EXERCISE 74.   **WHAT DO I REALLY VALUE?**

Purposes:
Affective—
To get students to examine what is truly important to them
To encourage students to spend more of their lives doing and saying
what is important to them

Linguistic—
To practice the conditional tense

Levels: Intermediate to advanced

Size of groups: Dyads

Materials needed: Dittoed handouts with questions to be answered

Procedures: Orient the class to this activity by saying:

"Every day that we live is in some way different from all other days. Do we make the most of every day of our lives? Do we say the things and do the things that mean the most to us? The answers to these questions are that we do not. What would we have to do to make life have its fullest meaning for us? The next activity is intended to help us see what is truly important to us in life.

"Imagine that you have been chosen to be one of a very special group of people to be sent to inhabit a new planet. You will be doing a great service for mankind by this mission by preparing this new territory for future settlement.

"Your family and friends are extremely proud of you. Life promises to be very exciting, adventurous, and rewarding on the new planet.

"Although many wonderful experiences await you as you serve your fellow man, you will never be able to return to earth, since man cannot readjust once he is on this new planet. This means you will never again see anyone you know or do any of the things you presently enjoy.

"You will be leaving for your new home in two weeks. Everything you need will be there when you arrive. Plan how you would spend your last two weeks in your present surroundings to make them the most memorable and meaningful to you."

Pass out a dittoed sheet with these questions:

1. Whom would you want to spend time with?
2. Which people would you spend the most time with and why?
3. What would you want to be sure to say to each of these people?
4. What activities and pastimes would you engage in?
5. What would be the most meaningful experience or contact of all for you during this time?

Now continue:

"To answer these questions will require careful thought. Therefore, spend time at home reflecting on these questions, and write out your responses. Be aware of the fact that you will be deciding what is truly meaningful in life to you. This is the essence of what we are searching for."

When the class meets to carry out the activity, ask the students to pair off with someone they would like to discuss these questions with.

End by having the total class discuss:

1. What did you learn from this experience?
2. How do you spend your time compared with how you would spend it more meaningfully?
3. Are there any changes you plan to make regarding what you say and do and whom you spend time with?

Comments: This activity should be done only after a good deal of trust has been built among students. Because it is a sensitive exercise, I have suggested the sharing be with only one person. However, if your class is quite cohesive, you could expand this to groups of three to four, if you wish.

EXERCISE 75.   **WHAT I WANT FROM LIFE[5]**

Purposes:
    Affective—
        To help students assess what they want to do with their lives
        To help students set goals for what they want to do now and in the
            future
    Linguistic—
        To practice a variety of verbs
        To practice free conversation and composition

Levels: Intermediate to advanced

Size of groups: Two to three

Materials needed: The assignment carried out by each student

Procedures: Orient the class to the assignment:

"The older we get, the faster time passes. There are many things we want to do, yet there never seems to be enough time to do them all. It can help us to know how to spend our time by examining what we actually want to do with our lives.

"As an assignment, I'm going to ask you to think about what you really want to do in your lifetime. What are your lifetime goals? Write a list of as many of these as come to your mind. Spend about fifteen minutes doing this and come up with as many as you can think of.

"Then spend the next fifteen minutes listing what you would like to do and accomplish during the next three years. When you finish both lists, decide on the top three in importance on each list. Mark them with a number one, two, or three.

"Next go back and mark which category each comes under: attitudes, career, education, family, finances, health, personal, personality, recreation, relationships, religion, socializing. Bring your list to class on (due date) Friday."

When the class meets to carry out the activity, divide the students into groups of two or three. Ask them to talk about any or all of the following questions:

1. What are your lifetime goals?
2. Which are your three most important lifetime goals?
3. What are your goals for the next three years?
4. Which are your three most important goals for the next three years?
5. Which categories do more of your goals come under?
6. Which categories do your six most important goals come under?
7. What can you do now to help you accomplish your goals for the next three years?
8. What can you do now to help you accomplish your lifetime goals?

With the entire class, ask the students to tell what they learned about themselves from this experience. You might wish to have a discussion on questions 7 and 8 also.

As a follow-up activity, the students can write about their three most important three-year and lifetime goals, why these have priority over the others, and how they will work toward fulfilling them. A summary of what they learned from doing this activity could also be included.

EXERCISE 76. AN EXTREME DREAM WARDROBE[6]

Purposes:
> Affective—
>> To determine the significance of clothing in our lives
> Linguistic—
>> To practice the vocabulary of articles of clothing
>> To practice the vocabulary of numbers

Levels: All levels

Size of groups: About four or five

Procedures: Discuss with students the importance or lack of importance that clothing has for us:

"To some people, what they wear is very important. The colors must go well with each other. The clothes must fit just right. They don't feel good unless they like how their clothes look on them.

"Others are more casual about their clothing. Anything is fine as long as it is comfortable. An outfit can be ripped or patched or old, but how it feels is what counts.

"Let's find out what clothing means to us. Imagine that you are on a quiz show on television. You have just won the grand prize of the wardrobe of your choice for five years. Here are the conditions attached:

1. You must give up all of your present wardrobe.
2. You can have any articles of clothing you want, no matter what the quantity or cost.
3. You have five minutes to write down exactly what you want: every article of clothing, the style or type, and the quantity of each. (As an example: one pair of boots, two pairs of sneakers, three pairs of casual shoes, two pairs of dressy shoes.)
4. You cannot buy or borrow any other clothing.
5. At the end of every year for five years, you'll be given an equal amount of new clothing in exchange for the old batch.

Take the next five minutes now to draw up your dream wardrobe for the year."

Call time after five minutes. Then announce:

"As you give your list to the master of ceremonies of the show, he tells you there is one other challenge you must meet before getting your dream wardrobe.

1. You will have to wait a year to receive the prize.
2. During that year you will not have any of your present wardrobe.
3. During that year, you will have only fifteen items of clothing of your choice.
4. You cannot buy or borrow any other clothing.
5. You have five minutes to write down which fifteen articles of clothing you want for the next year. (Each item counts as one garment unless it comes in pairs, such as gloves or socks.)"

Give the class five minutes to complete this task. Then divide the students into groups to discuss:

1. How did your two lists differ?
2. What kinds of clothing were eliminated from the second list? Why?

3. How would you feel about living for a year with only the fifteen items on your list?

4. What did you have to give up on your second list that you would miss?

5. What did you forget to include in the second list that you could not be without?

6. How important does what you wear seem to you now?

7. What benefits could result from your having to wear for a year only the items on your second list?

As each of these questions is discussed in small groups, ask for a few students to give their responses to the total class. In this way, the class will hear the reactions of the small group and some from other groups.

As a follow-up to the exercise, the students can write about "What Clothes Mean to Me." Or they can submit their two lists and respond to the discussion questions above, including what they learned from this experience.

EXERCISE 77. ONCE UPON A TIME, FIVE YEARS FROM NOW

Purposes:

    Affective—

        To have students think about what they want their lives to be like in the future

        To encourage students to live in the present in ways that help fulfill goals for the future

    Linguistic—

        To practice the future tense

        To practice the skill of writing

Levels: All levels

Size of groups: About four

Materials needed: The assignment completed by the class

Procedures: Introduce the activity by mentioning that we get so caught up with living from one day to the next that we may not think about or plan for the future. Sometimes the future feels so distant that we have no idea what it might be like.

As an assignment, ask the students to project into the future five years from now. Suggest that they consider a number of things:

1. Where will you live?

2. How will you spend much of your time?

3. How will you fill out the line on your income tax form that states "Occupation"?

4. Who will the people be that you will be closest to?

5. What will a typical day in your life be like?

6. What will you do for enjoyment?

7. What principles will guide your life?

8. What will be the most important thing in your life?

9. How will your life be different then from what it is now?

10. What can you do now to help achieve what you want five years from now?

You can guide the students into a fantasy first (see "Conducting Fantasies" on page 178) and then have them examine these questions about their future. This will act to stimulate the imagination and make it easier to come up with some answers for themselves. The composition can be written at home and discussed later in class. For advanced levels, where the fluency is greater, the reverse can be done: a spontaneous discussion follows the fantasy and the written composition is done afterwards.

EXERCISE 78.   **THE REMARKABLE GYPSY**

Purposes:

Affective—

To have students look at their hopes for the future and share them

To encourage students to examine their values of what is truly
            important to them

Linguistic—

To practice asking questions

To practice the future and the conditional tenses

Levels: All levels

Size of groups: Dyads or larger groups with two at a time taking turns to role play

Materials needed: Completion of the assignment by the students

Procedures: The written assignment will have to be completed by students before the exercise can be carried out. You can introduce it in this way:

"All of us wonder about the future and what it will bring. We hope good things are in store for us. Imagine that a gypsy caravan has just arrived nearby. The news has spread that there is an amazing fortune teller with the group. The woman is noted for seeing only the good events that will happen to people.

"The news travels fast and some of your friends go to see her. They are thrilled by her predictions. A few have already come true. You decide you'll go tomorrow, but you want to get your money's worth. So you will write down the questions you want answered by her before you go.

"You are allowed to ask only four questions of the gypsy: one regarding the immediate present and one each about your life two, five, and ten years from now. Write down the four most important questions you would ask the fortune teller." (Allow time to carry out these instructions.)

"Imagine that you have just asked her your four questions, and now you find out why she is so amazing, for she tells you: 'Give me the answers you would like to have to these questions, and they will come true.' You are delighted as well as shocked. Write what you would tell the gypsy, using the conditional tense in your responses: 'I would want to have excellent health' or 'I would like to have three children, two boys and a girl.' "

When the assignment is completed, divide the class into dyads. Each person will have the chance to be himself as well as the gypsy. The gypsy asks, "What would you like your answer to be?" The client gives the answer he wrote in the conditional tense. The gypsy responds by changing the request to the future tense as a forecast of what is to come. Here is how one might sound:

Gypsy: What do you want to know about your life two years from now?
Client: Will I go to a college away from home?
Gypsy: Tell me the answer you would like to hear and it will come true.
Client: I would like to go to a college in California and win a scholarship there.
Gypsy: You will be accepted to a well-known college in California and receive a scholarship to attend.

A way to initiate the activity is to enact a couple of samples before everyone. You can create a mysterious gypsy headgear and a crystal ball to use in role playing in front of the class to get everyone in the mood. Encourage the students to use the voice of an all-seeing gypsy clairvoyant.

The students will be interested in hearing what others wanted to know. Therefore, call on volunteers to ask one of their questions in front of the total class and their gypsy can role play with them. Summarize by determining what categories of concern the questions asked were, for example, health, financial welfare, occupation, love, marriage, family, and education. Ask what were some of the questions raised in each of these categories.

A certain amount of trust should have developed among students before this strategy is used. The role playing provides added enjoyment and laughter as this activity is carried out.

NOTES

1. I have encountered this activity at various workshops. The earliest version I could locate of this strategy is in the work of Herbert A. Otto; a later one is that of Daniel Malamud.

2. This exercise is adapted from an idea by Roberta Otto and a strategy subsequently developed by Herbert A. Otto.

3. This activity appeared in an unpublished mimeograph containing no title or author. I would appreciate learning of its origin.

4. Although a number of facilitators use the kernel idea of this exercise, usually called "Magic Box," the early origin can be traced to Hannah B. Weiner. This technique is an expansion of that activity.

5. The kernel idea for this exercise is based on the work of Alan Lakein.

6. This exercise is a variation of one developed by Elizabeth Flynn and John LaFaso.

Samples of Self-Collages

The Arts and Me

Art is a way to forget life and to become aware of it.

— Gertrude Moskowitz

There are many ways we can learn about ourselves, express our feelings, and discover new dimensions that exist within us. Through the arts we may enable students to open up and feel free enough to express themselves in ways they never knew were in them.

The exercises that follow combine humanistic techniques with the areas of art, sculpting, music, dance, and acting to help create insights, self-esteem, and fun.

EXERCISE 79.   **SELF-COLLAGE**[1]

Purposes:
> Affective—
>> To encourage greater self-awareness by asking students to think about what they are really like
>> To try to communicate creatively how one perceives himself
>> To get students in the class much better acquainted by means of a visual experience
>
> Linguistic—
>> To have students use words and expressions in the target language that they feel describe themselves and others

Levels: All levels

Size of groups: About six

Materials needed: A collage made by each student in the class

Procedures: Instruct the students to make a collage which will convey to the others in the class what they are like. Show at least one sample of a collage to be certain everyone understands what you mean. Ask them to use pictures and words in the foreign language to show where they are now in their thinking, feelings, and attitudes. Tell them to show what they are like and what they believe in.

Sample of a Self-Collage

Inform the students not to put their name on the front of the collage and not to put their picture on it so that it will not be obvious to anyone whose collage it is. Let them know that the collages will be posted and talked about.

Give the class one to two weeks to work on their collages. Tell the students to ask you for any words or expressions they don't know in the target language that they need for the collages. If they have access to newspapers and magazines in the target language, they can cut out the words they use from these.

How you carry out the activity will vary according to the size of your class and the amount of time you have. This activity can be spread over several periods with different phases each period.

Basic instructions are to have the collages hung up all around the room. Have an identical sheet of tablet paper placed beneath each one and number the sheets of paper consecutively with magic marker. Each student is to circulate around the room, study each collage, and note the impressions he gets of what the person is like. He writes these down in the target language, on the sheet of tablet paper which is adjacent to the collage. (The vocabulary list in Appendix B should be helpful in this part of the activity.)

When everyone has completed the cycle, the collages are taken down by each owner. The class is divided into groups. Each person reads over the comments made about his collage to see how others interpreted it. Each individual explains the meaning of the various parts of his collage and answers questions raised. He can share his reactions to the comments made on his tablet sheet and how accurate he believes they are and/or whether any comments surprised him. Each person in the class should get to see to whom the collage belonged.

Variations:

1. Ideally, everyone should get to hear about all of the self-collages of others. This can be done by having only a certain number brought in at a time and having the students, after receiving written comments, tell the total class about their collage and answer questions.

2. Break the class into moving groups while some students stand beside their collages. They can talk to each small group about the meaning of their collages as questions are asked. After about two minutes, a signal is given for the groups to move on to the next collage. The procedure continues until everyone has a turn talking with others about his collage.

3. Have the class try to guess whose collage each one is and write it on a piece of paper they have that is numbered to correspond with the numbers for each collage. Check out the accuracy on these lists.

4. Ask the students to find someone else's collage which most resembles how they perceive themselves. It will be interesting to find out whose collage it actually is.

Comments: There are many variations you can find for using these self-collages. They are very useful for vocabulary expansion, and you can pick up on points in each one to comment and ask questions on.

Figure out a system for having the collages hung up so that the true identity of the person is not revealed. One way is to have them turned in upon entering the class and assigning several students to hang them up arbitrarily.

If everyone's collage cannot be responded to in writing during a single class period, break it down into a manageable number but not so few that the activity becomes too repetitious before everyone is included. Don't forget to include your own collage in there.

This activity is good to use early in the year to help learn a great deal about others.

EXERCISE 80.   **THE BEST PRODUCT—ME^2**

Purposes:

Affective—

To get students to be introspective in a lighthearted way

To call on students' creativity and imagination

For fun

Linguistic—

To practice the use of superlatives

To practice the use of adjectives describing positive qualities

To practice forming interrogative sentences

Levels: All levels

Size of groups: Six to eight or the total class

Materials needed: A brochure or ad made by each student

Procedures: In giving the assignment to the class, say something similar to this:

"Wherever we turn, we are surrounded by advertisements. Every few minutes television broadcasts commercials. Magazines and newspapers are filled with ads. And even driving in a car, the radio and billboards on the highway overwhelm us with advertising. All of the products, we are told, are the best on the market.

Examples of commercials, an ad and a brochure, about oneself

"Since we are so familiar with advertising, we are going to write some commercials. The product each of you will write about is very special and very rare. The product is you!

"Think about yourself and what makes you so unique. Then design an ad or a brochure selling your product to readers. You can use colored paper on tag board. Magazine pictures, snapshots, sketches, and three-dimensional objects can help illustrate your commercial. Use (the foreign language) in writing your ad. Remember to rave about how great, how extraordinary, how remarkable your product is and what it can do for others.

"We will all get to see the ads or brochures you create, so use your imagination and remember how good your product is as you try to sell it." (Encourage creativity and you will get it.)

When the ads are brought in, divide the students into groups of six to eight. Have each student pass his ad to the person on his right. Everyone will then read the ad to himself to get the flavor of it. Then, one at a time, the students will read the ad aloud and show it to the group. (This means no one is reading his own ad, so embarrassment will be reduced.)

Next the groups should volunteer to have two of their advertisements read to the entire class. The owners of the ads could now read them before the class. Then instruct the students to hang their ads on the wall, and let the class circulate around the room reading them. As they do so, have the students each compose five questions based on the ads they read, and select some to ask before their former groups or the total class. This will keep the class actively rather than passively involved with the ads. It is fun and humorous to see whether you can remember "who the product is" in this follow-up quiz activity.

An alternate to dividing the class in groups at first is to have the class seated in a circle, with each person passing his ad to the one on his right to be read aloud and shown to the *total* class. The advertisements can still be posted around the room afterwards with the quiz following.

EXERCISE 81.   **BRANCHING OUT**

Purposes:
　　Affective—
　　　　To discover qualities about oneself through the medium of art
　　Linguistic—
　　　　To practice the first person singular
　　　　To practice the use of adjectives describing positive qualities
　　　　To practice the vocabulary of colors
　　　　To practice the use of possessive adjectives

Levels: All levels

Size of groups: About five or six

Materials needed: White sheets of drawing paper; a large assortment of crayons, magic markers, felt pens, and pastels; a record of relaxing music and a record player

Procedures: Tell the students:

"There are many ways that we can discover things about ourselves an
we are like. One is through our own drawings.

"I'm going to ask everyone to draw the same thing. You will each draw a
tree. Draw it any way that pleases you. Decide on the type of tree, the size, the
shape, the colors you will use. Although everyone will be drawing a tree, each will
be different from everyone else's. You will have five minutes to draw your tree.

Illustrates qualities the artists and their trees have
in common

"As you draw your tree, do not talk to anyone, but give all your attention
to creating *a tree that really pleases you.* Relax and enjoy yourself as you watch
the growth of your tree as it develops on your paper."

See that each student has a piece of white drawing paper in advance and
that there are ample crayons, felt pens, and pastels of various colors for all. Ask
class members who have coloring materials at home to bring them in to be shared
with those who have none available.

As the students create their trees, you can play some relaxing music in the
background to facilitate enjoying the art work they are producing.

At the end of five minutes, tell the students to study the tree they have
created and to think about the positive ways they can describe it. Then divide the

class into groups of five or six. Each student will have a turn at describing the tree he has drawn. He should hold up the drawing and speak in the first person, as though he were the tree. Tell the students to be aware that they are actually describing themselves. The others in the group can ask such questions as: "How are you like a tree, Polly?" or "What kind of tree are you, Rick?" The students should ask questions about things they see in the drawings that the "artist" hasn't mentioned, for example, "What does that red bird on this branch mean to you?"

When everyone has had a turn, all pictures in a group are held up at the same time. The students can comment on similarities and differences in the trees, using possessive adjectives to do so: "Your tree is full and my tree is full," "Our trees are short and their trees are tall."

As a closing activity, have the students write one or more sentences directly on the page with the drawing or on a separate sheet of paper, describing their trees in the first person. Each artist should autograph his creation. Hang a display of the trees around the room, and have the students "stroll through the forest" reading and appreciating the foliage.

The students can write compositions embellishing how they are like their trees and citing examples of when their similar characteristics can be seen.

EXERCISE 82.   **HAPPY ART TALK**[3]

Purposes:
    Affective—
        To get students to re-experience a pleasant memory of theirs
        To communicate good feelings through the medium of art
        To share pleasant memories
    Linguistic—
        To practice the vocabulary of feelings
        To practice free conversation

Levels: Upper intermediate to advanced

Size of groups: About six

Materials needed: Crayons, felt pens, magic markers, pastels, and paper

Procedures: See that students have crayons and colored paper available to them. They will select the colors they want later. Tell the class that they are going to experience something pleasant in this activity. And then get the group relaxed as is done prior to a fantasy (refer to "Conducting Fantasies" on page 178). In a quiet, soothing voice, say the following:

    "Close your eyes and relax . . . Get very, very comfortable . . . Breathe deeply and slowly and focus on your breathing . . . Your eyelids are growing heavier and heavier as you relax more and more . . . Every part of your body feels

Sketches of happy moments recalled from childhood

relaxed and comfortable . . . " (Take enough time to make certain that the group is feeling relaxed. Add comparable statements or repeat some of these.)

Continue in the same calming voice, pausing and not rushing:

And now I want you to think back to a time when you were a child. Picture a time or a day when something very pleasant occurred which meant a lot to you, something you really liked or enjoyed or appreciated . . . Keep your eyes closed and raise your hand slowly for a moment when you have recalled such a memory and then put it down . . . Raise your hand slowly if you are still trying to think of a pleasant time which meant a lot to you when you were a child . . . (If some students raise their hands, state the following.) . . . In the next minute decide on a pleasant event from your past, any one which came to your mind. It can be a simple happening but it meant a lot to you . . .

"Now with your eyes still closed, picture the situation you just thought of and recall it just as it happened. Think of how you felt then and let yourself feel now what you felt then. See if you can relive the experience . . . When you are finished, keep your eyes closed and wait for the others to finish . . . "

Allow about three to four minutes to pass. After several minutes tell the class:

"Bring the memory to a close in the next minute, but keep your eyes closed and just continue to feel the good feelings.

"Now open your eyes slowly and select a piece of paper and some coloring materials. Draw or sketch or use colors and shapes abstractly to capture this memory or your feelings about it on paper. You will have (give a time limit) seven minutes to do this. Do not concern yourself about producing a masterpiece. You are recording your feelings about a pleasant memory . . . "

Give the students notice when the time is almost up: "Finish up in the next minute."

Divide the students into groups to share this experience and to talk about how the drawing represents the event and/or their feelings about it. Adjust the size of the groups according to the time you wish to spend. Groups of three take less time than groups of six, but it is interesting to be able to hear a variety of memories from different students, if time permits.

The class members will be interested in seeing the drawings of the others in the class and knowing what the event was. You could have the students write about their memories that night for homework and have the compositions read the next day. Others in the group should ask questions. The drawings can be displayed in the room with the corrected compositions placed below them. You also can have each person hold up his drawing before the class and be requested to give a one- to two-sentence synopsis of the event.

EXERCISE 83.   **ARTISTRY IN FEELINGS**[4]

Purposes:
    Affective—
        To get students in touch with feelings through the medium of art
        To tap the creativity and imagination of students
    Linguistic—
        To practice the vocabulary of colors and feelings
        To practice asking and answering questions

Levels: All levels

Size of groups: About six

Materials needed: A wide variety of colored construction paper and a large assortment of crayons and other coloring utensils

Procedures: Mention to the students:
    "We have seen how feelings can be expressed in different ways. Music can help bring out our feelings, as can poetry and clay.
    "Today we're going to use colored paper and crayons to get to our feelings and communicate them. I'm going to mention two feelings which are opposites of each other. Each of you will then select any color or colors of paper that these

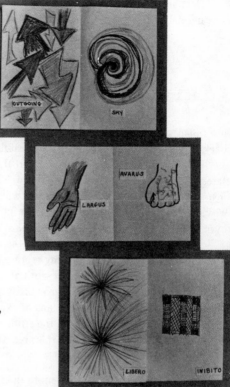

Impressions of contrasting feelings:
outgoing vs. shy, generous vs. selfish,
free vs. inhibited

feelings suggest to you. Then take appropriately colored crayons and draw
whatever images, sketches, lines, or abstract shapes come to you to express these
feelings."

Here are some suggestions of opposite feelings or moods that can be used in
this exercise. Select a pair that you think would be in keeping with the feelings
and interests of your own students:

daring — afraid
close — distant
free — inhibited
humorous — serious
outgoing — shy
trusting — cautious
generous — selfish
love — hate
relaxed — tense
enthusiastic — monotonous

Here are several conditions which suggest differences as well, although one is not necessarily the positive and the other the negative aspect of it:

separate — together
secure — risk-taking

The students may have ideas for moods, situations, or feelings to work with also. Check Appendixes A and B for other possibilities.

Divide the class into groups of about five to ask and answer questions related to how the feelings were portrayed. The questions can deal with why the construction paper colors were chosen as well as the colors used in the sketch: "Why did you choose blue to show 'peaceful'?" "Why does red mean 'enthusiasm' to you?" Other questions can relate to the sketches and symbols in the drawings.

The students will be curious about the drawings of those in other groups. An exhibit can be set up. The feeling represented should be written on each sheet. Half of the class can display the art work at a time, while the other half circulates and asks questions. Then the two groups reverse positions. Have the students discuss how they felt about this means of expressing themselves.

As a follow-up activity, have the students write a description of the feelings they illustrated. They can also tell their reactions to creating this type of art work.

Variations:

1. This activity can be done more than once by choosing a different set of feelings or situations for students to portray. For variety, you can give out a sheet of white paper. Have the students fold the paper down the center and sketch the positive feeling on the left and the negative on the right. If pastels or paint sets are available, these can be used to add a different flavor to the activity.

2. List a number of pairs of feelings on the board. Tell students to select a pair and draw these either on the two halves of one sheet of white paper or on two sheets of different colored paper, which have been cut in half. In groups, the students try to guess which feelings were depicted. Each person then states which feelings he tried to convey and why he represented them that way. The element of guessing the feelings portrayed lends added interest to the exercise.

As a total class, each person should hold up his drawings while the class guesses which pair of feelings the person sketched. This is particularly effective if the students can be seated in a large circle afterwards.

EXERCISE 84. **SCULPTURE IN FEELINGS**[5]

Purposes:

Affective—

To get students to express their feelings through the medium of clay
To tap the creativity and imagination of students

Linguistic—
> To practice the use of adjectives
> To practice the vocabulary of feelings
> To practice the vocabulary of shapes

Levels: Intermediate to advanced

Size of groups: About six or the total class

Materials needed: A piece of clay or play dough for every student

Procedures: Tell the students:

"There are different ways we can express ourselves and our feelings. Today we will illustrate some feelings by means of a piece of clay. You don't have to be an artist or a sculptor to express your feelings with clay."

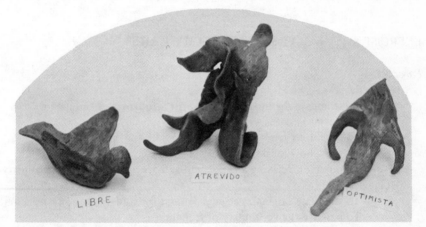

Created with the eyes closed, shapes expressing positive feelings: free, daring, optimistic

"I'm going to pass out the clay. When you get yours, mold it into a round ball first. Then wait for my instructions. (Distribute the clay. A small piece per student is sufficient.)

"Now close your eyes and continue to roll the clay into the round shape. As you do, I'm going to mention some feelings. Think about the feelings, and with your eyes closed, let your hands create a shape in clay to represent one of them. Later we will talk about what the shape you've made seems to mean to you as related to that feeling."

Decide on which feelings you want students to depict. Refer to Appendix A for a list of feelings to choose from, but select *positive* feelings. Or ask the students to think of a positive feeling themselves. Place the feelings you suggest on the board. Here are some examples:

confident   loved
daring   secure
close   peaceful
free   overjoyed
trusting   optimistic
exhilarated

Have the students form groups of six in which to describe the shapes they have molded and to share how these express the feeling depicted. If possible, have each student hold up his art work while the class guesses which feeling it is. A display of shapes can be placed around the room for all to see. If each person thought of a feeling on his own, the feeling can be written on a card with the name of the "sculptor." Half of the class can circulate to see the display, while the sculptors stand beside their creations and answer questions about them. Then the two groups can rotate being exhibitors and art gallery viewers.

EXERCISE 85.   **IT'S MUSIC TO MY EARS[6]**

Purposes:
  Affective—
    To stimulate the imagination to drift into fantasies and create
      pleasant images
    To tune in to one's feelings
    To show how music influences feelings
    To provide a relaxing and pleasant activity where feelings are primary
  Linguistic—
    To stimulate original, personal content for students to converse about
    To practice the vocabulary of feelings

Levels: Upper intermediate to advanced

Size of groups: Three (triads)

Materials needed: A record with a combination of peaceful, happy, and zestful melodies, preferably music that is unfamiliar to students. There should be no vocals to the music.

Procedures: Ask students to close their eyes and to get comfortable. Tell them you are going to play some music for them to listen to. Tell them to concentrate on the music and the feelings they get from it and to be aware of any images as well as feelings that come to them.

  Suggest that students do this in whichever way is best for them: either wait until the music is over and then jot down what they remembered feeling, thinking,

and seeing, or write down a few words as they go along to help them remember.
The latter should be done while keeping their eyes closed.

Play three pieces of music, without stopping, that have different tempos
and feelings to them. Use music with a tempo that will evoke good feelings, rather
than sad, tragic ones.

Have the students discuss the various feelings and fantasies they had in small
groups of three, so each person will have enough time to talk. (Each student will
have seen and experienced quite a bit.)

Process the experience with the total group, summarizing their reactions to
the experience.

EXERCISE 86. **MELODY ON MY MIND**[7]

Purposes:
> Affective—
>> To help develop the capacity to associate
>> To gain self-awareness through an unusual means
>> To help appreciate the intricate
> Linguistic—
>> For free conversation

Levels: Intermediate to advanced

Size of groups: Three

Procedures: Get your students still and relaxed. Then tell them:
"Today I'm going to ask you to do something before I tell you the purpose
of it. Close your eyes and be still a moment . . . Now see what song comes to your
mind (A longer pause) . . . Let it come to you without consciously trying . . . Keep
your eyes closed and raise your hand if a song has not occurred to you yet. (Wait
till everyone has thought of a song.)

"Now hum the song out loud for a minute and think about it as you do.
(You may have to encourage the students to do this aloud. After a minute ask
them to keep their eyes closed and think about these questions.) Does the title of
the song mean anything to you? . . . If there are words to the song, which lines
stand out as having particular meaning to you right now? . . . (A longer pause) . . .
What is the mood of the song? . . . What thoughts and feelings from your own
life are on your mind or preoccupying you that relate to this song, its title, any
of the words in it, or the mood it represents for you? . . . How does this song
relate to you right now?"

After the students have had time to reflect on the answers to these questions, mention that this exercise can help them become aware of their present
mood or the hidden thoughts and feelings that are utmost in their minds at this
time. Divide the students into groups of three, and ask them to tell each other

the name of the song that came to them and what associations they discovered in it.

Ask for volunteers to share with the total class the song that came to them and the associations they had. Tell the class about the song you thought of and what it means to you. Find out how many students discovered that the song which came to mind had some significance to what is actually in their thoughts right now or to the mood they are in. Conclude by saying that we all have the ability to associate extremely well, and we can use it to help our thinking and our self-awareness. Mention that they can do this exercise on their own to become more conscious of what they're thinking about and feeling at any given time.

Use this activity after some degree of trust has been built in the class, so that the students will be more willing to share the thoughts associated with their songs.

EXERCISE 87.   **SONGS THAT SAY A LOT**

Purposes:
    Affective—
        To connect pleasant memories with the medium of music
    Linguistic—
        To practice the vocabulary of feelings
        To practice the past progressive
        To practice the past tense(s)

Levels: Intermediate to advanced

Size of groups: Total class

Materials needed: Cassette recorders, record players, and/or a guitar or piano

Procedures: Mention to the class that many pieces of music unfold fond memories for us. Ask the students to think back from their earliest years up to the present and recall the melodies that bring back pleasant memories to them. Tell the students to try to think of several such songs and what their significance is. Ask them to bring in a cassette tape or a record if they have any for one of their songs.

You will need to know in advance how many will be bringing in a record or a tape. If you or one of your students play an instrument such as the guitar or the piano, this will be an asset to the exercise. If such talent is not available in the class, see if outside of the class you can find someone who is musically inclined. Then for any person who does not have a record or tape to present for one of his songs, have your musician play a few bars of one of the songs on the remaining individuals' lists and tape record it in advance, unless the person can come to your class with the instrument.

In carrying out the exercise, each student should tell the class what is special to him about the memory of his melody. Then a bit of the tune should be played via whatever medium is available, while everyone is asked to focus on the mood or feeling of the person whose selection it is. As the students listen to the music, ask them to try to capture for themselves some of the same feelings the person has whose memorable tune it is.

Have the students discuss how they felt about this experience. As a follow-up activity, they can write about the memories and associations of the songs on their lists.

EXERCISE 88. **SAY IT WITH MUSIC**

Purposes:
> Affective—
>> To get students acquainted with each other in an amusing way
>> To bring out good feelings in students through the vehicle of music
>> To energize the group
> Linguistic—
>> To practice giving one's name
>> To practice parts of speech such as verbs or adjectives
>> To practice tenses such as the future or the conditional

Levels: Beginning, but can be used with upper levels by practicing more difficult structures

Size of groups: Total class or groups of about twelve

Materials needed: A record with a fast, modern, lively, contagious beat which makes people feel like moving to it and which evokes good feelings. Examples of American songs of this sort are: "You Can Do It If You Really Want" by Jimmy Cliff in the album *The Harder They Come*; "Fly Robin Fly" and "Get Up and Boogie" by the Silver Convention; "That's The Way I Like It" and others on the album by KC and the Sunshine Band. Use music of the target culture if possible.

Procedures: This activity can be used at the start of school to introduce students to each other or at any time in the year. It should be used very early in the year only if you perceive that the class will be uninhibited in carrying it out. Here is how you can initiate the activity:

"There are many ways we can introduce ourselves to let others know about us. Today we're going to introduce ourselves in a way that is different and can be fun.

"I'd like everyone to get up, take one another's hands and form a circle. (Depending on the size of the class and the space available, decide on whether the total class should form a large circle or whether there should be smaller circles. Twelve is a good size for a smaller group. Do not make groups any smaller than ten.)

"I'm going to put on some music. Listen to it and feel the spirit of the music. Let it bring out good, happy, warm, excited feelings in you. As you hear the music, in your place move to the music and let yourself feel very happy.

"Then, one at a time, when you're feeling quite good, move into and around the circle. Move however the music makes you feel. You can dance, move around rhythmically, use gestures. Once you are in the circle call out: 'My name is _____ ' (and give your first name), 'and I like to _____ ' (and tell something you like to do, such as 'I like to swim.').

"Then return to your place in the circle. We all move differently to music and whatever any of us does to show these feelings will be fine. So let's listen to the music now and everyone start to move to it. When you're ready, start moving one at a time into the circle and tell us about yourself."

If there is music left on the piece being played after everyone has introduced himself, tell the group to keep moving in place till the end. A two and a half minute recording will probably suffice for groups of twelve. If the total class is in one group, either have consecutive pieces play without any break or copy a piece on tape twice and let it run through. Five minutes of music should be enough for most classes, but be prepared with extra music if it is needed. Join the group yourself, or if the class is in several groups, rotate to each group and step inside each circle yourself to take your turn.

Comments: This activity is useful in practicing numerous structures. They should all deal with something the students tell about themselves. Different tenses and parts of speech can be practiced by using statements such as these:

> In five years I will _____ . (Future tense.)
> If I had a wish, I would _____ . (Conditional tense.)
> My name is _____ , and I am _____ . (Give three positive adjectives that describe you.)

Use your imagination to make up statements that will be interesting to complete with structures or parts of speech needing practice. If the activity is well received, have a second or third round planned with a different structure and other music to be played.

EXERCISE 89.   **CURTAIN UP**[8]

Purposes:
>   Affective—
>   To encourage spontaneity, imagination, and humor
>   To get students actively moving and totally involved
>   For fun

Linguistic—
To encourage spontaneous conversation among students

Levels: Upper intermediate to advanced

Size of groups: Total class

Procedures: Explain to the students that they have studied a number of dialogs while learning a foreign language and that now they are going to create some themselves for a new type of use.

Ask each person to think of some particular setting in which a dialog can take place. Give a number of examples, including some unusual settings: a restaurant, a barber shop, a dentist's office, Macy's bargain aisle, an airport, a sports event, a gym class, a spaceship, a haunted house, a rock concert. Tell the students to think of a scene where some action is taking place and write about six lines that they could say to others present in this particular setting. In this case there might be only a few people or many. Give an example:

"Suppose you are in a supermarket and have a large cart full of groceries. You decide to go into the ten-package speed line. Here are some of the things you might say:

'Excuse me, but can I get in front of you? I only have a few things to buy . . . But I'm in a big hurry . . . But my dog is alone in the car waiting for me . . . I know this is the ten-package line, but I only have about twenty-five things!' "

Tell the class that they will be using their lines in a way that will be fun. Explain that the opening line should make clear to the class where the dialog is taking place.

When beginning the activity ask for two people to start. Have someone begin whose dialog can take place with only one other person being present. The other person should respond appropriately once he catches on to where the scene is taking place.

Instruct the class that after a few lines of dialog ensue, a third person should enter the "stage," at which time the actors in the present scene are to stop, freeze, and listen. Once they get the gist of the new scene from the opening lines of the new dialog, they begin to spontaneously participate in it. This process continues, with one person at a time coming on stage and all others already in the scene becoming the actors, until every person in the class is in the act. The students don't *have* to stick to the lines they wrote, but they will be a big help to them for the most part.

Be prepared yourself with a dialog and enter the action *early* to help keep the dialogs from dying when students run out of ways to respond in the scenes. Be certain that students allow a little time for each scene to develop before the next one starts and that the class does remain quiet when each new person changes the scene.

This lively, humorous activity serves as an energizer. It is fun to note where each change of scene will take the group dialog next.

EXERCISE 90.   **ANIMAL, VEGETABLE, FRUIT**[9]

Purposes:
> Affective—
>> To liven up the class at a time when energy is low or after something tedious or difficult to learn has just been concluded
>> To provide fun and physical action
> Linguistic—
>> To review the vocabulary of different categories of nouns
>> To review the vocabulary of nouns, verbs, adjectives, and prepositions (in a variation of this exercise)

Levels: All levels, especially beginning and intermediate

Size of groups: Divide the class into four groups

Procedures: Divide the class into four or five groups. Have the members of each group number off consecutively from one to the number in the group. Everyone will be standing up for this activity.

Some open space will be needed, with you, the teacher, in the middle of it. The groups should be spaced equidistantly from you in different parts of the room, similar to the diagram below:

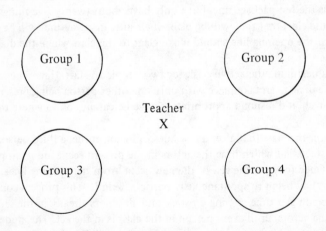

The students designated as number 1 in each group come to the center and huddle around you. You then whisper a word for them to act out nonverbally for their groups. The students return to their groups and silently enact hints to help in guessing the word. The members of the group call out, guessing the word they think is being enacted. When someone in a group gives the correct word, the student who acted out the word runs back to the teacher and touches his hand. Or you may prefer to hold a tablet or a book for students to touch. (Sometimes in the excitement students can be rough in trying to beat another team member to tapping the teacher first and a fast slap can occur.) For each round, give a point to the winning group.

Use three categories of words for students to act out in any given exercise. If the categories are "Animal, Vegetable, Fruit," the students should have a nonverbal signal to reveal to the groups so they know the category before they start guessing the actual word. The signals can be something acted out to represent each category, such as: making the hands look like claws and the mouth open and roaring to depict the category of "animal"; holding up one, two, or three fingers to mean the first, second, or third category; or using the fingers to form the first letter of the category, such as "A" for animal, "V" for vegetable, "F" for fruit. Use the letters for the words in the target language, of course.

If the class has been learning foods of all sorts and working with menus, other categories could be "Appetizer, Main Course, Dessert."

Parts of speech can be used as the categories also. "Nouns, Verbs, and Adjectives" are fun to act out. "Prepositions" and "Adverbs" can be added to make for even more challenging categories.

"Sports" and "Clothing" are other categories that can be included. If the latter is selected, state that it must be acted out nonverbally rather than merely pointing to the item someone is wearing.

This activity can be used on different occasions to drill and review categories of vocabulary and parts of speech. Use a different set of three whenever it is played. Include other categories that are appropriate for your class.

Comments: One very important ground rule is that the students must call out the words they are guessing in the target language or the teams do not score a point. Five to ten minutes of this exercise is sufficient for awakening a class with new energy and spirit to continue the lesson at hand. Expect laughter and excitement. It works with all ages, even adults.

NOTES

1. This is a very popular technique used by many facilitators. I was introduced to it being carried out in the way it is presented here by Marvin Levy.

2. This is another popular activity used by a number of facilitators. Original author unknown.

3. This technique is based on the type of activities used by art therapists.

4. This technique is similar to some used by art therapists.

5. The idea for this technique developed from some related to art therapy.

6. Thanks to George Isaac Brown for the idea underlying this exercise.

7. Credit for the origin of this technique belongs to William C. Schutz.

8. This activity is an adaptation of one experienced at a workshop. Originator unknown.

9. This technique is an adaptation of one experienced at a workshop. Original author unknown.

Me and My Fantasies

By nourishing and developing our capacity to fantasize,
we enrich and expand life itself.

— Herbert A. Otto

A common happening in all of our lives is to dream and to daydream. Yet taking advantage of these amazing capacities to learn about ourselves and to grow is not so common.

Fantasies are intended for just such purposes. We can discover a number of remarkable insights into ourselves by means of fantasies. The exercises in this section are intended to expose students to imaginative and intriguing journeys into themselves as their fantasies reveal what is meaningful to them at a conscious and unconscious level.

* * * * *

CONDUCTING FANTASIES

Before conducting fantasies, here are some words of advice. To begin with, the students must be introduced to what a fantasy is and what to expect when experiencing one. Never conduct your first fantasy without discussing these things first or some students may be worried that something mysterious or mystical is happening to them.

Explain to students that we all have dreams and daydreams and that these reveal to us what is on our minds: our hopes, ambitions, worries, and fears. Tell them that it is possible to learn about ourselves through a similar means called a fantasy, which is done while you are awake and relaxed and with your eyes closed. In order to get everyone feeling relaxed and peaceful, you will be giving some suggestions to get them in the mood for a fantasy.

Explain that a fantasy is like a dream or a daydream, except that you, the teacher, will be describing an imaginary situation that they are to try to visualize they are experiencing. At some points you will be talking and at other times you will be silent as they continue on their own with their fantasy. Tell the class that they will always have a positive experience during their fantasies.

Mention that even though everyone will start off with the same situation, all of their fantasies will be different. Their fantasies will represent some significant things about themselves and can give them insights into discovering more about what they are like. State that fantasies are fun, interesting, and unusual, as everyone creates his own personally meaningful story out of them. Let the students know that they will be sharing only what they want to from their fantasies and that you often will ask them to write something related to what they fantasize.

Tell the students that they may be surprised at how imaginative their fantasies are and how clever they are at gaining insights from them. Everything in their fantasies can potentially reveal to them something about themselves.

The fantasies included in this book are intended to focus on positive aspects for students and not on areas of great trouble or concern. Therefore, tell the students that although dreams can sometimes be scary, their fantasies will all be pleasant.

In conducting a fantasy, lowering the shades and turning off the lights help create a relaxed atmosphere. After orienting students as to what a fantasy is and what to expect, tell them that you are now going to help them feel relaxed. Then slowly start to give a number of relaxing suggestions in a *soft, calming* voice. Here are some ideas of what to say. You will find other things to add as you continue to conduct fantasies. Do not rush through this phase.

> Close your eyes now and relax . . .
> Breathe deeply and slowly and focus on your breath . . .
> Your eyelids are growing heavier and heavier . . .
> You are getting more and more relaxed . . .
> Feel your entire body getting very relaxed, deeply, deeply relaxed . . .
> From the top of your head to the tips of your toes, you are relaxing deeper
> and deeper . . .
> Notice your breathing—the slowness and deepness . . .
> With every breath you are getting more and more deeply relaxed . . .
> Your feet and your legs are relaxed . . .
> Your trunk and your stomach are relaxed . . .
> Your chest and your back are relaxed . . .
> You feel pleasantly peaceful and completely relaxed . . .
> Your arms and your shoulders are relaxed . . .
> Your neck and your face are relaxed . . .
> Your scalp is relaxed . . .
> Your entire body feels comfortable, peaceful, and relaxed . . .
> Focus on any part of your body that needs to relax . . .
> And it will now become relaxed . . .
> You are relaxed mentally and physically . . .
> All of the tension is gone . . .
> As you breathe deeply and slowly you are completely, totally relaxed . . .
> I am going to count slowly from ten to zero . . .
> As I say each number, you will become more and more deeply relaxed . . .

Ten ... nine ... eight ... seven ... six ... five ... four ... three ... two
... one ... zero ...
You are now very deeply, completely, and pleasantly relaxed.

Be sure to experience the fantasy for yourself before trying it with a class.
You can also re-experience it along with the class by closing your eyes and allowing yourself to drift into the mood. Your fantasy this time will probably differ
from the first one, and you, too, will be able to share with the class your fantasy
trip.

You will find that as time goes on, the class will look forward to new fantasy
journeys. For the second language teacher, fantasies provide a rich and motivating
vehicle for free conversation and composition. If a particular fantasy will not be
understood in the target language, use the native language to communicate it to
the class and the foreign language for the follow-up activities.

* * * * *

EXERCISE 91. **I HEAR HAPPINESS**[1]

Purposes:
    Affective—
        To stimulate the imagination to create pleasant images
        To tune in to one's feelings
        To listen to the environment in a new way
        To provide a pleasant activity where feelings are primary
    Linguistic—
        To practice the vocabulary of sounds and different things which
           produce them
        To practice the vocabulary of feelings

Levels: All levels

Size of groups: Three to five

Materials needed: A tape composed of relaxing, happy, joyful, peaceful sounds,
with each one lasting for about thirty seconds to a minute

Procedures: You will have to prepare a tape consisting of a number of distinctive
sounds. These can be taken from sound effects or environment records used by
theaters.*

*One source of environment and sound effects records is Thomas J. Valentino, 150 W. 46th
Street, New York, N.Y. 10036.

You also can produce and tape your own sounds. Select distinctive sounds which can be identified and are connected with positive events. The tape could be about five minutes long.

Some examples of sounds which can be included are: birds singing, bells ringing, a cuckoo clock, a train, the sound of the ocean, laughter, a plane taking off, the music from a carousel, a cheer at a football game, the striking of the chimes of a clock twelve times followed by the shout of "Happy New Year," the singing of "Happy Birthday to You," applause, rain on the roof, a doorbell with chimes ringing, an orchestra tuning up, the wind blowing through the trees, a champagne cork popping and the sound of pouring the beverage.

Explain to the class:

"We are surrounded by sounds wherever we go. Often we are not consciously aware of them. Yet they can affect our mood and the way we are feeling.

"I'm going to play a tape that has a number of sounds associated with good times and happy feelings. Listen to them with your eyes closed. Relax and let your imagination go. Notice the feelings you experience and any images or events that come to your mind. When the tape ends, you will discuss the feelings and images you experienced. Close your eyes now, get comfortable, relax, and enjoy yourself."

Play the tape for the class. Afterwards place the students into groups of three to five. Since advanced classes will be able to say more about the experience, put them into groups of three so there will be more time to express themselves.

Once the tape is over, place on the board or on the overhead projector, a list of the sounds just played. This will help the students to recall what was heard and experienced and will guide their discussion. Ask them to discuss the different feelings they had and the images, fantasies, or events they envisioned.

Process the experience with the total class and ask for their reactions to the exercise. Have the students suggest other happy sounds while in their small groups and compile a list of these for the total class.

As a follow-up activity, ask students to start listening more consciously to the sounds that surround them. Tell them to see whether they can become more aware of happy sounds they normally take for granted. Have them write down a list of the sounds they hear for a few days. Encourage students who may be interested to make their own tape of happy sounds to present to the class.

EXERCISE 92.   **MY IDEAL SCHOOL DAY**

Purposes:
>   Affective—
>>   To have students think about what their desires for school actually
>>   are
>>   To call on the imagination
>   Linguistic—
>>   To practice the future and the conditional tenses

Levels: Intermediate to advanced

Size of groups: About three or four

Procedures: This activity can be given as an assignment without any preliminaries. However, it will be much more enjoyable and easier to do if introduced by a fantasy. In the latter case, allow the students time to get comfortable and give some relaxing suggestions to get them ready for the fantasy. Then tell the class: (Pause wherever three dots appear.)

"You are now going to have an enjoyable fantasy. You are going to experience the ideal school day from the time you awaken in the morning until you leave for home at the end of the school day. So imagine that it is time to get up to go to school. You stretch and yawn and feel happy, for you know a good day is ahead . . . As you get dressed, you feel a new excitement in you and you dress faster than usual . . . You eat a delicious meal with all your favorite breakfast foods . . . And now you leave for school . . . On the way you see some of your best friends and you continue together, knowing a treat is in store for you . . .

"Yes, today school will be whatever you have always wanted it to be. Everything is going to go your way. However you plan it, that's what school will be—for one day.

"You enter the building now and walk through the halls. The bell rings for the school day to begin. Go to your regular classes one at a time and make the school day an ideal one for you. Go now and see what happens . . . (Allow five to seven minutes to pass.) The school day is drawing to a close so finish up your ideal school day shortly. When you are ready, come back to this room, open your eyes, and remain silent."

Divide the class into groups of three or, at the most, four. Have the students take turns telling what their ideal school day was like. Have everyone tell the total class the most important thing they envisioned in their ideal school fantasy. A number of these may be humorous.

As a follow-up activity, ask the students to write about the fantasy they experienced, using the future or the conditional tenses, for example, "In my fantasy school there will be no tests" or "In my fantasy school, teachers would not criticize students."

A discussion can follow as to what types of things the students in general would like to see changed and how many of these can actually be changed.

EXERCISE 93.   **JUNGLE BELLS[2]**

Purposes:
  Affective—
    To stimulate the imagination through the medium of music
    To gain insights into one's strengths by means of fantasy

Linguistic—
To practice the vocabulary of animals

Levels: All levels

Size of groups: About six

Materials needed: A record player and a record with modernistic music that gives the impression of sounds that animals make; the music should have a lot of range and variety to it—sounding clumsy, heavy, and raucous and also having high tones for birdlike chattering; an example of such music is the beginning of "King Lear" in the album *Four Overtures* by Hektor Berlioz (Forum, GLS-4304-B, conducted by Jean Martinon).

Procedures: Prepare the students for this fantasy trip:
"You will be going on a jungle safari soon. No harm will come to you on this trip. Our journey is through a distant jungle on a faraway continent where every animal imaginable is found. Listen to the sounds the different animals make as they come by and greet you. Enjoy the animals in their natural setting more than you ever have before."

(PUT ON THE RECORD)

Halfway through the record, lower the volume so the music is quietly in the background and now say:
"As you look at the different animals here in the jungle, go up to one and talk to it . . . Ask the animal where his strength lies and what is his secret for getting through a bad situation and surviving. Go ahead now and speak to one of the animals."

(TURN THE VOLUME OF THE MUSIC UP AGAIN)

When the record ends, place the students into groups of three. Have them discuss their reactions to their fantasy safari. Each should tell what animals he saw, which one he spoke with, and what the animal's message was. The students should talk about why they chose the animal they did and how the secret to their own survival and strength in difficult situations relates to that of this animal.

In the total class ask for the animals students spoke with to be named. See how many chose the same animal. Have some of the students tell the total group where the strength in their animal lies. Tell the students that through this fantasy and association, they have been in touch with learning about their own strengths in difficult situations.

As a written assignment, the students can name several animals they favor and have each one tell where its strength lies in surviving in a bad situation. This will provide additional insights to students in seeing their own means for taking care of themselves in times of stress or difficulty.

EXERCISE 94.　　　　**CURIOUS CURIO**[3]

Purposes:

    Affective—

        To call on the imagination

        To discover something each student is looking for

    Linguistic—

        To create a dialog using the first and second persons

        To focus on listening comprehension

Levels: Intermediate to advanced

Size of groups: About four

Procedures: Go through the steps of getting the class relaxed for a fantasy trip. Once they are ready, begin the story, which you can modify for the level of understanding of your students.

    "Imagine that you find yourself walking along a country road. It is a beautiful day, and you're enjoying your walk . . . You see flowers of all colors along the way. The wind is blowing gently through the branches of the trees.

    "The road seems endless ahead as you continue to walk. But then in the distance you seem to see a town . . . As you get closer and closer, the dirt road changes to cobblestones. You are approaching a quaint old street with shops on both sides . . .

    "The shops are very unusual looking . . . You stop to look in the windows to see the merchandise . . . Each shop looks more interesting than the one before. You have never seen such a variety of beautiful things for sale.

    "As you look in the window of the next shop, you can no longer resist. You decide to enter this shop and look around . . . As you open the door, a set of chimes rings, announcing your presence . . . The elderly shopkeeper greets you with a warm and pleasant smile.

    "You slowly gaze at every shelf and counter, at the interesting, unusual items on display. You decide that you must buy something before you leave as a remembrance of this lovely place. Look over all the merchandise in this very quaint shop, and decide what it is you wish to take with you . . . (Pause about a minute.) . . . When you decide on your purchase, take it to the shopkeeper to wrap for you, pay him, and leave the store . . . (Pause about thirty seconds.) You continue walking down the street until you come to the dirt road once more . . . You see a little bench along the way and decide to sit awhile and rest. As you do, you unwrap your package to look at your purchase once more.

    "There it is in your hands. You admire the article and are happy you bought it. Suddenly the article begins to speak to you. Have a conversation with it and listen carefully to what you say to each other . . . (Pause about two minutes.) . . . Now bring your conversation to a close . . . (Pause about thirty seconds.) . . .

Wrap the package once more and continue your journey until you are ready to come back to this class."

Place the students into groups of three or four. Have them discuss the following topics:

1. What were some interesting highlights of your fantasy journey?
2. What object did you purchase?
3. What was the nature of your dialog with the object you bought?
4. Why do you think you picked the object you did? What is its significance to you?

In the total class, the students could each tell what object they purchased and why it is significant to them. As a follow-up activity, have the students write the dialog they had with their object and discuss its meaning to them. They can also answer the other questions listed above, if you wish.

End the activity by stating that every part of a fantasy represents some element related to us. Ask the students to think about what they learned concerning themselves from their fantasy. This can be included in the written follow-up as well.

Reserve this fantasy experience for a time when the students are better acquainted and have gained more trust in each other.

EXERCISE 95. **SWAP SHOP**[4]

Purposes:
    Affective—
        To have students assess some areas in which they wish to grow and
            change
    Linguistic—
        To practice the vocabulary of measurements
        To practice the vocabulary of personality traits and characteristics
        To practice the imperative form

Levels: All levels

Size of groups: About six

Materials needed: The assignment completed by each student

Procedures: Tell the students to imagine that a brand new store has opened in the area. It is very unique because the merchandise consists of personality traits and characteristics. The only way to make purchases in this store is to give up some amount of a characteristic or personality trait you have more than enough of since no money is exchanged in this shop.

Ask the students to make out a shopping list of what characteristics they would like to have more of and what they can exchange for it. They should also specify the quantity they want to receive and what they will give in return. A shopping list might look like this:

WHAT I WANT	WHAT I WILL GIVE
Five pounds of lightheartedness	A bushel of seriousness
Six cans of energy	A family-size bottle of restlessness
A barrel of fun	A peck of work

The qualities being exchanged can be positive ones which the students know they can spare because they have so much of them:

Twenty-four fluid ounces of determination	A package of imagination
A gallon of assertiveness	A quart of charm

Ask the students to have a designated number of items on their shopping lists. When they come to class, put the students into groups of six to eight. In these groups, each person will have a turn at being the shopkeeper and the customer. The owner of the store will wait on the customer. The ensuing dialog can be elementary and thus highly structured or more open and spontaneous, depending on the level of the class. Basically, the customer will order what he wants:

Customer: Give me five liters of sensitivity.
Shopkeeper: What will you give me in return for it?
Customer: Take these three containers of enthusiasm.

In between, the two of them can admire or speak highly of the merchandise: "This is the finest brand of curiosity on the market" or "Your sincerity is very attractive." The shopkeeper can ask, "What else do you need?" or "Can you use some ___(patience)___ ? I have a special on it this week." Of course, they will greet each other as the customer enters and leaves the shop.

Demonstrate the role playing before the class with one or two students. The first time you should take one of the roles. The second time have two students do it on their own.

Conclude the activity with a discussion of how the students can acquire more of the traits and characteristics that they wish to have. This can be carried out as a written assignment as well.

EXERCISE 96. **THE GURU GIVES**[5]

Purposes:

    Affective—

        To tap the potential within us to answer our own questions in life

        To reveal to students how potentially wise we are

    Linguistic—

        To converse freely

        To practice listening comprehension

        To practice the past tense(s)

        To write a free composition

Levels: Intermediate to advanced

Size of groups: About four to five

Procedures: Tell the students that they are going to take a fantasy trip in which they will make some interesting discoveries. Have them close their eyes and give a number of suggestions in a soothing voice to get everyone relaxed. Then begin the fantasy:

"Picture yourself outdoors walking along a dirt road in India . . . It is a warm and sunny day . . . In the distance you see an elderly man in white walking along the road . . . A woman in a sari is going after water.

"You have come to this place because you are looking for answers to some questions. You have heard that a very unusual guru settled in this village after receiving enlightenment. People come from all over the world to the place the guru received his call.

"You approach the place where you find the famous tree . . . It fits the description . . . the huge rock nearby, the strange bend in the trunk of the tree . . . Yes, this is where the guru received enlightenment and now gives it to others.

"You approach the tree and sit on the ground, resting your back against the strong tree trunk. You close your eyes and sit quietly, meditating, and waiting to be enlightened.

"In the stillness you feel a breeze gently caressing your cheek. You open your eyes and see a brilliant light and within it the vision of the guru. He is about to tell you some things about yourself. Listen to what he has to say as he knows what is so . . . (Pause)

"Speak to the guru and answer him. Take a few minutes to have a talk with him . . . (Pause about two minutes.)

"Now is the time to ask the guru your important question. Tell him what it is that you need to know, the one question you want his help in answering—the one thing that will help you be an even happier person now. Ask the question and then listen to his answer, for he will tell you the solution . . . (Wait about two minutes.)

"Now say your closing words to each other, and when you are ready, come back to this room." (Pause about a minute longer.)

This can be a deep and moving experience for some students. They may wish to share only parts of this fantasy, such as what they saw visually and what the guru looked like. Some may not wish to discuss what they spoke to the guru about. The students may be much quieter and more reflective than usual. Do not be concerned about this. It means that these students got into something meaningful and they probably received the answers they needed to what is of concern to them.

Put the students into groups of about four and suggest that they share as much of the experience as they care to. In the total class, ask the students to react to this experience. See whether any students would like to share their experiences with the guru with the whole class. You can participate in this first to encourage others to do so.

Conclude the experience by asking how many felt that they received a meaningful response when they questioned the guru. Then ask, "Where did this wisdom actually come from?" Point out that we all know what we need and what is right for us. We just have to tune in to ourselves to find the answers. We are our own gurus.

To follow up the exercise, have the students write about their fantasies with the guru and what they shared with and found out from him. Tell them to be as specific or as general as they wish. Although there will be some things related to this fantasy that the students will prefer not to reveal in class, many will feel comfortable enough with you to write about it. Do not feel concerned if this is the case. The experience can be very worthwhile and rewarding, but deeply personal, as well.

Do wait until a good deal of trust has developed in the class before introducing this particular fantasy. You will have to shorten or modify it to meet the comprehension of your students.

EXERCISE 97.   **SCUBA DUBA**[6]

Purposes:
  Affective—
          To get in touch with things of beauty through the imagination
          To discover some things about oneself through the medium of music
          To show how music stimulates the imagination
  Linguistic—
          To stimulate original, personal content for students to converse about
          To practice the vocabulary of life under the sea

Levels: Intermediate to advanced

Size of groups: Triads

Materials needed: A record player and a record with impressionistic, classical modern music; the tempo should be slow, the melody going down the scale, with string instruments noticeable; "Poem Mystique" by Ernest Bloch (RCA Victor, LM 2089, violinist: Jascha Heifetz) would be such an example.

Procedures: This activity will be a fantasy induced by music. Introduce the idea by setting the scene:

"Close your eyes. Breathe slowly and deeply. Get comfortable and relax. You're going on a beautiful journey beneath the sea. You're going scuba diving. While you're under the water, observe and appreciate all the beautiful creatures and plant life you discover there. You know that it is safe here so enjoy your exploration under the sea."

(TURN ON THE MUSIC)

Part way through the record, lower the volume so the music is quietly in the background and tell the class:

"You've heard that something precious and valuable is hidden beneath the waters nearby. You decide to explore now and search for it. Watch for clues that lead you to this precious, hidden valuable under the sea, just waiting to be discovered. It might be something very large or small. What you find will be yours to keep."

(TURN THE VOLUME OF THE MUSIC UP AGAIN)

When the record ends, place the students into groups of three to describe their visit below the water and the precious hidden thing(s) of value they found there. Ask the students to discuss the significance of the particular treasure they found at the bottom of the sea. What does their valuable object seem to symbolize for them? Have some of the students share the treasure they found and its significance with the total group.

Afterwards they can write a description of their journey below the sea and/ or they may wish to pursue the topic of the precious object they found waiting for them.

EXERCISE 98.   **THE OBJECT IS ME**[7]

Purposes:
    Affective—
        To call on the imagination
        To call on students' ability to associate
        To enable students to discover some insights into themselves

Linguistic—
    To practice the present tense
    To practice the use of adjectives
    To practice the past, future, or conditional tenses if desired
    To practice listening comprehension

Levels: All levels

Size of groups: About four

Procedures: Explain the following to the class:

"Today we're going to take another fantasy journey to learn more about ourselves. Your journey will not be the same as anyone else's because it represents you and you alone. We will go to a faraway place on our trip today. Close your eyes now so we can relax and prepare to leave our surroundings. (Spend several minutes getting the class comfortable and relaxed as you speak to them softly.)

"And now imagine that you are in a beautiful foreign country near a body of water. It is a peaceful afternoon. The sun is dazzling in the sky. In the distance you can see several small boats, maybe fishing vessels. The landscape is more beautiful than any you have ever seen.

"You begin to walk along the shore . . . There are trees and flowers along the way. This is a very happy and peaceful moment for you . . .

"You decide to explore the country to see what you can find. You walk into the woods. The birds are chirping . . . The sun coming through the trees lights a brilliant path for you to follow . . . It's almost as though it is leading you somewhere . . . The birds seem to be flying in a path and directing you on your way.

"As you continue through the woods there is a clearing . . . You approach it and look beyond . . . The sun now directs its rays in the distance where you see . . . to your surprise . . . a beautiful castle . . . This is just what you always imagined a castle would look like . . .

"The birds chirp noticeably loud, as though they are excited, and fly in the direction of the castle. They seem to want you to follow . . . As you walk closer and closer to the castle, your heart beats a little faster with expectation . . . How wonderful to actually see a castle.

"You get closer and closer and now you are almost there. As you arrive the gates open, as though you are expected . . . You see the entrance to the castle and, as you get near, the beautifully decorated doors open for you . . . Somehow you know you are welcome . . . You enter the castle, but no one is there.

"You begin to explore the magnificent rooms. You admire the beauty of the rich and costly decor. Take some time now to visit the rooms of the castle . . . (Pause about two minutes.)

"Somehow you know the time you can spend in the castle is almost up. You see no one but you hear a soft friendly voice saying: 'Look at all the lovely things in my castle. I will give you a gift to remember your visit here. Decide on one thing you would like, and it will be yours.'

"Take a quick look around the castle and decide on the one thing you would like to take with you . . . (Allow about a thirty-second pause.) The voice bids you a warm good-bye and tells you to cherish the object you now have as a remembrance of your visit . . . You leave with the object, feeling very happy and content and knowing you have a very precious gift to treasure . . . Your journey has ended and it is time to come back . . . When you are ready to return to this class, open your eyes and remain quiet until everyone has returned."

When everyone's eyes are open, divide the class into groups of four. Ask the students to tell each other what gift they selected from the castle. Then instruct them to talk to the others in the group as though they are the object from the castle. They should speak in the first person and tell the group all the positive qualities and uses they can think of about this object. They should refer to descriptions of the object as well.

Tell them to start out by saying, "I am a _(name of the object)_ ," and then to continue by talking about themselves positively. Here is an example: "I am a golden apple. I am valuable. I am good for people. Everyone appreciates my beauty and my worth. I am little, but solid."

When everyone has finished, ask how many felt they were describing themselves as they gave their descriptions. Tell them that this is exactly what they were doing. The object each person selected was not accidental but was chosen for a purpose that had some meaning to him. Ask the students to think over the things they said as they talked about themselves through the voice of their objects. Tell them to decide on the one that is the most important to them and to share it, as well as the object they chose, with the class.

Conclude the processing phase by reinforcing how great is our capacity to learn about ourselves and that one way we can do this is through association. Follow up the activity by asking the students to write a composition as though the object they chose from the castle were talking about itself in the first person. State that if new things come to mind now, add them.

To practice other tenses, vary the assignment as follows: Suggest that in a past life, the students were the object selected. Tell them to write in the past tenses telling what they were like. Or ask the students to imagine that they had to select an object that they will become in a future life. In this case the class could write in either the future or the conditional tenses.

A good deal of description was included in this fantasy for very advanced classes. You can shorten this greatly to suit the comprehension of your classes.

EXERCISE 99. **MIRACULOUS MIRROR**[8]

Purposes:
    Affective—
        To gain insight into oneself at a different point of development

To compare one's development today with that at an earlier age
To call on the imagination to gain insight into oneself
Linguistic—
To practice conversing in the past tense(s)
To practice the use of adjectives

Levels: Intermediate to advanced

Size of groups: About four

Procedures: Tell the students that they are going to have an interesting fantasy experience and that you will help them to relax first. In a soothing voice give a number of the instructions presented for introducing a fantasy, to enable the students to be ready for the experience. Use any of the suggested statements and add your own for getting the class relaxed. Then begin presenting the fantasy, continuing in a calm, hushed voice:

"Picture yourself as a child at any age below seven . . . See yourself as you were at an age when you could talk but were quite young . . . (Allow time for them to picture this.) Observe what you are wearing . . . Notice how happy you seem to be . . . What are you doing? . . . Where are you? . . . What did you like to do then? . . .

"Wherever you are, notice that there is a full-length mirror nearby . . . Go over and look into the mirror . . . Notice your hair, the color of it, . . . the texture . . . See what you're wearing. What colors are your clothes? . . .

"And now, in the background of the mirror, you begin to see a person looking over your shoulder. You realize the person looking over your shoulder in the mirror is *you* as you are today . . . The two of you now stand side by side and look at each other in the mirror.

"Have a conversation with each other, the you as a child and the you of today, and get acquainted. You can continue to look at each other in the mirror or face each other . . . (Allow about three minutes to pass.)

"Let your conversation come to an end, and keep your eyes closed . . . (Wait about one minute.) Now the child and you as you are today look at each other in the mirror and very slowly begin to merge into one another, until they become the you of today . . . (Pause longer.) When they have merged into one, slowly open your eyes and return to this room, and remain quiet until everyone is ready."

In groups of four, have the students discuss the experience of meeting themselves as a child. In processing the activity with the total class, ask students to share what they learned about themselves from this fantasy. They can also tell a highlight that the experience had for them. Ask whether this was a happy or a sad fantasy for them.

In conducting the fantasy, you can tell them to picture themselves at a young age at a time when they felt happy, to assure that this side of their youth will be present. For almost everyone, the experience will be a pleasant and happy one. For several students it may be a little sad. By suggesting that they find a time when they were happy as a child, sad fantasies may be avoided. For some, the loss of innocence or naturalness caused by growing up is sad. Most will find that they enjoy the encounter with themselves and that they have warm feelings about the child they meet.

You can ask upper levels to write a summary of their fantasy and/or what they learned about themselves from it.

EXERCISE 100. **A DAY TO REMEMBER**

Purposes:

Affective—

To re-experience some very pleasant feelings from the past

To point out to students what gives them happiness and what they value

Linguistic—

To provide pleasant, personal material for students to write and converse about freely, using the past tense(s)

Levels: Upper intermediate to advanced

Size of groups: Three to five, depending on the amount of time available

Procedures: Ask the students to close their eyes. Suggest a number of things to relax them, as noted in how to introduce a fantasy. Then say something similar to this:

"I want you to think back to a very special day in your life, a day that had particular meaning to you. It doesn't have to be an exciting day, just one that meant a lot to you, a day you would like to relive all over again, just as it happened. It can be a recent day or one when you were much younger . . . (Give them some time to think.) Keeping your eyes closed, raise your hand if you still need time to recall such a day . . . "

Continue in this way: "Visualize yourself that day . . . What were you wearing? . . . Who was with you? . . . What things were around you? . . . Now go back in time and relive that special, meaningful day again, just as it happened, and let yourself feel it and re-experience it all over again . . . (Allow several minutes for this.) . . . When you're finished and are ready, open your eyes and quietly wait until everyone is finished."

Ask the students to discuss the experience in small groups. The mood set from this activity can be quiet, relaxed, enjoyable, refreshing, and conducive to warmth in sharing. In my own experience, I was very surprised at the day which came to my mind and that I felt what I did about it. I had never realized how sentimental this occasion was for me.

The content will provide good material for a written composition as a follow-up activity.

NOTES

1. The kernel idea for this technique can be found in the work of Elizabeth Flynn and John LaFaso.

2. June Bro was helpful in developing the idea for this fantasy.

3. This strategy is based on a common technique from Gestalt psychology.

4. The idea underlying this exercise is from the work of Hannah B. Weiner and Jacob L. Moreno and their noted strategy called "Magic Shop."

5. This fantasy is based on techniques used in Gestalt psychology. Beverly Galyean is noted for developing fantasies of a similar nature that draw upon one's inner wisdom.

6. The work in reverie done by June Bro helped in the development of this fantasy.

7. The basis for this fantasy comes from Gestalt psychology.

8. The underlying idea for this fantasy is from a warm-up technique used by Marcia Karp Robbins.

Chapter 4

All About Writing Your Own Humanistic Exercises

And now that you know so much about humanistic exercises, you're ready to write your own. One day, without any effort, the idea for a perfect activity will pop into your mind. You'll try it, your students will really like it, and you'll be inspired to create some more.

The time will come when you'll want to include an awareness exercise, but none you know of will relate to what your classes are studying now. And you know this is just where one is needed. Here's your chance to apply what you've learned and come up with some tailor-made exercises for the occasion. What follows are some hints for developing your own activities.

READ WIDELY

Read as many humanistic exercises as you can locate. Supplement the ones in this book with others. Values clarification exercises are quite well known and a number of them can be adapted for the foreign language class. Refer to the bibliography at the end of this chapter for a list of books containing affective strategies.

As you read a number of activities, they will *trigger some variations* to the exercises for you. Reading the values clarification exercise known as "Twenty Things You Love to Do"* can bring to mind "Twenty Things I Hope to Do in My Lifetime." Ideas beget ideas.

SEARCH THROUGH YOUR CURRICULAR MATERIALS

Start studying your present curricular materials with an eye to where affective strategies can be used. Search for the places where students seem to "turn off" or get bored.

*Sidney B. Simon, Leland W. Howe, and Howard Kirschenbaum. *Values Clarification: A Handbook of Practical Strategies for Teachers and Students.* New York: Hart Publishing Company (1972).

Find Grammar and Vocabulary
Requiring Practice

Which grammatical points do your classes have difficulty with that need to be reinforced in more vitalizing ways? Which vocabulary and idioms could be practiced more and expanded? These are the places where humanistic strategies can be included very effectively. Let's try brainstorming now to give you some ideas on how to generate your own exercises.

Suppose, for example, your classes find descriptive adjectives dreary or have difficulty with them in terms of agreement, number, and position. Here are some affective strategies for working with adjectives.

Draw up a list of adjectives that have been studied and ask your students to answer, in complete sentences, questions such as these:

Which ten adjectives describe you the most?
Which ten adjectives describe you the least?
Which ten adjectives do you think your mother (father or best friend) would say describe you the most? the least?
Which ten adjectives describe your mother (father or best friend) the most? the least?
Which five adjectives describe both you and your mother (father, best friend) the most? the least?

These questions could be responded to in writing and then orally in groups, having students conclude with any insights they have gained.

Another possibility for working with adjectives would be having each student write a response to this question:

Suppose a friend of yours wants to arrange a blind date for you with someone special. How would you like your friend to describe you to this prospective date?

If the target language has both masculine and feminine forms of adjectives, a variation of the blind-date theme could be used in this fashion:

Imagine that two good friends of yours, a boy and a girl, don't know each other. You think they would get along well and want to arrange for them to go out on a blind date. Think of two of your friends or acquaintances that you might want to have the chance to meet each other. Suppose that each has asked you to describe the other. Using a number of adjectives, write a paragraph describing each of your friends to the other in this situation.

With such exercises, the students can be reflective about themselves and others, making connections between the subject matter and their personal lives. Formulate themes of interest which will allow your students to gain some insights into themselves and others.

CONNECT THE CONTENT WITH THE STUDENTS' LIVES

In making up your own exercises, remember the key is to relate content from the dialogs, stories, or novels to the lives of your students in more involving, meaningful ways. Look for ways to make the material genuinely relevant to the students through making truly personal connections between their lives, feelings, beliefs, and desires and the subject matter at hand. Scan the textbook for potential topics of importance, interest, and significance to students.

By connecting the content with the students' lives, you are focusing on *what students know* rather than what they are ignorant of. From the learner's standpoint, there is quite a psychological difference in dealing with what is familiar to him rather than what is unknown.

Start where the students are—concentrating on areas of their daily lives in which they have thoughts, reactions, and experience. In foreign language teaching, we customarily begin with the lives of others, with whom students may not easily identify, and then expect students to transfer the material to their own lives. However, transfer to the textbook is easier when the content *starts* with the student himself and then leads into the materials to be learned. Rather than asking students "How does this relate or compare to our lives?" *after* they have dealt with some new content, reverse the process instead. Let the students first discover what they can generate on the subject from their own personal thoughts and feelings. By drawing on their own experiences and reactions, the transfer to the textbook will be more relevant and more apparent. Comparisons will be clearer between the target culture or characters in a story, novel, or film when students examine their own responses first.

SENTENCE STEMS AND LEADING QUESTIONS HELP

Two very useful ways to get started in creating your own awareness techniques are through the use of sentence stems or stubs and leading questions.

Sentence stems, or incomplete statements, can help the teacher develop a topic, open it up, summarize it, or put closure on it. Since sentence stems do not take long to complete, you can quickly assess the feeling tone of your students on a particular theme. In a few minutes, the entire class can complete the statement: "Right now I feel . . . " At the same time, students can discover where others in the class are compared to themselves.

And sentence stems are so easy to make up. If the theme deals with a "success" story, one way to initiate its introduction is with the statement: "I feel successful when . . . " Or if the element of surprise arises as a topic in the content, try: "The biggest surprise I've had was . . . "

Keep your ears open for interesting questions which can be utilized. Listen for questions that students ask while passing through the halls or in the cafeteria line. Interviews on television talk shows may reveal some leads to unusual, personally involving questions. Wherever you are, be alert to cues that inspire a possible humanistic strategy.

A thought-provoking question can form the basis of a brief or an extended exercise, a composition, or even a fantasy. Let me illustrate what I mean. Take Exercise 100, "A Day to Remember," found in Chapter 3. In one or more sentences a student could succinctly respond to the question: "What is one day that was so special, you'd like to relive it?" He could simply say, "I'd like to relive the day I made the winning point in the champion football game for our school." He could reveal even more of the details about it. Or he could write the entire story of what happened. Or the teacher could guide a fantasy for the class, enabling students to relive the experience and then talk and/or write about it.

FIND A THEME AND BRAINSTORM IT

Notice themes that come up in a dialog or a story which can be developed along humanistic lines. Brainstorm questions and sentence stems in keeping with these themes.

Here are some common topics which come up in foreign language dialogs and readings and a few suggestions of how to pursue them in this manner. The main characters in the dialog are happy because they are going to take a trip. Pick up the subject of "happiness" with such questions as: "What makes you happy?" "What words are 'happy' words for you?" "What sounds make you happy?" "Complete this popular statement for yourself: 'Happiness is . . . ' "

If a story or dialog mentions someone's birthday, deals with someone who is very young or elderly, or teaches telling how old you are, work with the theme of "age." In brainstorming questions, you might come up with: "What do you like about being your present age?" "What did you like about being younger?" "What will you like about being older?" "What do you think is the 'ideal' age to be and why?" (See Exercise 33, "Ageless.")

And in every foreign language class, the first names of people are learned. You can ask: "Which names do you like best and why?" "Which name would you pick for yourself?" "If you had been born the opposite sex, what name would you like to be called and why?"

Any of these questions can be developed into a full-blown exercise of some duration or used for shorter interludes, whichever is preferable.

Notice also that any question can be converted into a sentence stem for variety:

What is your best friend like?
My best friend is . . .

What makes you a good friend to others?
I'm a good friend to others because . . .

What do you and your best friend both like?
My best friend and I both like . . .

USE STUDENTS' RESPONSES IN THE LESSON

As the exercises you develop take form, plan to make use of the responses of students. Have the students note similarities and differences in each other's reactions or experiences and refer to them in processing the activity.

Since the students will be sharing of themselves, utilize what they share by asking the class questions related to what has been exchanged in the interaction. If the students have all told something they are personally proud of, ask the class questions such as: "Who remembers something that someone in the class feels proud of?" Then become more specific by asking questions based on responses that were just given. An example might be: "Who said he feels proud when he does something he didn't think he could do?" After a pupil answers, you can ask, "What did he say?"

Think of questions of this sort that you can ask related to the exercises you develop. Give the students an opportunity to follow your questions by asking their own questions, using the same pattern, or recalling the contributions of others. This type of practice not only reinforces the structure, but the students who are being remembered as well. Quite obviously, the skill of listening is brought into sharp play in such questioning. Further examples of this type of questioning practice can be found in Exercise 1, "Colorful Names"; Exercise 5, "Search for Someone Who . . . "; and Exercise 34, "I Like You, You're Different."

DETERMINE THE PURPOSES

For each exercise you create, there should be a set of purposes. Know in what ways you believe each activity will benefit the students' awareness and growth as well as ability in the target language. Remember that the exercises are not intended as gimmicks, but should enhance the personal and linguistic development of the learners.

YOUR STUDENTS HAVE IDEAS, TOO

Don't overlook an important resource of ideas for humanistic techniques. Who can tell you what interests them better than *your students themselves*? Invite them to share their thoughts on variations of exercises and any completely new ideas that strike them. You don't have to do it alone. You can even have your classes brainstorm activities, questions, and sentence stems in groups on themes that you suggest or on a particular assignment.

Intriguing pictures denoting feelings or a human-interest story with an emotion underlying it can be useful in starting a strategy. (See Exercise 44, "Talking Pictures," and Exercise 105, "Picture Me.") Ask the students to bring in such pictures when they find them. Show them some examples of what you mean. With your classes on the lookout for these pictures, you have the potential for a large collection. Be certain to use some of the pictures brought in, and mention the names of the students responsible for finding them.

If you include your students and encourage creativity, that's what you'll get!

When you make truly personal connections between learning a foreign language and the lives, feelings, and desires of students, the content will take on a new vitality. You will find your classes better-motivated and more willing to learn the target language.

Bringing the students' lives to the content brings life to the content!

TEACHER-MADE EXERCISES

And now for some activities dreamed up by creative foreign language teachers just like you. In methods courses on humanistic techniques of teaching foreign languages, I asked the teachers in my classes to develop some exercises for their own students. These could be variations of other exercises or completely new ideas.

The next section includes examples of the activities written by some of these teachers. The exercises appear here with the teachers' permission and their names are included for the credit they deserve. To be in keeping with the style and format of the exercises in Chapter 3, the techniques that follow have been rewritten, and at times embellished, for the purposes of inclusion in this book.

The exercises have been grouped according to the category headings used in Chapter 3 for classifying the strategies. Each main theme is stated before a set of exercises in that category. Remember that many of the activities overlap more than one of the humanistic themes.

Relating to Others
(Exercises 101-104)

EXERCISE 101.   **WHAT'S MY NAME?**

Purposes:
    Affective—
        To encourage students to observe others in the class more carefully

To note the perceptions others have of you
Linguistic—
To practice the use of adjectives describing positive qualities
To practice the vocabulary of parts of the body

Levels: All levels

Size of groups: About six to eight or total class

Materials needed: Completion of the assignment by students

Procedures: The day before the exercise is carried out, divide the class into groups. Have each student put his name on a slip of paper, fold it up, and place it in a container. The students each pick a slip of paper with the name of another student in the group. If the students pick their own name, tell them to put it back and select another. The assignment is then given to write a paragraph describing this person, his appearance and characteristics, without necessarily being obvious.

The following day the groups reconvene. Each student reads his description to the group. The others in the group try to guess the identity of the persons by writing the names down on a sheet of paper.

When everyone has had a turn, the group should go over the correct order of the list to see how many each had right. Where there were incorrect guesses, the descriptions can be reread. Instruct the groups not to call out their guesses aloud when the descriptions are initially read.

If there is more time for the activity, it can be done in the total class. This will make the guessing more difficult. However, the students should know each other fairly well when the exercise is used.

Jacqueline Johnson, teacher of Spanish

EXERCISE 102.   **LABEL ME**

Purposes:
Affective—
To have students give thought to describing themselves succinctly
To see whether others perceive you the same way you perceive
yourself
Linguistic—
To practice the use of adjectives describing positive qualities

Levels: Beginning and intermediate

Size of groups: Total class

Materials needed: Large cards on which students will be printing; magic markers for printing, if possible

Procedures: Tell the students to think of one adjective describing a positive quality that they feel fits them quite well. Each student should then *print* his adjective on a large card and turn it face down so no one can read it. Tell the students to print and make the letters very large so they can be held up and read by others in the class. If the students can use magic markers or felt pens, the letters will show up better.

Have about ten students take their cards to the front of the class, being careful to conceal what is written on them. They should exchange cards several times till each has someone else's card. The students should then stand in front of the class and hold up the cards so those seated can read them.

The remaining students are to write the names of those standing and try to match the adjectives with the correct person. When they are finished, the students who are seated can have the opportunity to guess who belongs to each adjective. You can conduct this phase by asking questions based on the adjectives on the cards, such as "Who is responsible?" or "Who do you think is trustworthy?"

After a number of guesses are made for each adjective, the ten students should retrieve their own cards and hold them up so those seated can check how well they were aware of their classmates' self-appraisals. Now have the next group go before the class and repeat the same steps.

You can have each student receive a list of the adjectives class members placed after his name by having those seated write each individual's name and adjective on separate slips of paper. The slips for each student can be collected separately and given to the individual to reflect on.

Robert Goldberg, teacher of Spanish

EXERCISE 103.   **WHAT'S MY SIGN?**

Purposes:
  Affective—
          To help students think about certain aspects of the personalities of
              their classmates
  Linguistic—
          To practice asking questions
          To practice the use of adjectives

Levels: Intermediate to advanced

Size of groups: Five

Materials needed: Dittoed handouts containing general horoscopes for each sign of the zodiac; this can be taken from an astrology book and translated.

Procedures: Divide the class into groups of five. Distribute copies of the handout on which descriptions are given for the horoscope signs. Allow time for students to read all the descriptions.

Instruct the class to try to discover the sign of each group member by means of questioning. Designate one student in each group to be the first person questioned by the others. Once the zodiac sign of this person has been guessed, the group continues around the circle, rotating the focus person, until everyone has been questioned.

Here are some samples of interaction that could take place during the questioning:

"Are you sentimental?"
"No, I am not sentimental."

"Do you have artistic talent?"
"Yes, I have artistic talent."

Barbara Mills, teacher of French

EXERCISE 104.   **GRAB BAG**

Purposes:
    Affective—
        To encourage interest in other members of the class
        To encourage thoughtfulness and the desire to give
    Linguistic—
        To practice the use of nouns, adjectives, and verbs followed by
            infinitives, prepositions, and superlatives

Levels: All levels

Size of groups: About six

Materials needed: A box with a lid for each group; either actual objects, 3- by 5-inch cards with magazine pictures or drawings on them, or slips of colored paper with sentences written on them

Procedures: Each group is given a box with a lid on it. Inside will be a number of "gifts" to be awarded or shared. The gifts may be *concrete* objects (that is, the actual object itself or a picture of it on a 3- by 5-inch card) or *abstract,* such as "popularity," in which case it will be written on a slip of paper. You can supply these "gifts" and/or have students do so.

Examples of concrete gifts are: a record by a favorite group, a camera, tennis lessons, a free dinner for two at a famous restaurant, sports equipment, etc. Abstract gifts might be: "You are getting your room cleaned by someone else,"

"You will make the most out of difficult situations," "You will get a long distance call from an important friend." Students could be asked to bring in small objects wrapped as gifts for the boxes rather than using the drawings or writings on slips of paper.

Each student picks a gift from his group's box. He first describes the gift. ("It's a record by Elton John, the popular singer.") He then gives the gift to the person in his group who he thinks would most likely enjoy receiving it and tells why. ("I'm giving the record to Sonia because she likes popular music a lot.") Everyone is to receive a gift from one person in the group.

The second time around "abstract" gifts are placed in the box. This time the person who picks a gift keeps it and says with whom he'd like to share the gift, basing his choice on the one he thinks would like to have it most.

When both rounds are completed, the students are to tell which gift was more meaningful to them. They will ask each other: "Which gift did you like more?" The students can tell the whole class about the presents they enjoyed receiving during the activity. A short composition can be written as homework related to one of the gifts they received or would like to have received. The students also can explore the topic of their abstract gift by writing about that theme. For someone receiving the abstract gift "You will make the most out of difficult situations," a composition could be written entitled "A Difficult Situation I Handled Well."

Angelica Eisenhardt, teacher of
French, German, and Spanish

Discovering Myself
(Exercise 105)

EXERCISE 105.　　　　　　　　**PICTURE ME**

Purposes:
　　Affective—
　　　　To gain introspection into oneself and to share it with others
　　Linguistic—
　　　　To practice the verb "to be"
　　　　To practice the vocabulary of adjectives

Levels: All levels

Size of groups: About six to eight

Materials needed: A number of large pictures, without captions, of scenery and objects and *without people* in them

Procedures: The pictures are placed all around the classroom. The students are told to circulate around the room and to study the pictures on display. They are to select one picture that depicts or symbolizes some aspect of their own personality.

Allow the students enough time to find a picture that suits them. A large assortment of pictures is necessary. There should be at least twice as many pictures as there are students to permit sufficient choices to be made. Tell the students not to interpret the pictures literally but imaginatively as they look for similarity between them and the scene or object in the picture. For example, a flame from a candle can mean warmth, brightness, contentment.

After the students make a selection, place them into groups where they will interpret the picture chosen for the others. When everyone is finished, the students can walk around the room holding their picture in front of them and stopping to ask and answer some who were in different groups: "How are you like (name the object or scene)?" Each partner can also add ways he sees the person is like the picture chosen.

After this phase, have the class seated, in a circle if possible, with each person holding his picture in front of him. For as many people as there is time, ask the class how different students are like their picture: "How is Judy like a cantalope?" "How is Andy like a car?" This will give students awareness that others listened to them, as well as provide the opportunity for review.

Dalia Podwol, teacher of Hebrew

My Self-Image
(Exercises 106-108)

EXERCISE 106.   **I SHOULD AND I WILL**

Purposes:
  Affective—
      To become aware of one's aspirations
      To help students feel that their aspirations can become reality
  Linguistic—
      To practice the future tense

Levels: Intermediate

Size of groups: About five to six

Materials needed: The assignment completed by students

Procedures: Introduce the activity by telling the class: "Often we say, 'I should do this' or 'I should do that.' How many of our 'shoulds' do we carry out? We may be unsure of ourselves and feel that we cannot make these goals or aspirations come true."

Either give the students a homework assignment or time in class to write a long list of the things they feel they should do. Examples are: "I should study more," "I should clean my room," "I should save money," "I should eat foods that are better for me."

In groups, have students take turns reading their lists of "shoulds." Next tell the class to say each statement again but change the word "should" to "will." Emphasize that they are to say each statement as though they know they can and will do it. Suggest that they have the power to make their aspirations come true.

When everyone finishes, have the students share their feelings as they said the statements the first and second times. In front of the total class, ask whether they experienced any feelings of strength or responsibility when the statements and tone of voice were changed the second time.

Ask the students to mark the statement that is the most important to them. Tell them to set a goal that they will try to reach during the coming week to help them start fulfilling this "should." The students should share the statement and goal with their group members. Tell the students they will meet with the same group in a week to report on the extent they reached this goal.

The following week, the students will relate to their group members the progress they made. Ask the total class how many were able to carry out their goal for the week. This procedure can be repeated for several weeks in a row, with another goal being set up in keeping with this most important "should" each week. The students can also decide to work toward several of their "shoulds" and set goals and report their progress to the group.

Gabrielle Cauvin, teacher of French and Spanish

EXERCISE 107.   **I AM MY BODY**

Purposes:
  Affective—
      To improve the students' self-image about their body by not thinking
          purely of physical characteristics
  Linguistic—
      To practice the vocabulary of parts of the body
      To practice the use of adjectives describing positive qualities

Levels: Beginning and intermediate

Size of groups: Four to five

Materials needed: Slips of paper for each group, each containing the name of a part of the body

Procedures: Introduce the activity by telling students that we are often critical of our physical appearance or body build. Tell them that they are going to think of their bodies in very positive ways.

Give each group a set of slips of paper on which a variety of parts of the body are written. Have the students pick one slip at a time with a body part on it and describe some positive traits of that body part. They should start by stating the part of the body as their own and describe that part using positive words, in this way:

"I am Sunny's heart. I am warm, kind, and gentle." "I am Ruth's eyes. I am sincere and sensitive." More advanced classes can expand the exercise by adding "because" to these statements and completing them. The students should all take a number of turns in their groups.

At the conclusion of the exercise, ask the students to discuss their reactions to this exercise.

Myra Friedman, teacher of ESL

EXERCISE 108. **IT'S IN THE STARS**

Purposes:
> Affective—
>> To help students explore and recognize their individual and unique characteristics in order to arrive at more precise, thoughtful assessments of themselves
> Linguistic—
>> To practice the vocabulary of months of the year, numbers, dates, and adjectives relating to personality traits

Levels: Intermediate to advanced

Size of groups: Two to four

Materials needed: Handouts with a description of personality traits, qualities, and talents for each sign of the zodiac; this can be taken from an astrology book and translated.

Procedures: Prior to this exercise, present students with appropriate vocabulary words and expressions that they will need to learn for this activity: signs of the zodiac, characteristics and personality traits, and things to do to improve one's personality.

Divide the class into groups according to their horoscope signs. Try to limit the number per group to no more than four. This may mean breaking a larger group into two smaller groups.

Give each student a handout containing the information about the zodiac signs. Have the students compare their "supposed" characteristics with the way they feel they actually are. Allow enough time for students to amply discuss this aspect.

In the total class, conduct a general discussion in which the students comment on their feelings during the activity and evaluate the conclusions they reach. After the discussion, allow time for the students to write their reactions and to comment on what they learned about themselves from this experience.

Domenica Falcione, teacher of French,
Latin, Italian, and Spanish

My Feelings
(Exercises 109-113)

EXERCISE 109.   **WEATHER FORECAST**

Purposes:
   Affective—
      To encourage students to be aware of their feelings in various
         situations
   Linguistic—
      To practice the vocabulary associated with the weather

Levels: Beginning and intermediate

Size of groups: About three or four

Materials needed: Dittoed handouts with a series of questions to be answered in groups

Procedures: Divide the class into groups. Then say that in every situation we are in, we have a number of feelings. Explain to the students that this activity will help them become aware of how they feel in different types of circumstances.

Tell the students that they are going to respond to a number of situations by describing how they would feel in each through the use of weather terms. For each question, the students are to include at least one temperature rating, that is, "hot," "warm," "cool," "chilly," "cold," "freezing," etc., and one weather term. Examples might be: "I am hot and stormy. I am thunder." For languages where it is not possible to use such terms with the first person, have the students give their responses as a weather forecast: "It is hot and stormy."

Tell the students to use a variety of terms in their responses. Some useful expressions for students to know for this exercise are: hot, warm, cool, chilly, freezing, bright, dark, quiet, windy, cloudy, sunny, foggy, clear, rain, snow, ice, wind, sun, cloud, fog, thunder, lightning.

Here are some sample questions to put on the dittoed handout for students to take turns answering in small groups:

How do you feel:
  1. when you see a good movie?
  2. when someone compliments you?
  3. when you have to get up early in the morning?
  4. when you're talking to someone of the opposite sex whom you like?
  5. when you come to class prepared with the assignment?
  6. when you come to class unprepared?
  7. right before an important test?
  8. when you've done well on an important test?
  9. when you're with your best friends?
  10. when you see two of your friends arguing with each other?
  11. when you return home from school?
  12. when you don't understand something explained in class?
  13. when others say you're wrong, but you know you're right?
  14. when you have a lot of homework?
  15. when you earn a lot of money?
  16. when you're alone?
  17. when a teacher scolds you?
  18. when you do a good deed for a stranger in need of help?

Larry R. Sauppe, teacher of German

EXERCISE 110. **FAVORITE TIMES**

Purposes:
  Affective—
      To reflect on the times when students are the happiest and to express the reason for this
  Linguistic—
      To practice the vocabulary of seasons, months, days of the week, and time of day (morning, afternoon, or evening)

Levels: Beginning and intermediate

Size of groups: Four

Procedures: Discuss with students that there are certain times when we feel the happiest. We usually have a favorite season, month, day, and even time of day. Place these four headings on the board. Ask the students to think about each category and write down when they are the happiest for each of these. For example:

Season	*Month*	*Day*	*Time of Day*
Spring	April	Saturday	evening

The students should also include why they are happiest at these times. Then place them in groups to discuss and compare their favorite times. With the total class, conduct a survey, putting the results on the board, to find out when people are the happiest under the four category headings.

Charles Ehrmann, teacher of German

EXERCISE 111.   **AND WHERE WERE YOU AT 9:00?**

Purposes:
    Affective—
        To have students focus on how their feelings change during the day
    Linguistic—
        To practice the past tense
        To practice the vocabulary of feelings

Levels: Beginning and intermediate

Size of groups: About three to four

Materials needed: A dittoed chart to be completed by each student

Procedures: Explain to students that what we do affects how we're feeling. The time of day can also influence our moods; some people feel better early in the day, while others function better at night.

Tell students that you want them to write down what was happening or what they were doing at a number of specific times of the day and night. For each time, they are to write down where they were, what they were doing, and how they felt. Tell them to keep the record for the next day and try to make an entry on the chart at the given times. Here is a sample of what the chart will look like:

Name_____   Date_____

Time	Where were you?	What were you doing?	How did you feel?
7:00 a.m.			
9:00 a.m.			
11:00 a.m.			
1:00 p.m.			
3:00 p.m.			
5:00 p.m.			
7:00 p.m.			
9:00 p.m.			
11:00 p.m.			

Have the students discuss their charts in small groups. They can ask each other the topic questions: "Where were you at 7:00 a.m.?" "What were you doing?" "How did you feel?"

With the total class, the teacher can take a survey to see how many students were happiest in the morning, in the afternoon, and in the evening. Other questions can be asked, such as: "What did you do that made you the happiest?"

Barbara Block, teacher of Spanish and Hebrew

EXERCISE 112.   **MY HOUSE AND ME**

Purposes:
> Affective—
>> To find out more about oneself by means of association
> Linguistic—
>> To review the vocabulary of rooms of a house
>> To practice the vocabulary of feelings

Levels: Beginning and intermediate

Materials needed: Dittoed handouts which students fill out as a homework assignment

Procedures: Announce to students that most of us have feelings about different rooms in the house or apartment in which we live. Usually we have one room in particular which is our favorite or in which we feel more comfortable. State that they are going to have the opportunity to write down and discuss their feelings about the rooms in their house. In some cases a room may be mentioned that is not in their own home, but they are to write a reaction to that also from whatever associations they have with that room. Here is a sample of the ditto to be given to students:

Name _____   Date _____

Beside each room in the house, write a word which sums up your feelings about that room or part of the house. In the "comment" column, explain why you associate this word with that part of the house.

At the bottom of the list, state what your favorite room or part of the house is and why it is special to you.

Part of House	Word Association	Comment
1. The living room		
2. The dining room		
3. The kitchen		
4. The bedroom		
5. The bathroom		
6. The den		
7. The porch		
8. The garage		
9. The basement		

10. The attic

11. The garden

12. The balcony

My favorite part of the house is the _____

because _____

_____

Divide the class into groups of six to discuss their word associations and comments for each part of the house. The students can ask each other questions related to their responses. They should discuss their favorite part of the house also.

As a close to the activity, regroup the students by having them mill around and locate others in the class that chose the same favorite part of the house. In this new group, the students should discuss why they like this part of the house best.

Anna Budiwsky, teacher of French and Spanish

EXERCISE 113. **MY FRIEND IS A PIECE OF FURNITURE**

Purposes:
    Affective—
        To gain insight into oneself, his family, and his friends
    Linguistic—
        To reinforce the vocabulary of furniture

Levels: All levels

Size of groups: About five

Procedures: Tell the students that often people have associations and feelings related to different objects. Direct them to complete the sentences you are going to give them by thinking of a person who reminds them of each piece of furniture you will mention. They are to state why they associate this piece of furniture with that friend or relative. Here are some sentences the students can be asked to complete and examples of responses some students gave to these:

My friend _____ is a sofa because . . .
    I am comfortable with her.
    he always rests in my living room.

My friend _____ is a television set because . . .
    I love to look at him.
    she is colorful.

My friend _____ is a refrigerator because . . .
    he doesn't show his feelings.
    he is well-organized.

My friend _____ is a table because . . .
    he supports a lot.
    he is hardy.

My mother is an armchair because . . .
    I can relax with her.
    her arms surround me.

Variation: Use rooms of the house to carry out the exercise. Have the students include themselves in the exercise as well.

Joan Weisberg, teacher of French

Sharing Myself
(Exercises 114-116)

EXERCISE 114. **READ ALL ABOUT ME**

Purposes:
    Affective—
        To help students focus on their aspirations
        To enable students to see how others see them
    Linguistic—
        To provide a meaningful situation for writing and general conversational practice

Levels: Advanced

Size of groups: Total class

Materials needed: A front page from the newspaper for each student in the class, with the headlines pasted over with plain white paper

Procedures: Tell the students to imagine that they could have any aspiration they might want for themselves come true. Instruct them to write a newspaper headline about themselves, based on their aspiration, which they would like to see come true.

They are not to use their names in the headline. Give them some examples to show what you mean:

> First Woman Astronaut Reaches Moon
> Former Philadelphian Discovers Cure for Cancer
> High School Graduate Writes Best Seller
> Nineteen-Year-Old Rookie Pitches No Hitter

Have the students write their headlines and turn them in to you to be certain they are correct. Then give each student a front page from the newspaper with the headline covered over with plain paper. (You could ask the students to provide their own front page.) Have the students print their headline in magic marker on the plain paper. This can be done at home or in class.

Collect the newspapers, number them consecutively with magic marker, and place them around the room. The students will need a sheet of paper numbered with the same number as there are headlines. On this sheet, they should write the name of the person they think might have written each headline.

After allowing sufficient time to complete this phase, everyone can stand beside his headline so the students can check to see how many they got correct.

The students can then be divided into groups to react to the headlines of others and to discuss their own.

As a follow-up activity, students can write the news story to accompany their headline.

Barbara Mills, teacher of French

EXERCISE 115. **FROM ME TO ME**

Purposes:
> Affective—
> > To express the ongoing feelings and thoughts of students
> Linguistic—
> > To practice writing, using the structure and form of a letter

Levels: Intermediate to advanced

Size of groups: An individual exercise between the teacher and the students if desired; it can be conducted in groups as well.

Procedures: The teacher can discuss with the class how most of us look forward to receiving letters, especially from those we like, our good friends. Suggest that we are one of our own best friends.

Then tell the class to write themselves a letter, sharing how they're feeling, what is happening to them, and expressing some good things they feel about themselves. The salutation can read "Dear Me," with the letter being written as though the writer were actually addressing another person.

This activity can be done over a period of time. The students can even answer their own letters. The letters would be handed in to you for corrections and some affective comments.

Talia Dunsky, teacher of Hebrew

EXERCISE 116.   **MY MOST IMPORTANT SYMBOL**

Purposes:
>Affective—
>>To clarify what a most important value of students is at the present time
>>To share the meaning of this value with others
>Linguistic—
>>To practice the vocabulary of colors, tangible objects, adjectives, and feelings

Levels: Intermediate or advanced

Size of groups: Five to six

Materials needed: Colored pipe cleaners

Procedures: Divide the class into groups of five or six. Place a selection of various colored pipe cleaners in the center of each group.

Tell the students to use the pipe cleaners to shape an object or symbol that is especially important to them right now. State that what they create can be (1) an actual *object* that is very important to them, such as a guitar; (2) an *event* that they can show through a symbol, such as a trip abroad by creating an airplane; (3) an *idea*, such as love, symbolized by a heart; or (4) a *friend* who is important to them, sharing something reminiscent of the person. Allow five to ·ten minutes for creating the symbols.

The students can then try to guess what the symbols of the others in the group are. Next have each person communicate to his group what the symbol is, what it represents to him, and why he values it so at this time. The others in the group can ask questions after each person shares the significance of his symbol.

Angelica Eisenhardt, teacher of French,
German, and Spanish

My Values
(Exercises 117-120)

EXERCISE 117. **HOW MANY TIMES?**

Purposes:
    Affective—
        To help students note some of their values and to make choices based
           on them
    Linguistic—
        To practice the use of numbers

Levels: Beginning

Size of groups: Five

Materials needed: Dittoed handouts of questions related to values

Procedures: Pass out the dittos. Ask the students to read the questions and answer them, making their choices carefully. When the students have answered the questions, have them discuss their responses in groups and tell why they made each choice. Then poll the class and place the results on the board. Stress that all responses given are valid and no one should feel he has to change his answer because he is the only one who responds a certain way.

    Here are some suggestions for questions to ask:

    1. If you could have ice cream for dinner, how many times would you have it in one week?

    2. If you could have spinach for dinner, how many times would you have it in one week?

3. If you could have French fries for dinner, how many times would you have them in one week?

4. If you could stay up until 1:00 a.m., how often would you stay up until then in a week?

5. If you could have as many best friends as you wanted, how many would you have?

6. If you could have a dog, how many would you have?

7. If you could have a cat, how many would you have?

8. If you could have as many pairs of blue jeans as you wanted, how many would you have?

9. If you could have as many brothers as you wanted, how many would you have?

10. If you could have as many sisters as you wanted, how many would you have?

Ellen Greenland, teacher of French

(Spanish) Humanistic Poster: "Love does everything!"

(Latin) Humanistic Poster: "If you want to be loved, then love."

EXERCISE 118. **PEOPLE I LIKE**

Purposes:
>   Affective—
>>   To have students examine what kinds of attributes about people
>>   attract them
>   Linguistic—
>>   To practice the use of adjectives describing positive qualities
>>   To practice vocabulary related to physical appearance

Levels: All levels

Size of groups: About six

Materials needed: A picture brought in by each student

Procedures: Discuss with the class the fact that there are certain things about some people that cause us to like them immediately. We may never have thought about what qualities or physical traits make us feel this way.

Then assign the students to look through magazines, newspapers, and books and search for a picture of someone they don't know but are sure they would like. Ask the students to decide what they see in the person selected that makes them feel this way. Designate a day to bring in the pictures.

Divide the students into groups and ask them to carry out the following steps. Give these directions one at a time:

1. Show your picture to the others in the group, and state why you were attracted to the person in the picture.
2. State the qualities you saw in the person in the picture, adding that you, too, have these qualities. Say, for example, "He is friendly and I am friendly, too."
3. The people in the group then tell which qualities they see in common between each person and the picture he selected.
4. Each student writes down a number of the qualities that he and the group members mentioned for the picture he brought in.
5. The class members now circulate with the picture and the list of words. As they approach others, each selects several of the words he feels are characteristic of the person, saying such things as, "He is humorous (referring to the picture), and you are humorous, too."

The pictures and the qualities listed can be posted around the room for all to see. Each student should sign his name on the sheet so the others can identify who chose each picture.

Susan C. Evans, teacher of French and German

EXERCISE 119.   **THE KEY THAT OPENS**

Purposes:
   Affective—
      To have students reflect on and talk about their wishes
   Linguistic—
      To practice indirect statements

Levels: Intermediate and advanced

Size of groups: About eight

Materials needed: A large key for each group; if possible, the keys should be unusual looking or in color (such as plastic toy keys are).

Procedures: Tell the students that we each have wishes we would like to come true. Some of them may seem as though they are only dreams and could never actually happen.

   Show the keys to the class and give one to each group. Ask the students to imagine that these keys can make their wishes possible by opening up what is needed to make them come true. Tell the students to take turns holding the key and stating their wish by mentioning what the key opens for them; for example: "This key opens a college education."

   As each student tells what the key opens for him, he must repeat what was said by everyone who preceded him in the group. One student might say, "Janet said that this key opens all the knowledge she needs, Mel said that this key opens the door to a new car, and as for me, this key opens the way to freedom."

   When everyone in the group has had a turn, the students should discuss whether their wishes are idealistic, realistic, practical, or certain to come true.

                                        Cathe Makem, teacher of French

EXERCISE 120.   **CAR CONSCIOUS**

Purposes:
   Affective—
      To allow students to gain insights into their values
   Linguistic—
      To practice adjectives of size, color, and personal qualities
      To practice nouns related to personal values

Levels: Intermediate to advanced

Size of groups: About five to six

Procedures: Tell students that many of us are "car conscious," especially when we first learn to drive or buy our first car. Mention that we can learn a lot about ourselves and our values by what appeals to us in cars.

Have the students take out a sheet of paper and fold it in quarters, lettering these from left to right: A, B, C, D. You will ask four sets of questions, which the students will respond to in the appropriate section. After the students write their responses, put the class into groups to discuss them.

Here are some suggested questions to ask:

Section A
1. What type of car does your family have?
2. Describe it. (color, size, model, etc.)
3. Does this model car reflect your parents' personality?
4. How do *you* feel about this car with reference to *your* personality?

Section B
1. What type of car would *you* like to drive?
2. Describe it or draw it.
3. How does this reflect your personality? (social status, success, etc.)

Section C
1. What type of car would you least like to drive?
2. Describe it.
3. Why? Is this directly opposing to your personality? Does this represent a negative symbol for you?

Section D
1. What type of car will you most likely buy?
2. Describe it.
3. Why? (money, position, family, etc.)

Other questions which can be discussed in the groups or the total class are:

Does the type of car you drive matter to you?

What external situations influence the type of car you drive? (money, family, age, etc.)

What are your personal desires and values in owning a specific car?

As a follow-up activity, have students write down the names of several close acquaintances they know who have cars. Ask whether their cars reflect the personality of their friends and whether they can make any generalizations now about cars and people's values related to them.

Gabrielle Cauvin, teacher of French and Spanish

REFERENCES ON HUMANISTIC EXERCISES FOR THE FOREIGN LANGUAGE CLASS

Boylan, Patricia C. and Alice C. Omaggio. *Strategies for Person-Centered Language Learning.* Detroit, Mich.: Advancement Press of America (1976).

Bruce, Douglas, Virginia Wilson, and Beverly Wattenmaker. *Real Communication in German.* Saratoga Springs, N.Y.: National Humanistic Education Center (1976).

Christensen, Clay B. *Explorando: Affective Learning Activities for Intermediate Practice in Spanish.* Englewood Cliffs, N.J.: Prentice-Hall (1977).

Galyean, Beverly. *Art and Fantasy: A Gestalt Approach to Counselling and Language Development.* Santa Barbara, Calif.: Confluent Education Development and Research Center (1973).

–––. *Human Teaching and Human Learning in the Language Class: A Confluent Approach.* Santa Barbara, Calif.: Confluent Education Development and Research Center (1973).

–––. *Language from Within: A Handbook of Teaching Strategies for Personal Growth and Self Reflection in the Language Class.* Santa Barbara, Calif.: Confluent Education Development and Research Center (1976).

Morel, Stefano. *Human Dynamics in French: A Teacher's Manual of Classroom-Tested Humanistic Activities for Advanced Classes.* Saratoga Springs, N.Y.: National Humanistic Education Center (1976).

–––. *Human Dynamics in German: A Teacher's Manual of Classroom-Tested Humanistic Activities for Advanced Classes.* Saratoga Springs, N.Y.: National Humanistic Education Center (1975).

–––. *Human Dynamics in Italian: A Teacher's Manual of Classroom-Tested Humanistic Activities for Advanced Classes.* Saratoga Springs, N.Y.: National Humanistic Education Center (1975).

–––. *Human Dynamics in Spanish: A Teacher's Manual of Classroom-Tested Humanistic Activities for Advanced Classes.* Saratoga Springs, N.Y.: National Humanistic Education Center (forthcoming).

Stoller, Phyllis H. et al. *Real Communication in French.* Saratoga Springs, N.Y.: National Humanistic Education Center (1974).

Wilson, Virginia and Beverly Wattenmaker. *Real Communication in Foreign Language.* Saratoga Springs, N.Y.: National Humanistic Education Center (1973).

–––. *Real Communication in Spanish.* Saratoga Springs, N.Y.: National Humanistic Education Center (1973).

OTHER SOURCES OF HUMANISTIC EXERCISES

Brown, George Isaac. *Human Teaching for Human Learning: An Introduction to Confluent Education.* New York: Viking Press (1972).

Canfield, Jack and Harold C. Wells. *100 Ways to Enhance Self-concept in the Classroom: A Handbook for Teachers and Parents.* Englewood Cliffs, N.J.: Prentice-Hall (1976).

Casteel, J. Doyle and Robert J. Stahl. *Value Clarification in the Classroom: A Primer.* Pacific Palisades, Calif.: Goodyear Publishing Company (1975).

Castillo, Gloria A. *Left-Handed Teaching: Lessons in Affective Education.* New York: Praeger (1974).

Chase, Larry. *The Other Side of the Report Card: A How-to-Do It Program for Affective Education.* Pacific Palisades, Calif.: Goodyear Publishing Company (1975).

Flynn, Elizabeth W. and John F. LaFaso. *Designs in Affective Education: A Teacher Resource Program for Junior and Senior High.* New York: Paulist Press (1974).

Harmin, Merrill, Howard Kirschenbaum, and Sidney B. Simon. *Clarifying Values through Subject Matter: Applications for the Classroom.* Minneapolis, Minn.: Winston Press (1973).

Hawley, Robert C. and Isabel L. Hawley. *A Handbook of Personal Growth Activities for Classroom Use.* Amherst, Mass.: Education Research Associates (1972).

———. *Developing Human Potential: A Handbook of Activities for Personal and Social Growth.* Amherst, Mass.: Education Research Associates (1975).

Hebeisen, Ardyth. *Peer Program for Youth.* Minneapolis, Minn.: Augsburg (1973).

Howe, Leland W. and Mary Martha Howe. *Personalizing Education: Values Clarification and Beyond.* New York: Hart (1975).

Hunter, Elizabeth. *Encounter in the Classroom: New Ways of Teaching.* New York: Holt, Rinehart, and Winston (1972).

James, Muriel and Dorothy Jongeward. *Born to Win: Transactional Analysis with Gestalt Experiments.* Reading, Mass.: Addison-Wesley (1971).

Johnson, David W. *Reaching Out: Interpersonal Effectiveness and Self-actualization.* Englewood Cliffs, N.J.: Prentice-Hall (1972).

Lacey, Richard A. *Seeing with Feeling: Film in the Classroom.* Philadelphia, Pa.: W.B. Saunders (1972).

Lewis, Howard R. and Harold S. Streitfeld. *Growth Games: How to Tune In Yourself, Your Family, Your Friends.* New York: Harcourt, Brace, Jovanovich (1970).

Livingston-Smith, Theresa. *Developing Human Potential: Structured Exercises in Awareness, Potency, and Relatedness.* Harleysville, Pa.: Institute for Personal Effectiveness (undated).

Lyon, Harold C. Jr. *Learning to Feel—Feeling to Learn.* Columbus, Ohio: Charles E. Merrill (1971).

Malamud, Daniel I. and Solomon Machover. *Toward Self-understanding: Group Techniques in Self-confrontation.* Springfield, Ill.: Charles C. Thomas (1965).

Otto, Herbert A. *Fantasy Encounter Games.* New York: Harper & Row (1974).

———. *Fourteen New Group Methods to Actualize Human Potential: A Handbook.* Beverly Hills, Calif.: Holistic Press (1975).

———. *Group Methods to Actualize Human Potential: A Handbook.* 3d ed. Beverly Hills, Calif.: Holistic Press (1973).

———. *Nine New Group Methods to Actualize Human Potential: A Handbook.* Beverly Hills, Calif.: Holistic Press (1973).

Pfeiffer, J. William and John E. Jones, eds. *A Handbook of Structured Experiences for Human Relations Training.* La Jolla, Calif.: University Associates, Vols. 1-3 (1972), Vol. 4 (1973).

Raths, Louis E., Merrill Harmin, and Sidney B. Simon. *Values and Teaching: Working with Values in the Classroom.* Columbus, Ohio: Charles E. Merrill (1966).

Saulnier, Leda and Teresa Simard. *Personal Growth and Interpersonal Relations.* Englewood Cliffs, N.J.: Prentice-Hall (1973).

Sax, Saville and Sandra Hollander. *Reality Games.* New York: Macmillan (1972).

Schrank, Jeffrey. *Teaching Human Beings: 101 Subversive Activities for the Classroom.* Boston, Mass.: Beacon Press (1972).

Schutz, William C. *Joy: Expanding Human Awareness.* New York: Grove Press (1967).

Silberman, Melvin L., Jerome S. Allender, and Jay M. Yanoff, eds. *Real Learning: A Sourcebook for Teachers.* Boston: Little, Brown and Company (1976).

Simon, Sidney B., Leland W. Howe, and Howard Kirschenbaum. *Values Clarification: A Handbook of Practical Strategies for Teachers and Students.* New York: Hart (1972).

Simon, Sidney B., Robert H. Hawley, and David D. Britton. *Composition for Personal Growth: Values Clarification through Writing.* New York: Hart (1973).

Stevens, John O. *Awareness: Exploring, Experimenting, Experiencing.* Moab, Utah: Real People Press (1971).

Chapter 5

All About Training Teachers in Humanistic Techniques

(Don't stop here. This chapter
is intended for *all* readers.)

And now I'd like to talk to those of you who are interested in teacher training and share with you the insights I've gained through instructing methods courses on humanistic techniques of teaching foreign languages. As I stated in the earlier chapters, it's highly desirable for teachers to get training of an experiential sort prior to using these activities in their classes. One way this can come about is if you, the person responsible for training teachers at the college level or within a school district, help provide that experience.

GET SOME EXPERIENCE FIRST

I'm taking for granted that you are the person who will actually do the training. I'll also assume that you'll attend workshops, conferences, and/or growth potential groups to pick up some personal experience yourself, just as I suggested that teachers do, before proceeding on your own to train others. This is the route I have taken myself. I have a background in group dynamics and sensitivity training and have participated in many related conferences, growth potential workshops, and courses through the years. It is based on these experiences and my work in foreign language education that I developed the courses on humanistic techniques of teaching foreign languages.

Since I knew no one in teacher training in foreign languages instructing a semester-long course on humanistic techniques, I proceeded on my own. It is what I learned before, during, and afterwards, which seems to work, that I'd like to share with you—the design, format, content, and suggestions for carrying out a training program of either long or short duration.

TRAINING HETEROGENEOUS GROUPS IS POSSIBLE

Let me begin by mentioning that the groups of teachers enrolled in the courses I taught were extremely heterogeneous. They represented most of the foreign languages instructed in our area: ESOL, French, German, Hebrew, Italian, Latin, Portuguese, Spanish, and Yiddish. The teachers were from urban, suburban, parochial, and private schools. And the grades ran the entire gamut: elementary and middle schools, junior and senior high schools, and college and adult education classes. The teachers ranged from those in their first years of teaching to some with over twenty-five years of experience.

Also enrolled in these courses were teachers who were natives of other countries: Arabia, Brazil, China, Germany, Haiti, Israel, Italy, Korea, and several Spanish-speaking countries. There was quite a conglomeration of interests and backgrounds to satisfy in these courses. Therefore, the suggestions I want to pass along to you are not designed for a single population, but can apply across-the-board.

BASIS FOR THE MODEL

And now for the key question: How can we prepare foreign language teachers to use humanistic techniques? I tried a certain approach, and it not only produced the results I hoped for, but surpassed my expectations. Because of this, I should like to describe for you the approach or model I used.

I designed two courses, each a semester long. They were based on two primary beliefs:

1. The only true way you learn something is to experience it yourself.
2. The course experiences and the instructor must be models of the message to be conveyed.

To implement these ideas in each course, there were three experiential phases. The teachers:

Phase 1. Experienced a number of humanistic activities
Phase 2. Tried out appropriate exercises in their own classes
Phase 3. Developed some exercises of their own and taught them to our class, as well as to their classes

PHASE 1

Experiencing the Activities

The key to the success of the program is conducting it workshop-style so that the teachers experience a good many humanistic exercises themselves *from the standpoint of the learner*. I took the role of the teacher and demonstrated the activities, and the teachers were involved in being participants. Approximately two thirds of the course time was devoted to this format.

The purpose of participating in the exercises is not only to demonstrate for teachers how to conduct the activities, but to allow them to develop the feelings of warmth and closeness which will follow. The feelings that develop cannot be communicated by words alone but must be experienced for oneself to fully understand. Only in this way will teachers truly see the benefits of using humanistic techniques and come to believe in the process.

The teachers were told to put their energies into being involved in the activities, enjoying them, and seeing what feelings resulted. They were asked not to focus on how to use the techniques in their own classes while the activities were in process. It was not until the following meeting that the strategies were discussed through the eyes of a "teacher." My concern was to have the teachers just be themselves and experience their reactions—to get into their feelings rather than their brains. I purposely separated in time *experiencing* the techniques and *discussing* their methodology, to avoid interfering with the emotions of the moment and to end the class on a feeling level, rather than an intellectual one.

The format I developed during Phase 1 was: (1) experience the techniques, (2) discuss and react to the exercises from the standpoint of being a *learner,* (3) collect written feedback about each activity, (4) discuss, at the following meeting, the purposes of the activities and how to conduct them through the eyes of a teacher, (5) present new strategies to be experienced, and (6) repeat the cycle. Refer to the flow chart for a graphic picture of this format.

The Importance of Feedback

At the end of every class, I requested written feedback about the activities experienced. I wanted to know how *everyone* was responding. In this way, I could hear from the less vocal and also get a truer, more intricate picture of what the members of the class were feeling.

From the written feedback, I not only learned a great deal about the reactions to the techniques, but about each person as well. I found the verbal feedback from the class not nearly as revealing as the written.

The feedback also helped me gain insights into what to point out at the next meeting during the discussion of the strategies. I discovered at times what points went past members of the groups or what I had not stressed sufficiently.

At the following meeting, I returned the feedback to the students with written comments which I made on each one, in response to their reactions. The

Format Teachers Experienced While Learning How to Use Humanistic Techniques

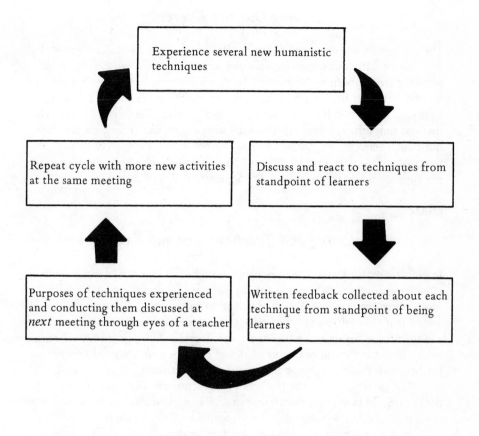

Experience several new humanistic techniques

Repeat cycle with more new activities at the same meeting

Discuss and react to techniques from standpoint of learners

Purposes of techniques experienced and conducting them discussed at *next* meeting through eyes of a teacher

Written feedback collected about each technique from standpoint of being learners

teachers responded very favorably to this aspect, and many expressed looking forward to reading my personal remarks to them.

Discussing the Activities

Each week the class began with a review of the activities which had been experienced the previous week, and it was then that I explained and we discussed the purposes, affective and linguistic, of each exercise. During the discussions, I asked for suggestions, variations, and modifications of the exercises and how they could be adapted for different levels. This aspect led to additional ideas for exercises.

With this book now available, I will have the teachers read the exercises just demonstrated for the next meeting and pick up the discussion from there. This will avoid having to go over the procedures in detail for carrying out the techniques while the teachers take copious notes.

PHASE 2

Trying Out the Exercises

The teachers were encouraged to try out the exercises they had experienced that were appropriate for their own classes and report back the results. Each week when the strategies from the previous week were discussed, the teachers brought up what they had tried out back home. Ideas, anecdotes, reactions, and suggestions were exchanged. Problems were also aired and possible alternatives offered. The first few times the teachers experimented with an exercise in their classes, they filled out a form for me, telling how they carried it out, the level of students it was used with, any supplementary vocabulary needed, the results they achieved, and suggestions for improvement. This gave me an idea of their progress.

PHASE 3

Developing and Teaching Original Exercises

In preparation for Phase 3, the teachers were asked to read books which contain affective exercises to get ideas about the varieties that already exist outside of foreign language teaching. They were asked to write up and duplicate for the class several that they felt could be effectively transferred to the foreign language class and to indicate the sources where these were located. A listing of such references can be found at the end of Chapter 4. These readings were intended to assist the teachers with Phase 3, creating their own original activities.

    The exercises which the teachers wrote themselves were also duplicated for the class. Since there were twenty-five in each class, you can imagine what a wealth of material the teachers went home with by the end of the course!

    In one of the courses, I had the teachers work with a partner to brainstorm and develop ideas for the exercises. They were to bring in their curricular materials as they worked on the strategies and to write exercises for different language levels.

    The teachers were then divided into groups and had an opportunity to demonstrate some of their original activities for the others and to get feedback on them. In addition, they were to try them out in their classes and get student reactions. The teachers truly enjoyed demonstrating their own exercises for one another. They each had a given amount of time in which to get the main ideas across, since most would take too long to go through in their entirety.

GETTING STARTED

Chapters 1 and 2 will be useful for you and your teachers to read and discuss. The material in the first chapter should be dealt with during the opening meetings and reinforced from time to time. Let the group know, for example, that you will be using positive focus, low-risk, high-involvement activities, and why.

Chapter 2 is beneficial in preparing the teachers to conduct exercises in their own classes and yours. There are more than enough techniques in Chapters 3 and 4 to be used by the class and you. Select some to present yourself, and ask the teachers to choose others to demonstrate, using peer teaching. In this way, the teachers will have an opportunity to try out and participate directly in many of the techniques in the book.

Chapter 4 may be used by the teachers and you to help in developing original strategies. This can be a very satisfying area for expressing the creative side we all have.

Get the Group Warmed Up

Don't present the material by lecturing. Remember this is an experiential approach. At the first few meetings, use warm-up exercises to get the teachers to feel comfortable and to get acquainted. (Refer to activities listed under "First Few Days of Class" and "Early in the School Year" in Appendix D-1 for selections to make.) Even if they already know one another, they will see each other in new and expanding ways.

Select activities for early meetings that will encourage the teachers to begin to feel close to each other. Exercise 68, "Cherished Object," and Exercise 79, "Self-Collage," are examples of such exercises. Also use some techniques which are fun, such as Exercise 5, "Search for Someone Who . . . " and Exercise 11, "Parts of Speech Like Me." Include enough variety in the early meetings to appeal to all tastes. The exercises you use will bring out different moods and feelings. Demonstrate how their feelings can change from the time they don't know each other to the end of the very first meeting by using a Feel Wheel, Exercise 41, to start and end with. At the closing meetings, use more sentimental activities such as "Priceless Gifts," Exercise 38, and "The Last Goodbye," Exercise 50.

Whether your contact with the teachers is for only a day or an entire semester, the principles are the same. The shorter the amount of time, the more careful you'll have to be to select strategies with appeal and obvious transfer.

Expect Some Worriers

Don't worry if some people do not see the transfer to the foreign language class at the initial meeting. Remember that this experience is quite new to most foreign language teachers. Encourage them at first to *focus on themselves* in the experience. The transfer will occur with time.

Do expect some of the teachers to be concerned about getting into problem areas or delicate situations. Remind them that using positive focus, low-risk activities gears the discussions away from such issues. In reality, any number of mundane and seemingly routine questions in a typical foreign language class can lead into a problem area for students. How often has a teacher asked a question related to a student's parents, assuming they are married, when they are divorced? Or a question may be posed about one's older brother, who it turns out was just recently killed. The world and the classroom are not insulated against such activities happening. When using humanistic strategies, you can deliberately enter the realm of the negative or avoid it.

Some Fears Are Instilled

I have seen teachers at affective workshops become apprehensive about stirring up anxious feelings in their students and getting into trying situations. Generally the reason these teachers become concerned is that an activity which was demonstrated was high-risk or promoted a negative focus. It may even have led them into a touchy area of their own. And so fears and misgivings arise.

What they do not realize and what was probably not pointed out, is that the nature of the exercises selected affects what follows. *They do not have to choose threatening, negative focus, or high-risk activities.* If the group leader has facilitated a negative or threatening focus, the point of view I am advocating usually is not apparent. Under these circumstances, teachers may "turn off" to using humanistic strategies, concluding that they can be "very dangerous."

Remember to model what you wish to convey. If the leader uses threatening activities, the message communicated is that all humanistic activities are like that. Once Pandora's box is opened, it leaves a lot of doubts not usually erased in the minds of some teachers.

This is not to say that higher risk topics cannot be handled very effectively and beneficially under a sensitive teacher who is skillful and highly qualified in human relations training. But since most foreign language teachers do not have this kind of training in their background, they can greatly reduce or avoid these concerns if both of you choose the activities wisely.

PRESENTING THE ACTIVITIES

In deciding on activities to demonstrate, select different types of exercises for each meeting. Choose exercises which evoke a lighter mood to combine with some that induce a more serious one. Vary the size of groups from dyads to larger groups, to the total class. At times mix strategies involving movement with others that are sedentary. On some occasions introduce an activity with physical contact of a nonthreatening nature, as you feel your teachers are ready for it. Exercise 6, "A Touching Experience," and Exercise 48, "Meditation on Us," are examples.

On other occasions run a related theme through the activities, such as one's physical appearance (Exercise 35, "I'm Attractive, You're Attractive," and Exercise 36, "Is That Me?") or family relationships (Exercise 54, "Family Album," and Exercise 59, "Birth Order"). Since most teachers instruct both beginning and more advanced classes, illustrate techniques for different language levels accordingly. You can introduce several exercises at one meeting, each suited for a different level. Or you can show how some of the activities can be used at all levels, indicating how the expectations will vary.

Mix shorter exercises with those requiring more time and thought. A number of activities need only be sampled rather than carried out fully because of the total time each takes to complete. This gives the teachers a "feel" for the activity while leaving enough time for you to present a variety of exercises.

If your group consists of teachers of different foreign languages, for some strategies put the teachers in groups based on their target language. For others, place the teachers into groups with those of various languages, and conduct the activity in the language that everyone speaks (this will probably be the native language for most people). I encourage this in mixed language groups only, to enable the teachers to get to know everyone else. This is a goal they should foster in their own classes. Of course, in that situation everyone will be expected to use the target language.

When the group seems to be getting tired, inject an energizing, fun-type activity (Exercise 90, "Animal, Vegetable, Fruit," or Exercise 89, "Curtain Up"), to get people livened up again. And when the teachers seem starry-eyed and dreamy, try a fantasy. Let them come to expect the unexpected.

Chapter 2 gives you background on how to carry out various types of exercises. Many of the activities I used in the methods courses I instruct appear in Chapter 3, so help yourself. The instructions for each will enable you to direct the activity, but don't forget to *try them out on yourself first.* To get some practice and feedback from their peers, as time goes on, have the teachers select some of the exercises in this book to demonstrate on each other and to discuss. This can be done in small groups. By dividing the class into groups of five to six, all of the teachers can gain experience in conducting strategies in much less time.

Get Involved Yourself

As I've said earlier, a main idea in training teachers in this area is to model for them what you advocate. One intention of humanistic approaches is to develop closeness through sharing. The person in charge should not be an exception.

Therefore, a very strong recommendation I'd like to pass along will make the class *better for you* and for the group—*participate in all the activities yourself.* Whatever you ask the teachers to do, do yourself. I strongly urge that the teachers do this as well in their classrooms. It will allow the class to see the "human" side of you, too, and they'll like that. And by your sharing and being included, you'll feel more involved in the action and will benefit from it as well. I'd like to share with you how I made this discovery.

The first semester that I taught one of the humanistic methods courses, I participated in some of the activities, especially when the class consisted of an uneven number and I was needed to form dyads or when the entire class as a group was involved in an activity. But my primary concerns were to circulate, to see how things were going and facilitate them, and to watch the time factor.

And then one evening, I clearly remember a teacher who had become an avid user of the humanistic exercises remarking with remorse, "I love using these activities with my students, and they're really excited about them, too. But somehow I'm disappointed that *I* don't have the same feelings when I use them with my students as I do when we try them here in our class."

I explained the reasons behind this. She was experiencing two distinct roles—being in charge of *leading* the activities and actually *participating* in them. The two are quite different and have different rewards. I knew what she meant because I had taken note right along of similar feelings I was experiencing and had discussed it with others who lead groups of a similar nature. They, too, felt as I did.

As I reflected on this further, a light bulb flashed for me. I knew that *I* wasn't getting a number of the benefits that the class was. I was able to facilitate some really great moments for others, but to some extent I was on the fringe of it all. I made the connection.

And so during the second course I taught, I participated in *every* activity, much to the class's surprise. They didn't seem to expect me to do the homework assignments, too. When they made a Self-Collage, so did I. When they brought in a Cherished Object, I did, too. What a difference it made for me!

At the end of the two courses, I spoke to a teacher who had been enrolled in both classes. I asked how she would compare the two. One of her observations was that I had been involved in all of the events the second semester. She thought that it was "really great" that I had shared so much about myself and had let the teachers get to know me even better. And really, I had to ask myself, "Why not?" I loved it! It just hadn't occurred to me at first that my preoccupation with "giving" the course did not preclude my "giving of myself," too.

Yes, for *me*, it was a far better experience. Even though I had participated in many of these or similar exercises before, being in on the *sharing* part of the class did make a difference to me. So I pass this knowledge along to you. And your participation will set an example for the teachers to become involved in the activities with their classes as well.

CREATE AN ATMOSPHERE

Working on the exercises in groups and sharing and processing the activities will create a climate of warmth and trust. In addition, I have found adding several elements to the environment also enhances the atmosphere.

Say It with Posters

To begin with, for the first meeting I designed some posters on which I wrote affective expressions or sayings, some original and others not, and used them to decorate the classroom. (A number of these quotes and sayings can be found in Appendix C.) Such themes as sharing, caring, living, giving, growth, love, friend-

(German) Humanistic Poster: "The rainbow is prettier than the pot at the end because the rainbow is *now*."

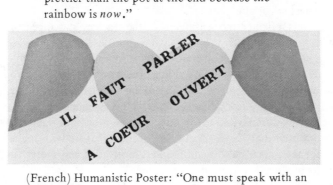

(French) Humanistic Poster: "One must speak with an open heart."

(Hebrew) Humanistic Poster: "You touch me and there is sunshine."

ship, feelings, self-concept, strength, and happiness were stressed in the posters. The intention was to arouse the interest of the teachers as they entered the classroom for the first time and to set an ambience of curiosity as to what was going to happen.

I designed six to eight posters for the first three meetings. After that, I asked the teachers to look for and think of beautiful, meaningful, affective messages which they would use to make posters. The expressions were to be put into their target language.

One semester I asked each person to make three posters to display. We began the class period with those who had made a poster reading and translating it for the benefit of those who did not understand the language, and telling what significance the statement had for them. In this way, the class was able to begin a collection of beautiful, witty thoughts and had a few posters ready for classroom use. The second semester I found it useful to have each teacher prepare a ditto master with his sayings (including translations), to avoid having the others get caught up in hastily copying them.

The posters reflected the sentiments of the teachers and appealed to their creative sides in designing them. This assignment inspired the teachers to "read between the lines" and to look all about them for meaningful messages. One teacher located a saying she really liked in a drugstore window! (The source of any quotation was to be included.) And thinking up original reflections was encouraged. I found very favorable reactions to this assignment.

The teachers were invited to try out the same process in their classes: to bring in posters that they designed and then request that students make some. A number of the teachers tried this and found it motivating and successful. Some of their students produced very artistic renderings.

The quotes in Appendix C await your use. Illustrations of some of these posters are included here and throughout the book to give you an idea of their potential.

Say It with Music

Another medium which I found invaluable is music. At each meeting I used a record player, and from the time the teachers entered the room until the class officially started, there was music in the background—happy, light, and relaxing. At break time and as the teachers wrote the evaluations of the exercises for the day, music played softly in the background. I also used soft music during certain activities which involved moving around but not speaking or writing. It helped create the mood I hoped to achieve. I prefer music without words for the most part since it doesn't tend to trigger off thoughts related to the words. Generally, I tried to use music that would be unfamiliar to most people.

I also requested that others bring in records for this purpose, which some did. One teacher, who has a huge collection of albums, taped excerpts of his favorite melodies for us. At the end of the course, another teacher mentioned to me that one of his favorite moments was entering our music-filled classroom. I'm sure you can see the carry-over of this activity in the school setting as well. It's not only a welcome change for the tired teacher who dashes to a course at the end of the day, but for the student who may have been facing a different kind of music all day, too!

Say It with Lights

A third element I used on occasions was lowering the lights. This was done when fantasies were being developed, to help relax the group. (In such ideal conditions expect one or two weary teachers to drift off to sleep during a fantasy!) When a topic was sentimental and during some nonverbal activities in which a mood of fun or quiescence was intended, less light was an aid.

Several teachers followed suit in their classes by lowering the shades and turning off the lights on appropriate occasions. One teacher who did this as he conducted his first fantasy with a class said that the next day the students were all ready for him. When he arrived in the classroom, the shades were down and the lights were out. The students in unison called out, "Let's do another one of those fantasies!"

COURSE ASSIGNMENTS

Some of the assignments in the courses are alluded to in different parts of this chapter, but they are all restated here to help summarize the nature of the expectations. I have varied the assignments from one semester to the next so a selection of these has been given each time:

1. The teachers had a reading list of books on humanistic topics. Some of the books contained affective exercises as well. Everyone was to read both types

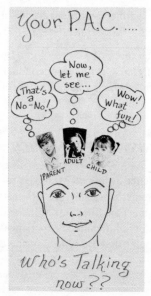

A poster created by a teacher to discuss a book read dealing with transactional analysis

of books, as well as several articles. (Refer to the references at the end of Chapters 1 and 4 and at the end of the book for suggested readings.)

2. Each teacher conducted a study in one class to determine the effects of using humanistic techniques. The variables assessed were achievement, attitudes toward learning a foreign language, attitudes toward classmates, and the self-concept.

3. The teachers kept a log related to their use of humanistic strategies. Included were the titles of the exercises used, the amount of time spent, how the activities were received, human interest stories that occurred, personal feelings they had while conducting the exercises, worksheets prepared to carry out certain activities, and samples of student work.

4. The teachers were asked to keep a log for themselves of their weekly reactions to each meeting. This was for their own benefit. I kept one, too. Feelings, insights, and reflections were to be recorded, just as one does in a diary or journal. The ultimate purposes were to heighten the teachers' awareness of the activities experienced, their reactions to them, and their own personal growth. The log served as a means of understanding and reflecting back on the cumulative learnings in the course. (The episode in which I came to realize the value of my own participation in the exercises is an example of an entry that was made in my journal.)

5. Each teacher was expected to write several original humanistic exercises and present them in his own classes as well as demonstrate a sampling of them to our class. These were to be duplicated and distributed to members of the class. As exercises were tried out, the teachers wrote a brief report to let me know how each went.

6. The humanistic sayings that were collected were duplicated and distributed to members of the class. Several posters illustrating the sayings were to be made and displayed in our class.

7. A number of weekly homework assignments in preparation for the following week's exercises were given as well.

Issuing grades, of course, becomes even more of a concern in a course based on closeness and good feelings. This type of course is therefore conducive to setting up a contract where the teacher decides which grade to work for.

IT'S REWARDING TO USE HUMANISTIC TECHNIQUES

A foremost result of having teachers experience awareness strategies for themselves is that strong convictions develop about the merit of using them to teach foreign languages. The anonymous evaluations the teachers filled out at the end of each semester are evidence of the value placed on the humanistic experiences and the learnings they derived. Here are a few examples that are typical of the comments made:

"From being total strangers at first, the group became a cohesive whole. The course proved what it was trying to teach."

"It helped me to be more aware of myself as a human being and to be a better teacher with a repertoire of exciting techniques."

"The relaxed atmosphere and tremendous encouragement strengthened my confidence in dealing with people."

"I have grown so much."

"This course improved the attitudes I had toward teaching, helped me better understand creative means of teaching a foreign language, and formed a more balanced self-image for me."

"This was my first experience with affective education. It is an absolute must for young people and adults."

"I am now a better teacher and a more feeling person."

"My students are truly enjoying the exercises we tried out in our class and I'm getting more out of teaching than ever before."

And It's Fun, Too

If you're worried about trying humanistic activities, relax. It's fun and rewarding, too. Just to give you an idea of what it can be like, let me share a few anecdotes with you.

At the end of each of my courses, the teachers didn't want to part. So the classes decided to have a party. And guess what we did? We played humanistic awareness games.

One teacher made up some clever humanistic questions for the midterm examination of her students. Her aim was to relax the students and help them think more clearly.

A teacher from another class I instruct came to see me during the break of one of my humanistic methods classes. She looked around the room, observing the posters, and said, "What do you do in here? It looks so interesting!"

On a couple of occasions, a teacher would bring a fellow teacher to visit the class. Can you imagine after teaching all day that teachers would give up three hours in the evening to observe a course? Well, they did, but, of course they didn't observe for long because they had to participate.

One teacher had a required course which met the same time as this class. He came into my classroom to return a book and to look over a few materials I had. The class started, he became interested, and wound up cutting his class. He also returned another evening to join us again.

But most important of all, the teachers themselves have very inspiring, touching stories to share of what they and their students experience as a result of the humanistic strategies. The result is that the teachers develop new excitement and zeal for teaching as they discover the powerfully motivating and valuable effects that studying about oneself has on the learner.

Everyone wants to be *a part* of the group, not *apart* from the group. Helping to bring this about is extremely rewarding for teachers and teacher trainers. Yes, this can be done by making your language a living, *loving* language.

Does this give you some encouragement to get involved in spreading humanistic awareness to the foreign language class? I sure hope so.

We
need
people
like
you!

APPENDIXES A, B, C

(Containing Enrichment in Seven Languages)

A FEW WORDS ABOUT APPENDIXES A AND B

The words and expressions in Appendix A and Appendix B are provided to enrich the vocabulary of students in carrying out a number of the humanistic exercises included in this book. Some of the vocabulary in Appendix A, Words and Expressions Indicating Feelings and Emotions, could be included under the heading of Appendix B, Words and Expressions That Describe Positive Qualities in People, and vice versa. Where more than one translation is given for an item, an attempt was made to list the most commonly used words first.

Certain words were difficult to translate since they do not presently exist in some languages. Examples of these are "accepting," "aware," and "colorful." In such cases, the meanings were interpreted and thereby translated. As the growth potential movement spreads, perhaps such words will be added to those languages where they do not as yet exist.

Words and Expressions
Indicating Feelings and Emotions

(Intended to be used to make such statements as "I feel _____ ."
or "Do you feel _____ ?"

English	German	Latin
adorable	anmutig, verehrungswürdig	venerandus
affectionate	liebevoll, herzlich	amans
afraid	ängstlich, besorgt, angstvoll	timidus, trepidus
aggressive	aggressiv, angriffslustig	hostilis
agitated	aufgeregt, aufgewiegelt, verärgert	turbatus
alert	aufgeweckt, aufmerksam, wachsam	promptus
alive	lebendig, voller Leben	vivus
aloof	zurückhaltend, hochnäsig	ab homine remotus
ambitious	ehrgeizig	gloriae adpetens
ambivalent	zwiespältig, in der Schwebe	ambiguus
angry	zornig, wütend, böse	iratus

Spanish	French	Italian	Hebrew
precioso, adorable	adorable	adorabile	חָמוּד
cariñoso, afectuoso	affectueux	affettuoso	מְחַבֵּב
tener miedo, asustado, espantado	peureux, craintif	impaurito	פּוֹחֵד
agresivo	agressif	aggressivo	תָּקְפָּנִי
agitado	agité	turbato	נִסְעָר
listo	alerte, éveillé	attento	עֵר
lleno de vida	plein de vie	vivace	מָלֵא חַיִּים, שׁוֹפֵעַ חַיִּים
apartado, reservado	distant, peu abordable	indifferente	מִתְבַּדֵּל
ambicioso	ambitieux	ambizioso	שְׁאַפְתָּנִי
ambivalente	ambivalent	ambivalente	דּוּ־עֶרְכִּי
enojado, enfadado	irrité, furieux	arrabbiato	כּוֹעֵס

APPENDIX A (continued)

English	German	Latin
animated	belebt, angeregt	animatus
annoyed	verärgert, verdrossen	vexatus
antagonistic	feindselig, gegnerisch	adversarius
anxious	besorgt, ungeduldig	sollicitus
apathetic	apathisch	hebes, lentus
appreciated	gewürdigt, anerkannt	aestimatus
ashamed	beschämt	pudore affectus
awkward	unbehaglich	inscitus, rusticus
bad	übel, schlecht, schlimm	malus, turpis
beautiful	schön, herrlich, hervorragend	formosus, pulcher
betrayed	verraten, betrogen	traditus
bewildered	verwirrt, verdutzt	conturbatus
bitter	verbittert	amarus, acerbus
blue	schwermütig, in trüber Stimmung (sein), deprimiert,	maestus

Spanish	French	Italian	Hebrew
divertido, animado	animé	animato	נִלְהָב
molesto, enfadado	contrarié	annoiato	נִרְגָּז
antagonista	antagonique	ostile, avversario	מִתְנַגֵּד
ansioso, desesperado, nervioso	soucieux, inquiet	preoccupato	מֻדְאָג
indiferente, apático	apathique, nonchalant	apatico	אָדִישׁ
apreciado	apprécié, estimé	apprezzato	מֻעֲרָךְ
avergonzado	honteux, avoir honte	vergognoso	מִתְבַּיֵּשׁ
incómodo	maladroit	maldestro	נָבוֹךְ
sentirse mal	de mauvaise humeur (être)	sentirsi male	רַע
precioso, hermoso	beau, joli	bello	יָפֶה
traicionado	trahi, trompé	tradito	מְרֻמֶּה
turbado, asombrado, confuso	déconcerté, désorienté	disorientato	נָבוֹךְ
amargo	amer	amaro	מַר־נֶפֶשׁ
melancólico, triste	triste, cafardeux	triste	מְדֻכָּא

APPENDIX A (continued)

English	German	Latin
	traurig, niedergeschlagen	
bold	kühn, gewagt	audax, confidens
bored	gelangweilt	defatigatus
bothered	belästigt	molestiā affectus
brave	tapfer, mutig	fortis
bugged	verärgert	vexatus
burdened	belastet	oneratus
calm	ruhig	quietus, placidus
capable	fähig	capax
captivated	gespannt, gefesselt	captus
cautious	behutsam, vorsichtig	prudens, cautus
challenged	„herausgefordert"	provocatus
cheated	betrogen, angeschwindelt, hintergangen	deceptus
childish	kindisch (nega- tive), kindlich	puerilis
clumsy	unbeholfen, linkisch	ineptus

Spanish	French	Italian	Hebrew
atrevido, bravo, valiente	hardi, décidé	audace, ardito	אַמִּיץ
aburrido	ennuyé	annoiato	מְשֻׁעֲמָם
molesto	tracassé	annoiato	מְטֹרָד
valiente, bravo	courageux, intrépide	coraggioso	אַמִּיץ לֵב
molesto, enfadado	on me tourmente	seccato	מְטֹרָד
agobiado, atareado	accablé	caricato	מֻדְאָג
tranquilo, calmado	calme	calmo	שָׁקֵט
capaz	capable, compétent	capace	מֻכְשָׁר
captivado	captivé	affascinato	מֻקְסָם
cuidadoso, cauto, cauteloso	prudent, avisé	prudente	זָהִיר
desafiado	provoqué, défié	sfidato	מְאֻתְגָּר
defraudado, engañado	trompé, dupé	imbrogliato	מְרֻמֶּה
aniñado, pueril	enfantin, puéril	puerile	יַלְדּוּתִי
torpe, descuidado	gauche, maladroit	sgraziato	מְגֻשָּׁם

APPENDIX A (continued)

English	German	Latin
comfortable	komfortabel, bequem	jucundus
compassionate	mitfühlend, mitleidsvoll	misericors
competitive	in Konkurrenz, im Wettbewerb	competitivus
conceited	eingebildet	mihi placitus
concerned	besorgt, bekümmert	versatus
confident	zuversichtlich, selbstsicher	confidens
confused	verwirrt	confusus, perplexus
conspicuous	auffallend, hervorstechend	conspicuus
content	zufrieden	contentus
cowardly	feige	ignavus
cozy	gemütlich	amoenus
crushed	niedergeschlagen	compressus
curious	neugierig	curiosus
cynical	zynisch	mordax

Spanish	French	Italian	Hebrew
cómodo	à l'aise	comodo	נוֹחַ
compadecido	compatissant	pieno di compassione	מִשְׁתַּתֵּף בְּרִגְשׁוֹת הַזּוּלַת
competitivo	avoir l'esprit de concurrence	competitivo	מִתְמוֹדֵד
engreído	vaniteux, prétentieux	vanitoso	יָהִיר
preocupado	soucieux	interessato	מֻדְאָג
seguro, confiado, confidente	confiant, assuré	confidente	בָּטוּחַ
confundido, confuso	désorienté, embrouillé	confuso	מְבֻלְבָּל
conspicuo, notable, visible	se faire remarquer	visibile	בּוֹלֵט
contento	satisfait	contento	מְרֻצֶּה
cobardemente, cobarde	lâche, peureux	codardo, vile	פַּחְדָּן
agradable, cómodo	resentir beaucoup de bien-être	comodo	נָעִים, נוֹחַ
desilusionado	terrassé	schiacciato	מָעוּךְ
curioso	curieux	curioso	סַקְרָן
cínico	railleur	cinico	צִינִי

APPENDIX A (continued)

English	German	Latin
daring	verwegen, kühn, waghalsig	audax
defeated	geschlagen, besiegt	vinctus
defensive	abwehrend	defensivus
dejected	niedergeschlagen	maestus
delighted	entzückt, erfreut, begeistert	delectatus
delirious	wahnsinnig, überschwenglich	laetissimus
depressed	niedergedrückt, deprimiert	adflictus
desirous	begierig, verlangend	avidus
despondent	deprimiert, verzagt	animo demissus
detached	abgetrennt, unbeteiligt	separatus
determined	entschlossen	constans
devilish	teuflisch	nefandus
disappointed	enttäuscht	frustratus
discouraged	entmutigt	animo fractus
disenchanted	desillusioniert, ernüchtert	animo mutatus

Spanish	French	Italian	Hebrew
atrevido, osado	audacieux	temerario	נוֹעָז
derrotado	vaincu	sconfitto	מוּבָס
defensivo	défensif, être sur la défensive	difensivo	מִתְגּוֹנֵן
aflijido, triste, despreciado	abattu	scoraggiato	מְדֻכְדָּךְ
encantado	enchanté	felicissimo	שָׂמֵחַ
delirante	énormément heureux	delirante	נִרְגָּשׁ מְאֹד
deprimido, desanimado	déprimé	depresso	מְדֻכָּא
deseoso	désireux	desideroso	חוֹמֵד
abatido, desalentado	désespéré	abbattuto	מְדֻכָּא
desapegado	indifférent, détaché	distante, riservato	מְנֻתָּק
determinado	déterminé	risoluto	תַּקִּיף, הֶחְלֵטִי
diabólico	diabolique	diabolico	שְׂטָנִי
decepcionado	désappointé, déçu	deluso	מְאֻכְזָב
desanimado, desalentado, descorazonado	découragé	scoraggiato	מְרֻתָּע
desencantado	désanchanté	disincantato	מְפֻכָּח

APPENDIX A (continued)

English	German	Latin
disgusted	angewidert	nauseatus
disillusioned	desillusioniert, enttäuscht	mente turbatus
displeased	unzufrieden	implacabilis
dissatisfied	unzufrieden, unbefriedigt	parum contentus
distant	entfernt	remotus
distracted	zerstreut, abgelenkt	conturbatus
disturbed	gestört, beunruhigt, unruhig	perturbatus
distrustful	misstrauisch, argwöhnisch	diffidens
dominated	beherrscht, dominiert	dominatus
doubtful	skeptisch, unsicher, im Zweifel	dubius
down	niedergeschlagen, bedrückt	maestus
downtrodden	unterdrückt, bedrückt	tristis
dumb	dumm	stultus

Spanish	French	Italian	Hebrew
disgustado	dégoûté	disgustato	מְגֹעָל
desilusionado	désillusionné	disingannato	מְאֻכְזָב
disgustado	mécontent, contrarié	scontento	בִּלְתִּי נָעִים
desatisfecho	insatisfait, peu satisfait	insoddisfatto	בִּלְתִּי מְרֻצֶּה
aislado	distant	freddo, riservato	מְרֻחָק
distraído	distrait	distratto, turbato	מְפֻזָּר
perturbado, preocupado	troublé	disturbato	מֻפְרָע
desconfiado	méfiant	diffidente	חַשְׁדָּן
dominado	dominé, subjugué	dominato	חוֹלֵשׁ עַל
dudoso	douteux	dubbioso	סַפְקָן
abatido	découragé, mal en point	giù, depresso	מְדֻכְדָּךְ, מְצֻבְרָח
pisoteado, oprimido	opprimé	oppresso	נִרְפָּף
estúpido, tonto	bête, stupide	stupido	אִלֵּם

APPENDIX A (continued)

English	German	Latin
eager	eifrig	studiosus
ecstatic	entzückt, verzückt	mente incitatus
elated	in gehobener Stimmung, begeistert	elatus
embarrassed	verlegen	impeditus
emotional	emotional, gefühlsvoll	animo motus
empty	leer	inanis
enchanted	bezaubert, entzückt	fascinatus
energetic	energisch, tatkräftig	impiger
enraged	zornig, ausser sich	irritatus
enthusiastic	begeistert	fervidus, ardens
envious	neidisch	invidus
exasperated	verärgert	exasperatus
excited	aufgeregt, erregt	excitatus
exhausted	erschöpft	defessus, effectus
exhilarated	erheitert, angeregt	exhilaratus

Spanish	French	Italian	Hebrew
deseoso	ardent, prêt à agir	ardente, desideroso	לָהוּט
extático	extatique, aux anges	estatico	אֶקְסְטָטִי
regocijado, excitado, alborozado	ravi	giubilante	מְרֻמָם
avergonzado	embarassé, gêné	impacciato	נָבוֹךְ
emotivo, emocional	émotionnable	emotivo	אֶמוֹצִיוֹנַלִי
perdido	vidé	insipido, vuoto	רֵיק
encantado	enchanté, ravi	incantato	מֻקְסָם
enérgico	énergique	energetico	נִמְרָץ
furioso, encolerizado	enragé	arrabbiato, infuriato	מְרֻגָּז
entusiasta, entusiástico	enthousiaste	entusiastico	מִתְלַהֵב
envidioso	envieux	invidioso	מְקַנֵּא
desesperado	exaspéré	esasperato	מֻכְעָם
excitado	excité	eccitato	נִרְגָּשׁ
agotado, cansado, desgastado	épuisé	esaurito	מֻרְדָּקן
exaltado, exitado	égayé, animé	esilarato	עַלִּיז, מְרוֹמָם

APPENDIX A (continued)

English	German	Latin
fantastic	fantastisch	mirus
fascinated	fasziniert, begeistert	captus
fearful	furchtsam, ängstlich	timidus, trepidus
fearless	furchtlos, mutig	impavidus
foolish	töricht, albern	stultus, ineptus
fortunate	begünstigt, glücklich	felix, beatus
frantic	ausser sich	furiosus
free	frei	liber
friendly	freundlich	amicus
frightened	erschreckt, beängstigt	territus
frustrated	frustriert, enttäuscht	ad vanum redactus
fulfilled	ausgelastet, erfüllt	confectus
furious	wütend	furibundus
generous	grosszügig	benignus
glad	froh, erfreut	laetus, hilaris

Spanish	French	Italian	Hebrew
fantástico	fantastique	fantastico	פַּנְטַסְטִי
fasinado	fasciné	affascinato	מְקֻסָּם
temeroso, tiene miedo	craintif	timido	פַּחְדָן
valiente	intrépide	intrepido	נוֹעָז
tonto	décontenancé, sot	sciocco, matto	טִפֵּשׁ
dichoso, afortunado	fortuné, chanceux	fortunato	בַּר־מַזָּל
frenético	frénétique, forcené	frenetico	נִרְעָשׁ
libre, despreocupado	libre	libero	חָפְשִׁי
amistoso	aimable, amical	amichevole	חַבְרִי
asustado	effrayé	spaventato	נִפְחָד
frustrado	frustré	frustrato	מְתֻסְכָּל
cumplido, realizado	comblé	soddisfatto	שְׂבַע־רָצוֹן
furioso	furieux	furioso	זוֹעֵם
generoso	généreux	generoso	נָדִיב
contento, alegre	content	lieto	שָׂמֵחַ

APPENDIX A (continued)

English	German	Latin
gloomy	trübselig, trübe	maestus
good	(in a good mood— in guter Stimmung)	bonus
grateful	dankbar	gratus
gratified	befriedigt	gratificatus
great	prima, grossartig	mirabilis
greedy	gierig	avarus
grief-stricken	in tiefer Trauer	tristis
gross	grob, derb, geschmacklos	horribilis
guilty	schuldig	sceleratus, nocens
happy	glücklich, guter Stimmung, froh	felix
hateful	gehässig	odiosus
heavenly	beglückt	caelestis
helpless	hilflos	inermis, inops
homesick	Heimweh haben	tecti mei cupidus
honored	geehrt	honoratus

Spanish	French	Italian	Hebrew
tristón, lóbrego, lúgubre	ténébreux, mélancolique	lugubre, triste	עָצוּב
sentirse bien	aller bien, de bonne humeur (être)	essere di buon umore	טוֹב
agradecido	reconnaissant	grato, riconoscente	אָסִיר תּוֹדָה
agradecido, complacido	satisfait, récompensé	appagato	מְרֻצֶּה
grandioso	en pleine forme	entusiasta, eccellente	מְצֻיָּן
codicioso	avide, rapace	avaro, bramoso	תַּאַוְתָן, חַמְדָּן
quebrantado	désolé, navré	angosciato	שָׁבוּר
horrible	grossier, indécent	volgare	גַּס
culpable	coupable	colpevole	אָשֵׁם
feliz	heureux	felice, contento	מְאֻשָּׁר, שָׂמֵחַ
odioso, aborrecible	haïssable, haineux, détestable	detestabile	שָׂנוּא
divino	aux anges	celeste	בַּשָּׁמַיִם
abatido	désemparé, sans ressort	indifeso	אוֹבֵד עֵצוֹת
nostálgico	nostalgique	sentire la nostalgia	מִתְגַּעְגֵּעַ הַבַּיְתָה
honrado	honoré	onorato	נִכְבָּד

APPENDIX A (continued)

English	German	Latin
hopeful	hoffnungsvoll	bonae spei
horrible	schrecklich	horribilis
hostile	feindlich	hostilis
humble	demütig, bescheiden	humilis
humiliated	gedemütigt	humiliatus
hurt	verletzt	injuratus
ignored	ignoriert, unbeachtet	neglectus, praetermissus
impatient	ungeduldig	impatiens
impetuous	impulsiv, ungestüm, gedankenlos	vehemens, violentus
important	wichtig	gravis, magnus
impressed	beeindruckt	motus
indecisive	unentschlossen	incertus, anceps
indifferent	gleichgültig	remissus
inferior	minderwertig	inferior
ingenious	klug, erfinderisch	ingeniosus
inhibited	gehemmt	cohibitus
inspired	inspiriert, angeregt	inspiratus

Spanish	French	Italian	Hebrew
esperanzado	optimiste, plein d'espoir	fiducioso	מְקַוֶּה
horrible	horrible	orribile	נוֹרָא
hostil	hostile	ostile	עוֹיֵן
humilde	humble	umile	עָנָו
humillado	humilié	umiliato	מֻשְׁפָּל
herido	blessé, offensé	offeso	נִפְגָּע
ignorado	rejeté, passé sous silence	ignorato	מְבֻטָּל
impaciente	impatient	impaziente	קְצַר רוּחַ
impetuoso	impétueux	impetuoso	נִמְהָר
importante	important	importante	חָשׁוּב
impresionado	impressionné	impressionato	נָתוּן לָרֹשֶׁם
indeciso	indécis	indeciso	הַסְּסָן
indiferente	indifférent	indifferente	אָדִישׁ
inferior	inférieur	inferiore	נָחוּת
ingenioso	ingénieux, habile	ingegnoso	חָרִיף
cohibido	inhibé, complexé	inibito	מְעֻכָּב
inspirado	inspiré	ispirato	מֻשְׁרֶה

APPENDIX A (continued)

English	German	Latin
intelligent	intelligent, klug	sapiens
interested	interessiert	studiosus, attentus
intimidated	eingeschüchtert, bedroht	territus
introverted	introvertiert, nach innen gerichtet	introvertus
involved	beteiligt	involutus
irritable	reizbar	irritabilis
irritated	verärgert, irritiert	irritatus
isolated	isoliert, allein	sejunctus
jealous	eifersüchtig	invidus, lividus
jolly	lustig, fidel, fröhlich	festivus, hilaris
joyful	freudig, fröhlich, froh	laetus
jumpy	sprunghaft, nervös	trepidus
lazy	faul	piger, iners
left out	übersehen, ausgeschlossen	separatus
lonely	einsam, allein	solitarius
lonesome	verlassen, einsam	solus
longing	sehnsüchtig, verlangend	cupidus

Spanish	French	Italian	Hebrew
inteligente	intelligent	intelligente	נָבוֹן
interesado	s'intéresser à	interessato	מְעֻנְיָן
amenazado, intimidado	intimidé	intimidito	מֻפְחָד
introvertido	introverti	introverso	מֻפְנָם
dinámico	engagé	incluso, coinvolto	מְעֹרָב
irritable	irritable	irritabile	נִרְגָּז
irritado	irrité	irritato	פּוֹעֵם
aislado	isolé	isolato	מְבֻדָּד
celoso	jaloux	geloso	קַנַּאי
jovial, agradable	gai, joyeux	allegro	עַלִּיז
alegre, gozoso	joyeux	allegro	מָלֵא שִׂמְחָה
nervioso, exaltado	nerveux	nervoso, eccitato	עַצְבָּנִי
perezoso	paresseux	pigro	עָצֵל
rechazado	délaissé, rejeté	escluso	נֶעֱזָב
solitario	seul, solitaire	solitario	גַּלְמוּד
solitario	isolé, délaissé	isolato	בּוֹדֵד
anheloso	désireux de . . .	anelante	מִתְגַּעְגֵּעַ

APPENDIX A (continued)

English	German	Latin
lost	verloren, einsam	perditus
lovable	liebenswert, nett	amabilis
loved	beliebt, geliebt	amatus
loving	liebevoll, warm	amans
low	niedergeschlagen	abjectus
manipulated	manipuliert, beeinflusst, gelenkt	tractatus
marvelous	wunderbar	admirabilis
mean	gemein, niederträchtig, raffiniert	crudelis
melancholy	melancholisch, schwermütig, bedrückt	tristis
mischievous	boshaft, schalkvoll, lausbubenhaft	perniciosus
miserable	miserabel, elend	infelix, miser
moody	launisch, launenhaft, verdriesslich	morosus

Spanish	French	Italian	Hebrew
perdido	perdu	perduto, smarrito	אָבוּד
encantador	attirant, très sympathique	amabile	חָבִיב
querido	aimé	amato	אָהוּב
cariñoso, afectuoso, amado	affectueux, aimant	amoroso	אוֹהֵב
abatido	déprimé, sans entrain	abbattuto	יָרוּד
manipulado	manipulé, malmené	maneggiato	מְנֻצָּל
maravilloso	merveilleux	meraviglioso	נִפְלָא
malo, cruel	méchant, malfaisant	cattivo, meschino	מֻשְׁחָת
melancólico	mélancolique	malincolico	מָרָה שְׁחוֹרָה
travieso	espiègle	malizioso, furbo	שׁוֹבָב
miserable	misérable, méprisable	afflitto, misero	עָלוּב
temperamental, caprichoso	changeant, maussade	malincolico	מְצֻבְרָח

APPENDIX A (continued)

English	German	Latin
naive	naiv	simplex
nasty	garstig, unangenehm	amarus
naughty	unartig, böse	improbus
negative	negativ, ungut	negativus
nervous	nervös	trepidus
numb	gefühllos, betäubt, ohnmächtig	torpidus, torpens
obnoxious	widerwärtig	noxius
odd	ungewöhnlich	novus, insolitus
optimistic	optimistisch	judicans omnia optima, optimisticus
outraged	entrüstet	violatus
overjoyed	hocherfreut	laetitiā exsultans
overwhelmed	überwältigt	oppressus
overworked	überarbeitet	immoderatus labore
panicky	in panischem Schrecken, nervös, unruhig	pavidus

Spanish	French	Italian	Hebrew
ingenuo, inocente, cándido	naïf	ingenuo, semplice	תָּמִים
grosero, antipático	mauvais, médisant	sgradevole, perfido	רָשָׁע, רָע
pícaro, desobediente	méchant, vilain	cattivo, disubbidiente	שׁוֹבָב
negativo	négatif	negativo	שְׁלִילִי
nervioso	nerveux	nervoso	עַצְבָּנִי
entumido, amortiguado, anestesiado	engourdi, gourd	intorpidito	רָדוּם
odioso, desagradable, ofensivo	désagréable, déplaisant	odioso	דּוֹחֶה, מַבְחִיל
extraño, raro	bizarre, étrange	strambo	מוּזָר
optimista	optimiste	ottimista	אוֹפְּטִימִי
violento, ultrajoso	outré, scandalisé	oltraggiato	מְזַעֲזֵעַ
alegre, regocijado	ravi, rempli de joie	lietissimo	שָׂמֵחַ בְּיוֹתֵר
colmado	accablé, débordé	sopraffatto, colmato	מְדֻכָּם
atareado	surmené	affaticato	תָּשׁוּשׁ
asustadizo, asustado	affolé	in preda al panico	נִפְחָד, מְבֹהָל

APPENDIX A (continued)

English	German	Latin
passive	passiv, friedlich, ruhig	passivus
peaceful	friedlich	pacatus, quietus
pensive	nachdenklich, tiefsinnig, ernst	cogitatione fixus
perplexed	verblüfft	perturbatus
pessimistic	pessimistisch	judicans omnia deterrima, pessimisticus
petrified	erstarrt, versteinert	territus, petrifectus
pity	Mitleid fühlend	misericors
pleased	erfreut	delectatus
powerful	mächtig	potens
precious	kostbar	splendidus, eximius
preoccupied	beschäftigt, in Anspruch genommen	praeoccupatus
pressured	bedrängt, unter Druck gesetzt	pressus
proud	stolz	superbus
puzzled	verwirrt, verdutzt	dubitatus

Spanish	French	Italian	Hebrew
pasivo	passif, inactif	passivo	סָבִיל
pacífico	paisible, calme	pacifico	שָׁלֵו
pensativo	pensif	pensieroso	מְהַרְהֵר
perplejo	perplexe	perplesso	נָבוֹךְ
pesimista	pessimiste	pessimista	פְּסִימִי
petrificado	pétrifié	pietrificato	מְהֻמָּם
lástima	plein de pitié	pietà	רַחֲמָנוּת
agradecido, complacido	content, satisfait	contento	מְרֻצֶּה
poderoso	puissant	forte	חָזָק
precioso, encantador	précieux, de valeur, avoir de la valeur	prezioso	יָקָר
preocupado	préoccupé	preoccupato	מֻטְרָד
oprimido	contraint, sous pression	pressato, (to be) essere sotto pressione	בְּלַחַץ
orgulloso	fier	orgoglioso	גֵּאֶה
confundido, asombrado	intrigué, étonné	sconcertato	תָּמֵהַּ

APPENDIX A (continued)

English	German	Latin
quarrelsome	zänkisch	jurgiosus, rixosus
quiet	ruhig	quietus
rebellious	rebellisch, aufsässig	rebellis, seditiosus
reckless	waghalsig, rücksichtslos	temerarius
refreshed	erfrischt	redintegratus
regretful	voller Bedauern, bedauerlich	paenitens
rejected	abgelehnt, verschmäht	rejectus
relaxed	entspannt	relaxatus
relieved	erleichtert	relevatus
resentful	ärgerlich, verärgert, ablehnend	iracundus
reserved	zurückhaltend, reserviert	taciturnus
restless	rastlos, unruhig	inquietus

Spanish	French	Italian	Hebrew
riñoso, pendenciero	querelleur	litigioso	קַנְטְרָן
tranquilo, pacífico	silencieux, tranquille	tranquillo	שָׁקֵט
rebelde	rebelle, insubordoné	ribelle	מַרְדָּנִי
atolondrado	imprudent	temerario	פּוֹחֵז
refrescado	reposé, délassé	ristorato	רָגוּעַ
arrepentido, deplorable	plein de regrets	pentito	מִתְחָרֵט, מָלֵא חֲרָטָה
rechazado, despreciado	rejeté, éconduit	respinto	פָּסוּל
relajado, descansado	détendu, décontracté	riposato, rilassato	רָגוּעַ
aliviado	soulagé	sollevato, alleviato	מִשְׁהָרָר
resentido	rancunier, plein de rancoeur	risentito	נֶעֱלָב מְאֹד
reservado	réservé	riservato	מָאְפָּק
inquieto	agité	irrequieto	חֲסַר מְנוּחָה

APPENDIX A (continued)

English	German	Latin
restrained	beherrscht	repressus
revolted	empört, abgestossen, angeekelt	motus
rewarded	belohnt	remuneratus
ridiculous	lächerlich, närrisch	ridiculus
righteous	gerecht, rechtschaffen	probus, aequus
rude	unhöflich, grob	rudis
sad	traurig	maestus, tristis
safe	sicher	tutus
satisfied	zufrieden, genügsam	satisfactus, contentus
scared	ängstlich	territus
secure	sicher	securus
self-confident	selbstsicher	mihi fidens
self-conscious	befangen	pudibundus
selfish	selbstsüchtig, egoistisch	avarus

Spanish	French	Italian	Hebrew
restringido	refréné	limitato	מַבְלִיג
repugnado	révolté	ribellato	מִגְעָל
premiado	récompensé	premiato	נִשְׂכָּר
ridículo	ridicule	ridicolo	מְגֻחָךְ
recto, correcto	droit, vertueux	giusto, virtuoso	צַדִּיק
rudo, descortés	grossier, mal élevé	rudo, maleducato	גַּס
triste	triste	triste	עָצוּב
seguro	en sécurité, sauf	sicuro	בָּטוּחַ
satisfecho	satisfait	soddisfatto	שְׂבַע רָצוֹן
temeroso	effrayé, avoir peur	spaventato	פּוֹחֵד
seguro	en sûreté	sicuro	בָּטוּחַ
confiado en sí mismo	sûr de soi	sicuro di sé	בָּטוּחַ בְּעַצְמוֹ
consciente en sí mismo	gêné, emprunté	imbrazzato, vergognoso	רָגִישׁ לְעַצְמוֹ
egoísta	égoïste	egoista	אָנוֹכִי

APPENDIX A (continued)

English	German	Latin
sentimental	sentimental	mollis, effeminatus
serene	gelassen, erhaben, ruhig	serenus, tranquillus
serious	ernst	gravis
shocked	schockiert, empört	percussus
shy	scheu, schüchtern	timidus
sick	krank	aeger, infirmus
silly	albern, kindisch	fatuus
skeptical	skeptisch	scepticus
sleepy	schläfrig	somniculosus
smart	klug	sollers, callidus
solemn	ernst	sollemnis
so-so	so-so, unentschieden	mediocris
special	besonders, auserlesen, ausgesondert	eximius
spiteful	gehässig	lividus, malevolus
stimulated	angeregt, erregt	excitatus
stingy	geizig	sordidus, avarus

Spanish	French	Italian	Hebrew
sentimental	sentimental	sentimentale	רִגְשִׁי
sereno	serein	sereno	רָגוּעַ
serio	sérieux	serio	רְצִינִי
sobresaltado, sorprendido	choqué	scandalizzato	מְזֻעֲזָע
tímido	timide	vergognoso, timido	בַּיְשָׁן
enfermo	malade	malato	חוֹלֶה
tonto, bobo	sot	sciocco	טִפְּשִׁי
escéptico	incrédule	scettico	סַקְפְּטִי
soñoliento	somnolent, avoir envie de dormir	assonatto	רָדוּם
inteligente, brillante	intelligent	bravo, intelligente	חָרִיף, פִּקֵּחַ
solemne	sérieux, solennel	solenne	רְצִינִי
así, así, regular	ni bien, ni mal	così-così, passabile	כָּכָה כָּכָה
especial	spécial	speciale	מְיֻחָד
rencoroso, despechado	rancunier	dispettoso	זָדוֹנִי
estimulado	stimulé	eccitato	מְמֻרְץ
tacaño, avaro	avare	tirchio	קַמְצָן

APPENDIX A (continued)

English	German	Latin
strong	stark	validus, fortis
stubborn	halsstarrig, stur	obstinatus
stupid	dumm, dämlich	stultus
submissive	unterwürfig	submissus
supported	unterstützt	sustentatus
sure	sicher	certus
surprised	überrascht	attonitus
suspicious	misstrauisch	suspicax
sympathetic	mitfühlend, ähnlich fühlend	concors, sympatheticus
taken advantage of	übervorteilt, ausgenutzt	violatus
temperamental	temperamentvoll	inconstans, mutabilis
tempted	versucht	temptatus
tense	gespannt	intentus
terrible	schrecklich, furchtbar	terribilis
terrific	grossartig, prächtig	terrificus
thankful	dankbar	gratus

Spanish	French	Italian	Hebrew
fuerte	fort	energico, forte	חָזָק
testarudo, terco, obstinado	têtu	testardo	עַקְשָׁן
estúpido	stupide	stupido	טִפְּשִׁי
sumiso	soumis	sottomesso	נִכְנָע
apoyado	soutenu	sostenuto	נִתְמָךְ
seguro	sûr, sûr de soi, certain	sicuro	בָּטוּחַ
sorprendido	surpris	sorpreso	מֻפְתָּע
sospechoso	soupçonneux	sospettoso, diffidente	מְעוֹרֵר חָשָׁד
compasivo	compatissant	simpatetico	אוֹהֵד
aprovechado	abusé	esserne approfittato	מְנֻצָּל
temperamental	coléreux	emotivo, capriccioso	בַּעַל מֶזֶג
tentado	tempté	tentato	מְפֻתֶּה
nervioso, tenso	tendu	teso, attento	מָתוּחַ
terrible	terrible	terribile	אָיֹם
magnífico	extraordinaire, mirobolant	spaventoso	יוֹצֵא מִן הַכְּלָל
agradecido	reconnaissant	riconoscente	אֲסִיר תּוֹדָה

APPENDIX A (continued)

English	German	Latin
threatened	bedroht	minatus
thrilled	begeistert	laetitiā elatus
timid	schüchtern, ängstlich	timidus, tremidus
tired	müde	fessus, lassus
touchy	empfindlich	difficilis
trapped	eingefangen, eingeschlossen, in der Falle	inlaqueatus
troubled	bedrückt, beunruhigt	agitatus
trusting	vertrauensvoll	fidem habens
uncertain	unsicher	incertus, dubius
uncomfortable	unbequem	incommodus
uneasy	unbehaglich	inquietus
unhappy	unglücklich	infelix
uninhibited	unbefangen	non cohibitus
upset	empört, ausser sich	adflictus
up tight	verklemmt, verkrampft	anxius

Spanish	French	Italian	Hebrew
amenazado	menacé	minacciato	מְאָיָם
excitado	emballé	emozionato	נִלְהָב, נִרְגָּשׁ
tímido	timide	timido	בַּיְשָׁנִי
cansado	fatigué	stanco	עָיֵף
sensible, temperamental	susceptible	suscettibile	רָגִישׁ
atrapado	pris au piège, attrapé	intrappolato	נִלְכָּד
perturbado	troublé	inquieto, disturbato	מֻטְרָד
confiado	confiant	fiducioso	מַאֲמִין
inseguro, incierto	incertain	incerto	מְפַקְפֵּק
incómodo	mal à l'aise, incommodé	scomodo	בִּלְתִּי נוֹחַ
inquieto, incómodo	inquiet, malaisé	preoccupato	מֻדְאָג
infeliz	malheureux	scontento	אֻמְלָל
no cohibido	sans inhibition, sans complexes	privo d'inibizioni	בִּלְתִּי מְעֻצָּר
perturbado, afligido	contrarié	sconvolto, turbato	מֻדְאָג
nervioso, tenso	tendu	nervoso, teso	מָתוּחַ

APPENDIX A (continued)

English	German	Latin
used	gebraucht, ausgenützt	fraudatus
vehement	heftig, hitzig	vehemens
vivacious	lebhaft, munter	vividus
vulnerable	verwundbar	vulnerabilis
warm	warm, herzlich	calidus
weepy	weinerlich	lacrimosus
wise	weise, klug	sapiens, prudens
withdrawn	zurückgezogen	avocatus
wonderful	wunderbar	mirabilis
worried	besorgt	vexatus

Spanish	French	Italian	Hebrew
aprovechado, usado	utilisé	essere usato	מְשֻׁמָּשׁ
vehemente	véhément, emporté	veemente	עַז
vivaracho, alegre	animé	vivace	עֵרָנִי
vulnerable	vulnérable	vulnerabile	פָּגִיעַ
sentirse en casa, sentirse como en familia	sentiments chaleureux	caloroso	נָעִים
lloroso	pleurnichard, avoir la larme à l'oeil	piangente	בַּעַל רֶגֶשׁ חַם בַּכְיָן
sabio	sagace, au courant	prudente	חָכָם
retirado	renfermé	ritirato	נָסוֹג
maravilloso	merveilleux	meraviglioso	נִפְלָא
preocupado	inquiet	preoccupato	מֻדְאָג

Appendix B

Words and Expressions that Describe Positive Qualities in People

English	German	Latin
accepting	empfänglich	accipiens
active	aktiv, tätig, rührig	activus, impiger
adventurous	abenteuerlich, unternehmungslustig	audax
affectionate	liebevoll, herzlich, warmherzig	benevolus
amiable	liebenswürdig, liebenswert	amabilis
amusing	amüsant, unterhaltsam	facetus
animated	lebhaft, munter	animatus
appreciative	verständnisvoll	gratus
artistic	künstlerisch	artificiosus, elegans
assertive	selbstsicher	assertivus
authentic	echt, wirklich	verus, ratus

Spanish	French	Italian	Hebrew
comprensible	tolérant, compréhensif	comprensivo	בַּעַל הֲבָנָה
activo	actif	attivo	פָּעִיל
aventurero	aventureux	audace, avventuroso	הַרְפַּתְקָנִי
afectuoso	affectueux	affettuoso	מְחַבֵּב
amable, bonachón	aimable	simpatico	חָבִיב
divertido	amusant	divertente	מְשַׁעֲשֵׁעַ
animado	animé	animato	עֵרָנִי
apreciativo	reconnaissant, capable d'apprécier	grato, apprezzativo	מוֹקִיר
artístico	artistique, artiste	artistico	אוֹמָנוּתִי
asertivo	affirmatif, péremptoire	assertivo	תַּקִּיף
auténtico	autentique	autentico	אוֹתֶנְטִי,

APPENDIX B (continued)

English	German	Latin
aware	bewusst	sciens
capable	fähig, tüchtig	capax
carefree	sorglos	securus
careful	vorsichtig, achtsam	attentus, diligens
caring	fürsorglich, sorgend	curans
charitable	wohltätig, barmherzig, uneigennützig	beneficus
cheerful	heiter, fröhlich, frohgemut	hilaris
clever	klug, schlau	sollers, ingeniosus
colorful	vielseitig, farbig	facetus
comical	drollig, spasshaft	comicus
compassionate	mitfühlend	misericors
competent	fähig, kompetent	congruens, peritus
confident	zuversichtlich	confidens
congenial	übereinstimmend, angenehm, symphathisch	consentaneus, concors
considerate	rücksichtsvoll	humanus

Spanish	French	Italian	Hebrew
consciente	avisé, informé	consapevole	נֶאֱמָן לְעַצְמוֹ מוּדָע
capaz	capable	capace	מֻכְשָׁר
libre, despreocupado	insouciant	spensierato	חֲסַר דְּאָגָה
cuidadoso	prudent, soigné	prudente	דּוֹאֵג
cariñoso, esmerado	se soucier de, s'intéresser à	premuroso	זָהִיר
caritativo	charitable	benevolo	נַדְבָנִי
alegre	gai, plein d'entrain	allegro	עַלִיז
listo, hábil, diestro	adroit, habile, malin	ingegnoso, bravo	פִּקֵּם
llamativo	pittoresque, vif	affascinante	סַסְגּוֹנִי
cómico	comique	comico	מְבַדֵּם
compasionado	compatissant	pieno di compassione	מִשְׁתַּתֵּף בְּרִגְשׁוֹת הַזּוּלָת
competente	compétent	capace, abile	מֻכְשָׁר, מֻסְמָךְ
confiado, seguro	confiant, assuré, sûr de soi	sicuro	בָּטוּחַ
congenial, simpático, compatible	sympathique, agréable	simpatico	נָעִים
considerado	prévenant, complaisant	gentile, cortese	מִתְחַשֵּׁב

APPENDIX B (continued)

English	German	Latin
cooperative	hilfsbereit	unā agens, cooperativus
cordial	herzlich, aufrichtig	comis
courageous	mutig, tapfer	fortis
courteous	höflich	urbanus
creative	schöpferisch	creatrix
dependable	zuverlässig	fidus
devoted	ergeben, verpflichtet	deditus
earnest	ernst	intentus
easygoing	nicht schwerfällig, unbekümmert	neglegens
efficient	leistungsfähig, wirtschaftlich	efficiens, aptus
empathetic	mitfühlend	concors, empatheticus
energetic	energisch, tatkräftig	strenuus
enthusiastic	begeisterungsfähig, begeistert	ardens, fervidus
expressive	ausdrucksvoll	significans
fair	fair, gerecht	mediocris

Spanish	French	Italian	Hebrew
cooperativo	solidaire	cooperativo	קוֹאוֹפֶּרַטִיבִי, מְשֻׁתָּף פְּעוּלָה
cordial	cordial	cordiale	לְבָבִי
valiente, valeroso	courageux	coraggioso	אַמִּיץ
cortés	courtois	cortese	נִמּוּסִי
creativo	inventif, créateur	creativo	יוֹצֵר
confiable, seguro	sûr, digne de confiance	leale, fidato	מְהֵימָן
dedicado	dévoué	devoto	מָסוּר
diligente, honrado, serio	sérieux, empressé, sincère	serio	רְצִינִי
calmado	accomodant, peu exigeant	incurante, facilone	נִנּוֹחַ, שָׁלֵו
eficiente	compétent, à la hauteur	efficiente	יָעִיל
comprensivo	pénétré de sympathie	comprensivo	אֶמְפַּתִי
enérgico	énergique	energico	נִמְרָץ
entusiasta	enthousiaste	entusiastico	מִתְלַהֵב
expresivo	expressif	espressivo	מָלֵא הַבָּעָה
justo, imparcial	juste, équitable	giusto, imparziale	הוֹגֵן

APPENDIX B (continued)

English	German	Latin
fascinating	faszinierend	fascinans
flexible	beweglich, biegsam	flexibilis
forgiving	vergebungsbereit, nicht übel-nehmend	clemens
friendly	freundlich	amicus
funny	belustigend, amüsant, lustig	jocularis
generous	grossherzig, grosszügig	largus, liberalis
gentle	sanft	lenis, clemens
genuine	echt, wahr, aufrichtig	verus, purus
giving	hingebend, gebend	largus, liberalis
goodhearted	gutherzig	benignus
good-humored	humorvoll	laetus
good listener	aufmerksam, ein guter Zuhörer	qui bene audit
good-natured	gutmütig	bonae naturae
gracious	gütig	humanus
happy	glücklich, fröhlich, froh	felix

Spanish	French	Italian	Hebrew
fascinante	fascinant	affascinante	מַקְסִים
flexible	flexible, souple	flessibile	גָּמִישׁ
clemente	clément, indulgent	clemente	סַלְחָן
amistoso	amical, aimable	amichevole	יְדִידוּתִי
cómico, divertido	amusant, drôle, comique	divertente	מַצְחִיק
generoso	généreux	generoso	נָדִיב
gentil	doux	tenero, buono, mite	עָדִין
auténtico, genuino	sincère, naturel	schietto	אֲמִתִּי
generoso	donnant, généreux	magnanimo	נוֹתֵן
de buen corazón	bonne pâte	di buon cuore	טוֹב לֵב
de buen humor, jovial	enjoué, de bonne humeur	di buon umore	עַלִּיז
buen escucha	attentif	buon ascoltatore	נוֹטֶה אֹזֶן
de buena naturaleza, afable	affable, cordial	bonario, pieno di bontà	טוֹב מֶזֶג
amable, gentil	gracieux, courtois	gentile, cortese	אָדִיב, נוֹחַ לַבְּרִיּוֹת
feliz, contento	heureux	felice, contento	מְאֻשָּׁר

APPENDIX B (continued)

English	German	Latin
happy-go-lucky	unbeschwert	sine curā
hard-working	arbeitssam, strebsam	impiger
helpful	hilfreich, hilfsbereit	utilis
heroic	heroisch, tapfer	heroicus, fortissimus
honest	ehrlich	sincerus, probus
honorable	ehrbar	honestus
hospitable	gastfreundlich	hospitalis
humane	menschlich	humanus
humorous	humorvoll	facetus, jocularis
idealistic	idealistisch	exemplaribus motus, idealistcus
imaginative	fantasievoll	ingeniosus
independent	unabhängig, selbständig	liber
industrious	fleissig	industrius, sedulus
informal	informell, ungebunden	relaxatus

Spanish	French	Italian	Hebrew
siempre alegre, imperturbable	insouciant, que rien ne tracasse	spensierato	חֲסַר דְּאָגָה
laborioso, hacendoso	travailleur	laborioso	חָרוּץ
servicial	serviable	servizievole, utile	מוֹעִיל
heroico	héroïque	eroico	אַמִּיץ, נוֹעָז
honesto	honnête	onesto	הָגוּן
honrado, honorable	honorable, convenable	persona d'onore	מְכֻבָּד
hospitalario	hospitalier	ospitale	מַכְנִים אוֹרְחִים
humano	humain	umano	אֱנוֹשִׁי
de humor, humorístico	plein d'humour	spiritoso, comico	מְשַׁעֲשֵׁעַ, מְבַדֵּח
idealista	idéaliste	idealistico	אִידֵיאַלִיסְטִי
imaginativo, soñador	imaginatif	immaginativo	בַּעַל דִּמְיוֹן
independiente	indépendent	indipendente	עַצְמָאִי
aplicado, laborioso	travailleur, diligent	diligente	שַׁקְדָן
natural, informal	sans formalisme, sans cérémonie, qui ne se formalise pas	senza cerimonie	בִּלְתִּי פוֹרְמָלִי

APPENDIX B (continued)

English	German	Latin
initiative	Initiative	incipiens
insightful	einsichtsvoll	intellegentiam monstrans
inspiring	begeisternd, anregend, motivierend	inspirans
intelligent	gescheit, intelligent	sapiens, argutus
interesting	interessant	studium habens
inventive	erfinderisch	ingeniosus
jovial	jovial, heiter, lustig, gemütlich	hilaris, jovialis
joyous	fröhlich	festivus
just	gerecht, gerechtfertigt	justus
keen	scharfsinnig	sagax, acer
kind	freundlich, gütig	benignus
kindhearted	gutherzig	benevolus
lighthearted	leichtherzig	hilaris cordis

Spanish	French	Italian	Hebrew
iniciativo	entreprenant, qui prend l'initiative	pieno d'iniziativa	בַּעַל יָזְמָה
perceptivo	perspicace	penetrante	מַבְחִין
inspirador, inspirante	capable d'inspirer quelqu'un	ispirante, incoraggiante	מַלְהִיב
inteligente	intelligent	intelligente	נָבוֹן
interesante	intéressant	interessante	מְעַנְיֵן
inventivo	inventif	inventivo	מַמְצִיא
jovial	jovial	gioviale	שָׂמֵחַ
alegre	joyeux	allegro, gioioso	עַלִּיז
justo	juste, équitable	giusto	צוֹדֵק
agudo, mordaz	pénétrant, perspicace	profondo	חָרִיף
bondadoso	bon, bienveillant	benevolo, compiacente	חָבִיב, נָעִים, אָדִיב
bondadoso, de buen corazón	généreux	di buon cuore	טוֹב לֵב
libre de cuidados, alegre	insouciant, au coeur léger	gaio, allegro	חֲסַר דְּאָגָה

APPENDIX B (continued)

English	German	Latin
lively	lebendig	vivus, vividus
logical	logisch	logicus, dialecticus
lovable	liebenswürdig	amabilis
loving	liebevoll	amans
loyal	treu, loyal	fidus, fidelis
mature	reif	maturus, adultus
merciful	gnädig, vergebend	misericors
natural	natürlich	naturalis
nourishing	fördernd, stärkend	alens
nurturing	hegend	nutriens
objective	objektiv, sachlich	objectivus, verus
observant	beobachtend, aufmerksam, achtsam	attentus
open-minded	aufgeschlossen	docilis
organized	geordnet, systematisch	ordinatus

Spanish	French	Italian	Hebrew
animado	animé, plein de vie	vivace	מָלֵא חַיִּים
lógico	logique	logico	הֶגְיוֹנִי
encantador, precioso	très sympathique	amabile	חָבִיב
afectuoso, cariñoso, amoroso	aimant, affectueux	amoroso, affettuoso	אוֹהֵב
leal	loyal	fedele	נֶאֱמָן
maduro	mûr, fait, réfléchi	maturo	מְבֻגָּר
misericordioso	compatissant, clément	misericordioso, pietoso	רַחוּם
natural	naturel	naturale	טִבְעִי
nutritivo	nourrissant	nutriente	מֵזִין
alimenticio	nourricier	sostenente	מְטַפֵּח
objetivo	objectif	obiettivo	אוֹבְּיֶקְטִיבִי
observador, observativo	observateur	perspicace	מִתְבּוֹנֵן
receptivo, razonable, imparcial	large d'esprit	liberale	רְחַב אֲפָקִים, פָּתוּחַ
organizado	organisé	organizzato	מְאֻרְגָּן

APPENDIX B (continued)

English	German	Latin
original	original, ursprünglich	pristinus, originalis
outgoing	gesellig	amicus
patient	geduldig	patiens, tolerans
perceptive	aufmerksam, einsichtsvoll	sentiens
persistent	beharrlich	pertinax
playful	spielerisch	jocosus, ludibundus
pleasant	angenehm, nett	amoenus
poised	ausgeglichen	urbanus
polite	höflich	comis
practical	praktisch	utilis
productive	produktiv	ferax, fecundus
profound	tiefschürfend, gründlich	altus, subtilis, abstrusus
progressive	fortschrittlich	proficiens

Spanish	French	Italian	Hebrew
original	original	originale	מְקוֹרִי
amigable, extrovertido	extraverti	attivo	חַבְרוּתִי
paciente	patient	paziente	סַבְלָן
perceptivo	perceptif	perspicace	בַּעַל כֹּשֶׁר הַבְחָנָה
persistente	persistant	persistente	מַתְמִיד
juguetón	badin, espiègle	scherzoso	אוֹהֵב שְׂחוֹק
agradable, simpático	agréable	piacevole	נָעִים
bien presentado	pondéré	ben comportato	יַצִּיב
cortés, bien educado	poli	cortese	נִמּוּסִי
práctico	pratique	pratico	מַעֲשִׂי
productivo	productif	produttivo	פּוֹרֶה
profundo	profond	profondo	מַעֲמִיק
progresista	progressif	progressivo	פְּרוֹגְרֶסִיבִי

APPENDIX B (continued)

English	German	Latin
rational	vernünftig, verständig	ratione praeditus, rationalis
realistic	realistisch	verisimilis
reasonable	verständnisvoll	aequus, justus
reflective	nachdenklich	cogitabundus
reliable	zuverlässig	fiduciam habens
resourceful	findig	facultates habens
respectful	ehrerbietig, respektvoll	reverens
responsible	verantwortlich	reus
responsive	ansprechbar, empfänglich	respondens, responsivus
self-reliant	voll Selbstvertrauen, selbstsicher	liber
self-respect	voll Selbstrespekt	pudorem habens
sense of humor	Sinn für Humor, humorvoll	facetias habens
sensible	vernünftig, verständig	prudens
sensitive	empfindlich	sensilis

Spanish	French	Italian	Hebrew
racional	rationnel, logique	ragionevole	רַצְיוֹנָלִי
realista	réaliste	realistico	מְצִיאוּתִי
razonable	raisonable	ragionevole, giusto	הֶגְיוֹנִי
reflexivo	réfléchi	riflessivo	נוֹהֵג לַחֲשֹׁב וְלִשְׁקֹל
confiable	sûr, sur qui on peut compter	fidato	מְהֵימָן
ingenioso, listo	plein de ressources	intraprendente, pieno di risorse	בַּעַל תּוּשִׁיָּה
respetuoso	respectueux	rispettoso	בַּעַל דֶּרֶךְ אֶרֶץ
responsable	responsable, digne de confiance	responsabile	אַחְרָאִי
sensible, responsivo	responsable	responsivo	מֵגִיב בְּחִיּוּב
confiado en sí mismo	sûr de soi, assuré	fiducioso in sè	בָּטוּחַ בְּעַצְמוֹ
digno de sí mismo	se respecter (to respect oneself)	dignità, amor proprio	בַּעַל כָּבוֹד עַצְמִי
sentido de humor	qui a le sens de l'humour	una vena d'umorismo	חוּשׁ הֻמוֹר
sensato	sensé, raisonnable	assennato, saggio	הֶגְיוֹנִי
sensible, susceptible	impressionnable	sensibile	רָגִישׁ

APPENDIX B (continued)

English	German	Latin
sincere	ernst	sincerus
skillful	geschickt	peritus, scitus
sociable	umgänglich, gesellig	sociabilis
spontaneous	spontan, schlagfertig	voluntarius, sponte meā
stable	standhaft, solid	stabilis, solidus
supportive	verständnisvoll	sustinens
sympathetic	mitfühlend	concors, sympatheticus
tactful	taktvoll	judiciosus, dexteritatem habens
tender	zart	tener, mollis
thorough	gründlich	perfectus
thoughtful	rücksichtsvoll, gedankenvoll, nachdenklich	cogitabundus
trustworthy	vertrauenswürdig	fidus
truthful	ehrlich, wahrhaftig	verax

Spanish	French	Italian	Hebrew
sincero	sincère	sincero	כֵּן
experto, hábil	adroit, habile	abile, esperto	מֻכְשָׁר
sociable	sociable	socievole	חַבְרוּתִי
espontáneo	spontané	spontaneo	סְפּוֹנְטָנִי
estable	stable	risoluto, costante	יַצִּיב
apoyador	qui est un soutien	sostenitore	תּוֹמֵךְ
compasivo	compatissant, qui marque de la sympathie	comprensivo	אוֹהֵד
discreto	délicat, plein de tact	premuroso, pieno di tatto	טַקְטִי
tierno	tendre	tenero, dolce	עָדִין
cabal, completo, concienzudo, cuidadoso	consciencieux	completo	יְסוֹדִי
considerado	prévenant, plein d'attention	premuroso	רְצִינִי
confiable	digne de confiance	fidato	רָאוּי לְאֵמוּן
verídico, veraz	sincère	veritiero	אֲמִתִּי

APPENDIX B (continued)

English	German	Latin
unaffected	unbeeinflusst, gefühllos, unberührt	simplex, candidus
unbiased	unvoreingenommen, vorurteilsfrei	incorruptus, integer
understanding	verständnisvoll	prudens, sapiens
unique	einmalig	unicus, singularis
unselfish	selbstlos	liberalis, suae utilitatis immemor
versatile	beweglich, vielseitig	versatilis, agilis
warm	warm, freundlich	calidus
warm-hearted	warmherzig	fervido corde
wholesome	ausgeglichen, gesund	saluber, salutaris
wise	weise	sapiens
witty	witzig	facetus, salsus
zestful	eifrig, energievoll	gustatosus

Spanish	French	Italian	Hebrew
inafectado	sans affectation	disinvolto	טִבְעִי
imparcial	impartial, sans préjugé	imparziale	בְּלִי מִשְׁפָּט קָדוּם
comprensivo	compréhensif	comprensivo	בַּעַל הֲבָנָה
único	unique	unico	יָחִיד בְּמִינוֹ
desinteresado, altruísta	dévoué, désintéressé	altruistico	לֹא אָנוֹכִי
hábil, versátil	versatile	versatile	רַב־צְדָדִי
sentirse en casa, sentirse como en familia	chaleureux	caloroso, cordiale	לְבָבִי
afectuoso, bondadoso	généreux	di sentimenti calorosi	חַם לֵב
saludable, lozano	sain	salubre	בָּרִיא
sabio	expérimenté, au courant	saggio	חָכָם
ingenioso, ocurrente, chistoso, agudo	spirituel	spiritoso	פִּקֵּחַ
entusiasmado	piquant, intéressant	vivace	מָלֵא חַיִּים

A FEW WORDS ABOUT APPENDIX C

The humanistic quotes included here are intended to be displayed around the classroom in the form of posters. They can also be treated the same way that proverbs are in the foreign language class.

To illustrate the universality of humanistic ideas through the ages, quotes from ancient to modern times and from different cultures have been included. Because of the differences in languages and the difficulties therefore in saying exactly the same thing in all languages, some variations exist in the way a number of the quotes have been translated.

An interesting discovery was made in translating these quotes. Some expressions and words commonly used in the vernacular of the growth potential movement do not presently exist in certain languages. Words such as "growth" and "sharing" are examples of difficult terms to translate in some languages. As the humanistic potential movement spreads, perhaps such expressions will find their way into these languages.

In order to be able to locate each language efficiently, the first letter of the name of the language has been used prior to the translation of each quote. You will therefore find the languages contained in Appendix C after the following letters: G—German, L—Latin, S—Spanish, F—French, I—Italian, H—Hebrew.

Wherever the source of a quote is known, it is given. Where it is not known, "Source unknown" is stated. Where no credit is listed, the quote is my own.

A heart-shaped poster made for an ESOL class

(Latin) Humanistic Poster: "While we live, let us live."

(German) Humanistic Poster: "Accept me as I am so I can learn what I can become."

(French) Humanistic Poster: "Touch the heart, find the friend."

Appendix C

Humanistic Quotes
for the Foreign Language Class

Discovering Myself

1. The greatest discovery is finding yourself.
    G — Die grösste Entdeckung ist, sich selbst zu finden.
    L — Teipsum invenire maximum est.
    S — El descubrimiento más grande es encontrarse uno mismo.
    F — La plus grande découverte c'est de se connaître.
    I — Il ritrovare se stessi è la più grande scoperta.
    H — ‏הַגִּלּוּי הַגָּדוֹל בְּיוֹתֵר הוּא לִמְצֹא אֶת עַצְמְךָ.‎

2. The most important ideas any man ever has are the ideas he has about himself.—*Robert Bills*
    G — Die wichtigsten Gedanken, die ein Mensch jemals hat, sind seine Gedanken über sich selbst.
    L — Omnia in opinione de teipso sita.
    S — Las ideas más importantes que un hombre tiene son aquellas de sí mismo.
    F — Les idées les plus importantes que l'homme peut avoir sont celles qu'il a sur lui-même.
    I — Le idee più importanti sono le idee che un uomo ha di se stesso.
    H — ‏הָרַעֲיוֹנוֹת הַחֲשׁוּבִים בְּיוֹתֵר שֶׁל אָדָם הֵם הָרַעֲיוֹנוֹת שֶׁיֵּשׁ לוֹ עַל עַצְמוֹ.‎

3. Speak to your own self and let it teach you.—*Dagobert D. Runes*
   G — Sprich mit deinem eigenen „Ich," und lass es dich belehren.
   L — Tibi dic et te doceas.
   S — Háblate a ti mismo y deja que eso te enseñe.
   F — Parle à ton coeur et laisse-le te guider.
   I — Parla a te stesso e imparerai.
   H — דַּבֵּר אֶל הָ"אֲנִי" שֶׁלְּךָ וְיֹשָׁה"אֲנִי" יְלַמְּדְךָ.

4. It is more necessary to study men than books.—*La Rochefoucauld*
   G — Es ist wichtiger, Menschen zu studieren als Bücher.
   L — Homines quam libri.
   S — Es más necesario estudiar al hombre que los libros.
   F — Il est plus nécessaire d'étudier les hommes que les livres.
   I — È più necessario imparare dagli uomini che dai libri.
   H — נָחוּץ יוֹתֵר לִלְמֹד אֲנָשִׁים מֵאֲאֶׁר סְפָרִים.

5. I observe myself, and so I come to know others.—*Lao-tzu*
   G — Ich beobachte mich selbst und lerne dadurch andere Menschen kennen.
   L — Meipsum video et sic alteros invenio.
   S — Al observarme llego a conocer a los demás.
   F — C'est en m'observant que je parviens à connaître les autres.
   I — Osservando me stesso vengo a conoscere gli altri.
   H — אֲנִי מִתְבּוֹנֵן בְּעַצְמִי וְכָךְ אֲנִי מַגִּיעַ לְהַכָּרַת אֲחֵרִים.

Feelings

6. Your feelings are your true strength. Be in touch with them.
   G — Deine Gefühle sind deine wahre Stärke. Höre auf sie.
   L — Sentire vis vera est. Senti.
   S — Tus sentimientos son tu verdadero valor. Mantén contacto con ellos.
   F — **Tes émotions sont ta vraie force. Mets-toi en contact avec elles.**
   I — I sentimenti sono la tua vera forza. Stai in contactto con loro.
   H — רִגְשׁוֹתֶיךָ הֵם כֹּחֲךָ הֲיֶה אִתָּם בְּקֶשֶׁר.

7. Let us say what we feel.—*Seneca*
   G — Lasst uns unsere Gefühle zum Ausdruck bringen.
   L — Quod sentimus loquamur.
   S — Digamos lo que sentimos.
   F — Exprimons ce que nous ressentons.
   I — Diciamo quello che sentiamo.
   H — נֹאמַר אֶת אֲשֶׁר נַרְגִּישׁ.

8. I talk because I feel, and I talk to you because I want you to know how I
   feel.—*Hugh Prather*

   G — Ich spreche, weil ich Gefühle habe. Und ich spreche mit dir, weil
   ich möchte, dass du meine Gefühle kennst.

   L — Dico quia sentio et tibi dico quia volo te scire affectūs meos.

   S — Hablo porque siento, y te hablo porque quiero que sepas lo que
   siento.

   F — Je parle parce que je sens, je te parle parce que je veux que tu
   saches ce que je sens.

   I — Parlo perchè sento, e io parlo a te perchè voglio farti sapere quello
   che provo.

   H — אֲנִי מְדַבֵּר מִפְּנֵי שֶׁאֲנִי מַרְגִּישׁ וַאֲנִי מְדַבֵּר אֵלֶיהָ כְּדֵי שֶׁאַתָּה תֵּדַע
   אֵיךְ אֲנִי מַרְגִּישׁ.

9. Thought is deeper than all speech,
   Feeling deeper than all thought.—*Christopher Pearse Cranch*

   G — Denken ist tiefgehender als alles Reden,
   Fühlen tiefgehender als alles Denken.

   L — Putare altius quam dicere.
   Sentire altius quam putare.

   S — El pensamiento es más profundo que la palabra.
   El sentimiento es más profundo que el pensamiento.

   F — La pensée est plus profonde que toute parole,
   Les sentiments plus profonds que toute pensée.

   I — Il pensiero è più profondo delle parole,
   Il sentimento è più profondo del pensiero.

   H — הַמַּחְשָׁבָה עֲמוּקָה מִכָּל דִּבּוּר
   הַהַרְגָּשָׁה עֲמוּקָה מִכָּל מַחְשָׁבָה.

10. Being deprived is not being aware of how you feel.

    G — Man ist benachteiligt, wenn man seine eigenen Gefühle nicht
    versteht.

    L — Nescire quae sentis privatio est.

    S — Estar deprivado es no saber como uno siente.

    F — Etre dépourvu, c'est ne pas comprendre ce que l'on ressent.

    I — Essere privi significa non essere consapevoli di quello che sentiamo.

    H — לִהְיוֹת מְקֻפָּח פֵּירוּשׁוֹ לֹא לָחוּשׁ בְּהַרְגָּשׁוֹתֶיךָ.

11. There are two worlds, the world that we can measure with line and rule, and
    the world we feel with our hearts and our imagination.—*Leigh Hunt*

    G — Es gibt zwei Welten: die Welt, die wir mit Richtschnur und Lineal
    messen können, und die Welt, die wir mit unseren Herzen und
    unserer Phantasie empfinden.

L — Sunt duo mundi: observandus, atque sentiendus.

S — Hay dos mundos, el que medimos con metro y regla y el que sentimos con nuestros corazones e imaginación.

F — Il y a deux mondes, le monde de la limite, et le monde du coeur et de l'imagination.

I — Ci sono due mondi: il mondo che possiamo misurare e il mondo che possiamo toccare con il cuore e la fantasia.

H — יֵשׁ שְׁנֵי עוֹלָמוֹת: הָעוֹלָם שֶׁאֶפְשָׁר לְמָדְדוֹ בְּמַו וּבְסַרְגֵּל וְהָעוֹלָם שֶׁאוֹתוֹ אָנוּ מַרְגִּישִׁים בְּלִבֵּנוּ וּבְדִמְיוֹנֵנוּ.

Friendship

12. The only way to have a friend is to be one.—*Ralph Waldo Emerson*

    G — Um einen Freund zu haben, muss man selbst ein Freund sein.

    L — Debet amare si vis amari.

    S — La única manera de tener un amigo es ser un amigo.

    F — Pour avoir un ami il faut en être un.

    I — L'unico modo di avere amici è di essere amico.

    H — לִרְכֹּשׁ חָבֵר פֵּרוּשׁוֹ לִהְיוֹת חָבֵר.

13. I have begun to be a friend to myself.—*Hecato*

    G — Ich habe begonnen, mich mit mir selbst anzufreunden.

    L — Amicus esse mihi coepi.

    S — He comenzado a ser amigo de mí mismo.

    F — J'ai commencé à être mon propre ami.

    I — Ho incominciato ad essere un amico a me stesso.

    H — הִתְחַלְתִּי לִהְיוֹת חָבֵר לְעַצְמִי.

14. Where there are friends, there is wealth.—*Plautus*

    G — Wo Freunde sind, da ist auch Reichtum.

    L — Ubi amici, esse ibidem opes.

    S — Donde hay amigos, hay riqueza.

    F — Les amis sont la richesse.

    I — Dove c'è amicizia c'è ricchezza.

    H — בְּמָקוֹם שֶׁיֵּשׁ חֲבֵרִים, יֵשׁ עֹשֶׁר.

15. A friend is a person with whom I may be sincere. Before him, I may think aloud.—*Ralph Waldo Emerson*

    G — Ein Freund ist ein Mensch, mit dem ich offen sein kann. In seiner Gegenwart darf ich laut denken.

L — Amicus persona coram quo sincerus sim et vivā voce cogitem.

S — Un amigo es una persona con quien yo puedo ser sincero. Ante él
yo puedo pensar en alta voz.

F — Un ami est quelqu'un avec qui je peux être sincère. Devant lui je
peux penser à haute voix.

I — Un amico è una persona con cui si può essere sinceri. Con lui posso
pensare apertamente.

H — חָבֵר הוּא אָדָם שֶׁאִתּוֹ מֻתָּר לִי לִהְיוֹת כֵּן, לְפָנָיו מֻתָּר לִי לַחֲשֹׁב בְּקוֹל.

16. The bird a nest,
The spider a web,
Man friendship.—*William Blake*

    G — Ein Nest für den Vogel,
Ein Gewebe für die Spinne,
Freundschaft für den Menschen.

    L — Avis nidum,
aranea araneum,
homo amicitiam.

    S — El pájaro un nido,
La araña una tela,
El hombre la amistad.

    F — L'oiseau le nid,
L'araignée la toile,
L'homme l'amitié.

    I — L'uccello un nido,
Il ragno una ragnatela,
L'uomo l'amicizia.

    H —
הַצִּפּוֹר—הַקֵּן

הָעַכָּבִישׁ—הַקּוּרִים

הָאָדָם—הַחֲבֵרוּת.

17. Life is nothing without friendship.—*Cicero*

    G — Das Leben ist nichts ohne Freundschaft.
    L — Sine amicitiā vita nihil.
    S — La vida no vale nada sin la amistad.
    F — La vie n'est rien sans l'amitié.
    I — La vita è niente senza l'amicizia.
    H — הַחַיִּים הֵם אֶפֶס בְּלִי יְדִידוּת.

18. Ah, how good it feels!
The hand of an old friend.—*Henry Wadsworth Longfellow*

    G — Ah, wie tut das gut!
Die Hand eines alten Freundes.

L — O quam bonum et jucundum,
manum amici tenēre.

S — ¡Oh, que bien se siente!
La mano de un viejo amigo.

F — Ah! Comme c'est bon!
La main d'un bon copain.

I — Ah! Com'è bello!
Il tocco di una vecchia mano amica.

H — אַה, אֵיזוֹ הַרְגָּשָׁה טוֹבָה!

יָדוֹ שֶׁל חָבֵר וָתִיק.

Giving

19. In giving a man receives more than he gives.—*Source unknown*

    G — Durch Geben bekommt man mehr, als man gibt.

    L — Dans recipit plus quam dat.

    S — Al dar, el hombre recibe más de lo que da.

    F — C'est en donnant que l'homme reçoit le plus.

    I — Dando un uomo riceve di più di quello che dà.

    H — בְּתִתּוֹ אָדָם מְקַבֵּל יוֹתֵר מֵאֲשֶׁר הוּא נוֹתֵן.

20. If you continually give, you continually have.—*H. H. Hart*

    G — Je mehr man gibt, desto mehr erhält man.

    L — Dare continenter, continenter habēre.

    S — Si siempre das, siempre tendrás.

    F — Plus tu donnes, plus tu as.

    I — Se dai sempre, avrai sempre.

    H — אִם פַּתְמִיד לָתֵת, יִהְיֶה לְךָ תָּמִיד.

21. Give to others what you long for yourself, and you'll find you have it already.

    G — Gib anderen Menschen das, wonach du dich selbst sehnst, und du wirst erkennen, dass du es schon besitzt.

    L — Da alteribus quod cupis et invenies te hoc jam habēre.

    S — Da a los demás lo que anhelas para tí y verás que ya lo tienes.

    F — Donne aux autres ce que tu désires pour toi, tu verras que tu l'as déjà.

    I — Dà agli altri quello che desideri per te stesso, e vedrai che lo possiedi già.

    H — תֵּן לַאֲחֵרִים מַה שֶׁאַתָּה מִשְׁתּוֹקֵק לְקַבֵּל לְעַצְמְךָ וּתְגַלֶּה שֶׁהַדָּבָר

כְּבָר בִּרְשׁוּתְךָ.

22.   To receive well is to give.

   G — Mit Freude zu empfangen, bedeutet zu geben.
   L — Bene recipere dare est.
   S — El bien recibir es también dar.
   F — Bien recevoir c'est donner.
   I — Accettare bene, é dare.
   H — לְקַבֵּל בְּסֵבֶר פָּנִים יָפוֹת פֵּרוּשׁוֹ לָתֵת.

Growth

23.   To grow is to change, and to have changed often, is to have grown much.—
   John H. Newman

   G — Wachsen heisst, sich zu ändern. Und sich oft geändert zu haben,
         bedeutet, viel gewachsen zu sein.
   L — Crescere mutare; saepe mutavisse valde crevisse.
   S — Crecer es cambiar y el haber cambiado a menudo es haber crecido
         mucho.
   F — Evoluer c'est changer, et avoir changé souvent c'est avoir beaucoup
         évolué.
   I — Maturarsi significa combiare, e aver cambiato spesso vuol dire aver
         maturato molto.
   H — לִגְדוֹל פֵּרוּשׁוֹ לְהִשְׁתַּנּוֹת, וּלְהִשְׁתַּנּוֹת תְּכוּפוֹת, סִמָּן שֶׁגָּדַלְתָּ מְאֹד.

24.   We grow through sharing ourselves.—*Herbert A. Otto*

   G — Wir wachsen, indem wir von uns selbst geben.
   L — Nosmetipsos partiendo crescimus.
   S — Crecemos al compartirnos.
   F — On se développe en partageant son essence avec les autres.
   I — Si matura dando di noi stessi.
   H — אֲנַחְנוּ גְדֵלִים ע"י שִׁתּוּף הֲדָדִי.

25.   Growth involves taking risks.—*Source unknown*

   G — Wachstum bedeutet Risiko.
   L — Crescere periculosum.
   S — Para crecer hay que arriesgar.
   F — La maturité ne vient pas sans prendre de risques.
   I — La maturità non si ottiene senza correre dei rischi.
   H — צְמִיחָה גּוֹרֶרֶת הִסְתַּפְּנוּת.

Happiness

26. Happiness seems made to be shared.—*Pierre Corneille*
    G — Glück soll man doch teilen.
    L — Laetitia partienda videtur.
    S — La felicidad parece ser hecha para compartirse.
    F — Le bonheur semble fait pour être partagé.
    I — La felicità è fatta per essere condivisa.
    H — הָאֹשֶׁר נוֹצַר לְהִתְחַלֵּק בּוֹ.

27. Happiness is not having what you want, but wanting what you have.—*Rabbi Hyman Judah Schachetl*
    G — Glücklich sein bedeutet nicht zu haben, was man will, sondern zu wollen, was man hat.
    L — Laetitia quod cupis habēre non est sed quod habes cupere.
    S — La felicidad no es tener lo que uno desea, sino desear lo que uno tiene.
    F — Le bonheur n'est pas d'avoir ce que l'on veut mais de vouloir ce que l'on a.
    I — La felicità non vuol dire avere quello che vuoi, ma volere quello che hai.
    H — אֹשֶׁר אֵין פֵּרוּשׁוֹ שֶׁיִּהְיֶה לְךָ מַה שֶׁתִּרְצֶה אֶלָּא שֶׁתִּרְצֶה מַה שֶׁיֵּשׁ לְךָ.

28. The greatest happiness is to be (yourself).—*Theodor Herzl*
    G — Man selbst zu sein, ist das grösste Glück.
    L — Maxima beatitudo est sua propria agere.
    S — La mejor felicidad es ser uno mismo.
    F — Le plus grand bonheur c'est d'être soi-même.
    I — La più grande gioia è di essere te stesso.
    H — הָאֹשֶׁר הַגָּדוֹל בְּיוֹתֵר הוּא לִהְיוֹת "עַצְמְךָ".

29. Happiness is a habit—cultivate it.—*Elbert Hubbard*
    G — Glücklich zu sein ist eine Gewohnheit—pflege sie.
    L — Beatitudo consuetudo est; eam cole.
    S — La felicidad es una flor—cultívala.
    F — Le bonheur est une habitude—cultive-le.
    I — La felicità è un'abitudine—coltivala.
    H — הָאֹשֶׁר הוּא הֶרְגֵּל— טַפַּח אוֹתוֹ.

30. Happiness can be measured by how many people you love.—*Adapted from Dagobert D. Runes*
    G — Glück kann daran gemessen werden, wieviele Menschen man liebt.
    L — Quot homines amati tot gaudia.

S — La felicidad puede medirse por el número de personas que amas.

F — Le bonheur se mesure au nombre de gens que l'on aime.

I — La felicità può essere misurata secondo il numero di persone che ami.

H — .הָאֹשֶׁר יָכוֹל לְהִמָּדֵד לְפִי מִסְפַּר הָאֲנָשִׁים שֶׁאַתָּה אוֹהֵב

31. Happiness comes from making others happy.

G — Man wird glücklich, wenn man andere Menschen glücklich macht.

L — Alteros facere laetos est fons laetitiae.

S — La felicidad se tiene haciendo felices a otros.

F — Le bonheur s'obtient en rendant les autres heureux.

I — La vera felicità si ottiene rendendo felici gli altri.

H — .הָאֹשֶׁר פֵּרוּשׁוֹ לְשַׂמֵּחַ אֲחֵרִים

Identity and Self-Image

32. I love myself when I am myself.—*Hugh Prather*

G — Ich liebe mich selbst, wenn ich „ich selbst" bin.

L — Me amo quando ego sum ego.

S — Me amo a mí mismo cuando soy yo mismo.

F — Je m'aime bien quand je suis moi-même.

I — Amo me quando sono me stesso.

H — ."אֲנִי אוֹהֵב אֶת עַצְמִי כַּאֲשֶׁר אֲנִי "עַצְמִי

33. Think of yourself as you wish others to think of you.—*Dagobert D. Runes*

G — Sieh dich selbst, wie andere Menschen dich deiner Meinung nach sehen sollen.

L — Cogita de te sicut cupis alteros de te cogitare.

S — Piensa acerca de ti mismo como deseas que los demás piensen de tí.

F — Pense de toi-même ce que tu veux que les autres pensent de toi.

I — Pensa di te stesso come vuoi che gli altri pensino di te.

H — .חֲשֹׁב עַל עַצְמְךָ כְּפִי שֶׁהִנְּךָ רוֹצֶה שֶׁאֲחֵרִים יַחְשְׁבוּ עָלֶיךָ

34. It is more important to be the right person than to find the right person.—*Ken Keyes, Jr.*

G — Es ist wichtiger, die richtige Person zu sein, als die richtige Person zu finden.

L — Pluris momenti est esse bonus quam invenire bonum.

S — Es más importante ser LA persona que encontrar a LA persona.

F — Il vaut mieux être idéal soi même que de chercher l'être idéal.

I — È più necessario aspirare alle perfezione in noi stessi che cercarla negli altri.

H — יוֹתֵר חָשׁוּב לִהְיוֹת הָאָדָם הַנָּכוֹן מֵאֲשֶׁר לִמְצֹא אֶת הָאָדָם הַנָּכוֹן.

35. To be nobody-but-myself . . . means to fight the hardest battle which any human being can fight.—*E. E. Cummings*

G — Nur „man selbst" zu sein, bedeutet, den schwersten Kampf zu kämpfen, den ein Mensch bestreiten kann.

L — Mea propria agere est maximum proelium quod pugnari potest.

S — Al ser uno mismo y no otro es luchar la batalla más dura que un ser humano puede luchar.

F — N'être que soi-même c'est livrer la plus grande bataille humaine.

I — Essere nessuno all'infuori di me stesso, significa lottare la battaglia più difficile che si possa combattere.

H — לֹא לִהְיוֹת אַחֵר אֶלָּא אֲנִי עַצְמִי, פֵּרוּשׁוֹ לִלְחֹם אֶת הַמַּאֲבָק הַקָּשֶׁה בְּיוֹתֵר שֶׁאָדָם יָכוֹל לִלְחֹם.

36. You are a much nicer person than you think you are.—*Herbert A. Otto*

G — Du bist eine viel nettere Person, als du glaubst.

L — Suavior es quam putas.

S — Eres mucho mejor de lo que tú crees.

F — Tu es meilleur que tu ne le penses.

I — Sei molto migliore di quello che credi di essere.

H — הִנְּךָ הַרְבֵּה יוֹתֵר נֶחְמָד מִמַּה שֶׁאַתָּה חוֹשֵׁב.

37. Love thyself.

G — Liebe dich selbst.

L — Ama teipsum.

S — Amate a ti mismo.

F — Aime-toi toi-même.

I — Ama te stesso.

H — אֱהַב אֶת עַצְמְךָ.

38. I just want to be me.

G — Ich will nur ich selbst sein.

L — Solum volo mea propria agere.

S — Sólo quiero ser yo.

F — Je ne veux être que moi-même.

I — Voglio solamente essere me stesso.

H — בִּרְצוֹנִי רַק לִהְיוֹת עַצְמִי.

Life and Living

39. Live as you want to be remembered.—*Dagobert D. Runes*
    G — Lebe so, wie du in Erinnerung behalten werden möchtest.
    L — Vive ut cupis memoriam tui esse.
    S — Vive como quieres ser recordado.
    F — Vis comme tu veux qu'on se souvienne de toi.
    I — Vivi come vuoi essere ricordato.
    H — חֲיֵה בְּאֹפֶן שֶׁהִנְּךָ רוֹצֶה לְהִזָּכֵר.

40. Life is an exciting business and most exciting when it is lived for others.—
    Helen Keller.
    G — Das Leben ist eine aufregende Sache, und es ist am wunderbarsten,
        wenn man es für andere Menschen lebt.
    L — Vivere res excitans et alteribus vivere excitantissima.
    S — La vida es excitante y es aún más cuando se vive por otros.
    F — La vie est une aventure passionnante, et encore plus quand elle est
        vécue pour les autres.
    I — La vita è meravigliosa ma lo è ancora di più se è vissuta per gli altri.
    H — הַחַיִּים הֵם מְאֹד מַלְהִיבִים וּמַלְהִיבִים בְּיוֹתֵר אִם חַיִּים עֲבוּר אֲחֵרִים.

41. Living is not getting more but being more.
    G — Zu leben bedeutet nicht, mehr zu bekommen, sondern mehr zu
        sein.
    L — Vivere non plura obtinēre sed plura esse.
    S — El vivir no es obtener más, sino ser más.
    F — Vivre ce n'est pas obtenir davantage mais être davantage.
    I — Vivere non significa avere di più ma essere di più.
    H — לִחְיוֹת אֵין פֵּרוּשׁוֹ לְהַשִּׂיג יוֹתֵר אֶלָּא לִהְיוֹת יוֹתֵר.

42. Feeling alive is getting in touch with what you really are.
    G — Sich am Leben zu fühlen bedeutet, mit sich selbst in Berührung zu
        kommen.
    L — Sentire et vivere est noscere teipsum.
    S — Sentirse vivo es saber lo que uno realmente es.
    F — Se sentir vivre c'est de se mettre en contact avec soi-même.
    I — Sentirsi vivi vuol dire essere in contatto con quello che sei
        veramente.
    H — לְהַרְגִּישׁ שֶׁהִנְּךָ מָלֵא חַיִּים, פֵּרוּשׁוֹ לָבוֹא בְּמַגָּע עִם מַה שֶׁהִנְּךָ בֶּאֱמֶת.

43. The best way to live is to love.—*Adapted from Herbert A. Otto*
    G — Zu lieben ist die beste Art zu leben.

L — Optimus modus vivendi amare est.
S — El mejor modo de vivir es amando.
F — La meilleure façon de vivre c'est d'aimer.
I — Il migliore modo di vivere è di amare.
H — הַדֶּרֶךְ הַטּוֹבָה בְּיוֹתֵר לִחְיוֹת הִיא לֶאֱהֹב.

Love

44. Love is always lovely.—*Plautus*
G — Liebe ist immer lieblich.
L — Lepidumst amare semper.
S — El amor es siempre hermoso.
F — L'amour est toujours beau.
I — L'amore è sempre bello.
H — הָאַהֲבָה תָּמִיד נִפְלָאָה הִיא.

45. Whoever you are, I love you.—*From the walls of a subway*
G — Wer du auch bist, ich liebe dich.
L — Quisquis tu es ego te amo.
S — Quienquiera que seas, te quiero.
F — Qui que tu sois, je t'aime.
I — Non importa chi sei, io ti amo.
H — הֱיֵה מִי שֶׁתִּהְיֶה, אֲנִי אוֹהֵב אוֹתְךָ.

46. Love is contagious.—*Susan Evans*
G — Liebe ist ansteckend.
L — Amare contagiosum.
S — El amor es contagioso.
F — L'amour est contagieux.
I — L'amore è contaggioso.
H — הָאַהֲבָה מִדַּבֶּקֶת.

47. If you want to be loved, then love.—*Anonymous* (from Latin)
G — Wenn du geliebt werden willst, dann liebe.
L — Vis amari, amas.
S — Si quieres ser amado, ama.
F — Si tu veux être aimé, eh bien aime!
I — Se vuoi essere amato, ama.
H — אִם בִּרְצוֹנְךָ לִחְיוֹת נֶאֱהָב, אֱהַב.

48. By Living Love, (we) can make our planet a here and now paradise.—*Ken Keyes, Jr.*

    G — Gelebte Liebe kann unseren Planeten heute in ein Paradies verwandeln.

    L — Vere amando, possumus facere terram hīc et nunc paradisum.

    S — Viviendo con amor, hoy podemos hacer de nuestro planeta un paraíso.

    F — L'amour vécu c'est le paradis terrestre assuré dès maintenant.

    I — Con una vita d'amore possiamo costruire un paradiso in terra.

    H — בְּחָיוֹתֵנוּ אֶת הָאַהֲבָה אֲנַחְנוּ יְכוֹלִים לַהֲפוֹךְ אֶת כַּדּוּר הָאָרֶץ בְּיָמֵינוּ
    לְגַן־עֵדֶן.

Relating to Others

49. The more we talk, the more we know ourselves. The more we know ourselves, the more we understand life.—*Ellen Greenland*

    G — Je mehr wir sprechen, desto besser erkennen wir uns selbst. Je mehr wir uns selbst erkennen, desto besser verstehen wir das Leben.

    L — Plus dicimus, plus nosmetipsos scimus. Plus nosmetipsos scimus, plus vivere comprehendimus.

    S — Al hablar más, más nos conocemos. Al conocernos más, más comprendemos la vida.

    F — Plus on parle plus on se connaît. Plus on se connaît, plus on comprend la vie.

    I — Più parliamo, più ci conosciamo. Più conosciamo noi stessi, più veniamo a capire la vita.

    H — כָּל שֶׁאֲנַחְנוּ מְדַבְּרִים יוֹתֵר אֲנַחְנוּ מַכִּירִים יוֹתֵר אֶת עַצְמֵנוּ. כָּל
    שֶׁאֲנַחְנוּ מַכִּירִים אֶת עַצְמֵנוּ אֲנַחְנוּ מְבִינִים יוֹתֵר אֶת הַחַיִּים.

50. Do unto others as you say you do.—*Dagobert D. Runes*

    G — Behandle deine Mitmenschen so, wie du behauptest, sie zu behandeln.

    L — Age alteribus ut dicis te agere.

    S — Haz con los demás lo que dices que haces.

    F — Fais pour les autres ce que tu prétends faire.

    I — Fà per gli altri ciò che dici di fare.

    H — נְהַג בַּאֲחֵרִים כְּפִי שֶׁאַתָּה אוֹמֵר שֶׁאַתָּה עוֹשֶׂה.

51. I hear and I forget;
    I see and I remember;
    I touch and I understand.—*Chinese proverb*
    > G — Ich höre, und ich vergesse;
    >   Ich sehe, und ich erinnere mich;
    >   Ich berühre, und ich verstehe.
    > L — Audio et obliviscor;
    >   Video et memini;
    >   Tango et comprehendo.
    > S — Oigo y olvido;
    >   Veo y recuerdo;
    >   Toco y comprendo.
    > F — J'entends et j'oublie;
    >   Je vois et je me souviens;
    >   Je touche et je comprends.
    > I — Sento e dimentico;
    >   Vedo e ricordo;
    >   Tocco e capisco.

    H — אֲנִי שׁוֹמֵעַ וְשׁוֹכֵחַ

    אֲנִי רוֹאֶה וְזוֹכֵר

    אֲנִי נוֹגֵעַ וּמֵבִין.

52. You touch me and there is sunshine.—*Elaine Baer*
    > G — Du berührst mich, und die Sonne scheint.
    > L — Me tangas et sol lucet.
    > S — Me tocas y hay sol.
    > F — Tu me touches et voila! Le soleil brille.
    > I — Mi tocchi e c'è sole.

    H — הִנְּךָ נוֹגֵעַ בִּי וְהִנֵּה זָרְחָה הַשֶּׁמֶשׁ.

53. The most precious thing a man can lend is his ears.—*Dagobert D. Runes*
    > G — Die Gabe des Zuhörens ist etwas ganz Besonderes.
    > L — Pretiossimum hominis audire est.
    > S — Lo más valioso que se puede prestar es el oído.
    > F — Le prêt le plus précieux est celui d'une oreille.
    > I — Il prestito di un orecchio è il dono più prezioso.

    H — הַדָּבָר הַיָּקָר בְּיוֹתֵר שֶׁאָדָם יָכוֹל לְהַשְׁאִיל הוּא הָאֹזֶן.

54. The same heart beats in every human.—*Matthew Arnold*
    > G — Das gleiche Herz schlägt in jedem Menschen.
    > L — Idem cor omnes vivificet.
    > S — El mismo corazón late en todo ser humano.
    > F — Le même coeur bat dans toutes les poitrines.

I — Lo stesso cuore batte in ogni essere umano.

H — אוֹתוֹ הַלֵּב הוֹלֵם בְּתוֹךְ כָּל אָדָם.

55. I'm so glad you are here. It helps me realize how beautiful my world is.–
Source unknown

    G — Ich bin so froh, dass du hier bist. Deine Nähe hilft mir einzusehen,
wie schön meine Welt ist.

    L — Gaudeo te adesse. Coram te incipio intellegere quam formosum
mundum meum esse.

    S — Me alegro que estés aquí. Me ayuda a comprender cuan bello mi
mundo es.

    F — Je suis si content que tu sois là. Cela m'aide à voir comme le monde
est beau.

    I — Sono contento che tu sia qui. Mi aiuti a capire la bellezza del mio
mondo.

    H — אֲנִי שָׂמֵחַ מְאֹד שֶׁהִנְּךָ פָּאן. זֶה עוֹזֵר לִי לְהָבִין כַּמָּה יָפֶה הוּא עוֹלָמִי.

56. The power of remembering may be a gift, but the power to forget is a
blessing.–*Dagobert D. Runes*

    G — Die Fähigkeit sich zu erinnern mag ein Geschenk sein, doch die
Fähigkeit zu vergessen ist ein Segen.

    L — Meminisse donum sit, sed oblivisci benedictio est.

    S — El poder de recordar es un talento, pero el poder de olvidar es una
bendición.

    F — Pouvoir se souvenir est un don, mais pouvoir oublier est une
bénédiction.

    I — La capacità di ricordare è un dono, ma la capacità di dimenticare è
una benedizione.

    H — כֹּחַ הַזְּכִירָה הִיא מַתָּנָה אוּלָם כֹּחַ הַשִּׁכְחָה הִיא בְּרָכָה.

57. Minds are like parachutes. They only function when open.–*Source unknown*

    G — Der Verstand ist wie ein Fallschirm. Er funktioniert nur, wenn er
offen ist.

    L — Mentes similes umbellis adapertilibus. Aperiendae.

    S — La mente es como el paracaídas. Sólo funciona cuando se abre.

    F — L'esprit est un parachute. Tous les deux ne fonctionnent que
quand ils sont ouverts.

    I — La mente è come un paracadute. Funziona solamente quando si
apre.

    H — הַמַּחְשָׁבָה דּוֹמָה לְמִצְנָח, שְׁנֵיהֶם פּוֹעֲלִים רַק כְּשֶׁהֵם פְּתוּחִים.

58. Our greatest deprivation is touch starvation.

    G — Die grösste Entbehrung besteht darin, von niemandem berührt zu
werden.

L – Maxima prīvatio vivere sine tangendo.
S – Nuestra mayor privación es la falta de tocarnos.
F – Le plus grand dénuement c'est de ne pas se toucher l'un l'autre.
I – La più grande privazione è la mancanza di un tocco umano.
H – הַמַּחְסוֹר הַגָּדוֹל בְּיוֹתֵר הוּא לַסְבֹּל מַחֲסוֹר בְּמַגָּע.

Smile

59. A smile is the shortest distance between two people.—*From a radio commercial*
G – Ein Lächeln ist der kürzeste Abstand zwischen zwei Menschen.
L – Subrisus inter duos brevissima distantia.
S – La sonrisa es la distancia más corta entre dos seres.
F – Le sourire est le plus court chemin entre deux personnes.
I – Un sorriso è la distanza più corta fra due persone.
H – הַחִיּוּךְ הִנֵּהוּ הַמֶּרְחָק הַקָּצָר בְּיוֹתֵר בֵּין שְׁנֵי אֲנָשִׁים.

60. Your smile gives me the desire to grow.—*Ellen Greenland*
G – Dein Lächeln gibt mir das Verlangen zu wachsen.
L – Subrisus tuus mihi desiderium dat ut crescam.
S – Tu sonrisa me inspira a madurar.
F – Ton sourire me donne l'envie de croître.
I – Il tuo sorriso mi da il desiderio di sviluppare.
H – חִיּוּכְךָ נוֹטֵעַ בִּי אֶת הָרָצוֹן לִגְדֹּל.

61. If you see someone who needs a smile, give him one of yours.—*Cathe Makem*
G – Wenn du jemanden siehst, der ein Lächeln braucht, dann lächle ihn an.
L – Subride quando maestum vides.
S – Si ves a alquien que necesite una sonrisa, dale una de las tuyas.
F – Si tu vois quelqu'un qui a besoin d'un sourire, donne-lui un des tiens.
I – Se qualcuno ha bisogno di un sorriso, sorridigli.
H – אִם תִּרְאֶה אָדָם הַזָּקוּק לְחִיּוּךְ, תֵּן לוֹ אֶחָד מִשֶּׁלְּךָ.

62. Laugh and be well.—*Matthew Green*
G – Lache und sei gesund.
L – Rideas et valeas.
S – Ríete y siéntete bien.
F – Ris et tu iras bien!
I – Ridete e starete sani.
H – צְחַק וְתַרְגִּישׁ טוֹב.

63. Don't lose your smile. It may help others find themselves.—*Source unknown*

   G — Verliere nicht dein Lächeln. Es kann anderen helfen, sich selbst zu finden.

   L — Subride ut alteri se sciant.

   S — No pierdas tu sonrisa. Puede ayudar a otros encontrarse a sí mismos.

   F — Ne perds pas ton sourire. Il peut aider les autres à se retrouver.

   I — Non perdere il tuo sorriso. Sorridendo aiuterai gli altri a scoprire loro stessi.

   H — אַל תְּאַבֵּד אֶת חִיּוּכְךָ אוּלַי יַעֲזֹר לַאֲחֵרִים לִמְצֹא אֶת עַצְמָם.

Strength and Confidence

64. Nothing is so strong as gentleness, and nothing is so gentle as real strength.—*The Reverend Ralph W. Sockman*

   G — Nichts ist so stark wie Sanftmut, und nichts ist so sanft wie wirkliche Stärke.

   L — Lenitas robusta et robur verum lene.

   S — Nada es tan fuerte como la nobleza, y nada tan noble como la fortaleza.

   F — Rien n'est plus fort que la douceur et rien n'est plus doux que la vraie force.

   I — Non c'è niente più forte della tenerezza e niente più tenero della vera forza.

   H — אֵין דָּבָר פֹּה חָזָק כַּעֲדִינוּת, וְאֵין דָּבָר פֹּה עָדִין כֹּה כְּחֹזֶק אֲמִתִּי.

65. Strength comes from contacting people, not from having power over them.

   G — Stärke kommt vom Kontakt mit Menschen, nicht davon, dass man Macht über sie hat.

   L — Robur communicare, non dominare.

   S — La fortaleza viene del contacto humano y no del poder sobre los humanos.

   F — La force vient du partage et non pas de la domination.

   I — La vera forza viene dal contatto umano, non dal potere sugli uomini.

   H — פֹּח נוֹבֵעַ מִמַּגָּע עִם אֲנָשִׁים וְלֹא מִשְׁלִיטָה עֲלֵיהֶם.

66. Self-confidence is the first requisite for great undertakings.—*Samuel Johnson*

   G — Selbstvertrauen ist die erste Voraussetzung für grosse Unternehmungen.

   L — Sibi federe primum mobile rerum magnarum.

   S — Tener confianza en sí mismo es el primer requisito para lograr grandes empresas.

F — La confiance en soi est à la base de toute grande réalisation.

I — La fiducia in sè è il primo requisito per ottenere grandi imprese.

H — בִּטָּחוֹן עַצְמִי הוּא הַצֹּרֶךְ הָרִאשׁוֹנִי לְמַעֲשִׂים גְּדוֹלִים.

Appendixes D-1, D-2, D-3, D-4, D-5

(Containing Cross-References to the Humanistic Exercises)

Recommended Time for Using Each Exercise *⁎⁎*

First Days of Class	Early in the School Year	When the Group is Better Acquainted		End of the School Year	As an Energizer
1	3	8	30	10	6
2	5	9	36	28	13
22	7	10	37	38	47
23	13	14	74	39	88
40	41	15	78	48	89
41	43	20	86	49	90
42	60	21	94	50	
	68	28	96	67	
	79	29	99		
	88				

*The numbers correspond to those given to the humanistic exercises in Chapters 3 and 4.

**All exercises not listed can be used at any time of the year.

Appendix D-2

Levels of Language in Which Each Humanistic Exercise Can Be Used ***

All Levels				Beginning	Intermediate			Advanced		
1	18	40	58	79	13	2	66	100	2	57	92
3	19	41	62	80	88	13	74	102	16	59	94
4	20	43	63	81	102	16	75	103	21	60	96
5	22	44	64	83	107	23	82	106	23	61	97
6	24	46	65	85	109	26	84	107	26	66	99
7	25	47	67	90	110	27	86	108	27	71	100
8	28	48	68	91	111	31	87	109	31	74	103
9	29	49	69	93	112	32	88	110	32	75	108
10	30	50	70	95	117	37	89	111	37	82	114
11	33	51	72	98		39	92	112	39	84	115
12	34	52	73	101		42	94	115	42	86	116
14	35	53	76	104		45	96	116	45	87	119
15	36	54	77	105		57	97	119	55	89	120
17	38	56	78	113		61	99	120			
				118							

*The numbers correspond to those given to the humanistic exercises in Chapters
3 and 4.

**Proper structuring on the part of the teacher can enable exercises to be used
at levels other than those suggested here.

Appendix D-3

Parts of Speech Emphasized in Specific Exercises *, **

Nouns		Verbs			Adjectives			Comparative Superlative	Adjectives Describing Positive Qualities		Possessive Adjectives	Prepositions	Adverbs
3	91	2	30	81	11	25	99	26	28	81	53	104	11
11	93	11	46	87	12	32	103	31	29	88	64		
17	95	9	49	88	16	36	104	55	30	98	81		
23	97	10	50	90	18	39	105	59	50	101			
46	104	16	56	91	19	65	108	80	54	102			
53	116	18	57	94	20	69	116		62	107			
65	120	22	58	104	22	72	120		79	118			
90		28	59	105	23	84			80				
		29	75		24	90							

*The numbers correspond to those given to the humanistic exercises in Chapters 3 and 4.

**This is a suggestive rather than an exhaustive list of parts of speech which can be practiced in various exercises.

Appendix D-4

Tenses, Moods, and Sentence Forms Emphasized in Specific Exercises * **

Two or More Tenses	Past Tense(s)		Future	Conditional	Interrogative		Imperative	Subjunctive	Negative
5	27	61	8	17	2	55	6	8	5
7	31	62	77	69	3	61	14	17	47
33	32	63	78	70	4	64	95	47	
34	39	66	88	74	5	66			
37	49	67	92	78	6	68			
47	52	87	98	88	7	78			
64	53	96	106	92	27	79			
98	54	99		98	37	80			
	57	100			47	83			
	60	111			53	103			

*The numbers correspond to those given to the humanistic exercises in Chapters 3 and 4.

**This is a suggestive rather than an exhaustive list of tenses, moods, and sentence forms which can be practiced in various exercises.

Appendix D-5

Vocabulary Emphasized in Specific Exercises * **

Feelings			Parts of the Body		Colors/ Shapes		"I Like" Statements		Giving One's Name	"Because" Statements
1	48	87	6	101	1	83	35	64	1	41
40	50	91	29	107	6	84	36	88	40	51
41	59	111	35	118	12	116	58		45	68
43	82	112	36		52	120			51	89
45	83	116			81				88	
46	84									
47	85									

Numbers	Members of the Family	Giving One's Age	Months, Dates	Rooms of the House
76	54	54	106	112
106	59	63	110	113
117				

Furniture	Weather	Seasons, Months, Days	Telling Time	Measurements
113	109	110	13	95

*The numbers correspond to those given to the humanistic exercises in Chapters 3 and 4.

**This is a suggestive rather than an exhaustive listing of vocabulary and expressions which can be emphasized in various exercises.

Selected Bibliography

Ashton-Warner, Sylvia. *Teacher.* New York: Bantam Books (1963).

Avila, Donald L., Arthur W. Combs, and William W. Purkey. *The Helping Relationship Sourcebook.* Boston: Allyn and Bacon (1971).

Berne, Eric. *Games People Play.* New York: Grove Press (1964).

———. *What Do You Say After You Say Hello?* New York: Grove Press (1964).

Blank, Leonard, Gloria B. Gottsegen, and Monroe G. Gottsegen, eds. *Confrontation: Encounters in Self and Interpersonal Awareness.* New York: Macmillan (1971).

Borton, Terry. *Reach, Touch, and Teach: Student Concerns and Process Education.* New York: McGraw-Hill (1970).

Boy, Angelo V. and Gerald J. Pine. *Expanding the Self: Personal Growth for Teachers.* Dubuque, Iowa: Wm. C. Brown (1971).

Briggs, Dorothy C. *Your Child's Self-Esteem: The Key to His Life.* Garden City, N.Y.: Doubleday (1970).

Bry, Adelaide. *The TA Primer.* New York: Harper & Row (1973).

Clark, Don and Asya Kadis. *Humanistic Teaching.* Columbus, Ohio: Charles E. Merrill (1971).

Cullum, Albert. *Push Back the Desks.* New York: Citation Press (1967).

———. *The Geranium on the Window Just Died and Teacher You Kept Right on Teaching.* New York: H. Quist (1971).

Daniels, Steven. *How 2 Gerbils, 20 Goldfish, 200 Games, 2,000 Books and I Taught Them How to Read.* Philadelphia, Pa.: Westminster Press (1972).

Davis, David C. L. *Model for a Humanistic Education: The Danish Folk High-School.* Columbus, Ohio: Charles E. Merrill (1971).

Dennison, George. *The Lives of Children: The Story of the First Street School.* New York: Random House (1969).

Disick, Renee S. and Laura Barbanel. "Affective Education and Foreign Languages," in *The Challenge of Communication.* Gilbert A. Jarvis, ed. Skokie, Ill.: National Textbook and ACTFL (1974), pp. 185-222.

Ernst, Ken. *Games Students Play (and what to do about them).* Milbrae, Calif.: Celestial Arts (1972).

Friedenberg, Edgar. *Coming of Age in America.* New York: Random House (1965).

Galyean, Beverly. "Humanistic Education: A Mosaic Just Begun," in *An Integrative Approach to Foreign Language Teaching: Choosing Among the Options.* Gilbert A. Jarvis, ed. Skokie, Ill.: National Textbook and ACTFL (1976), pp. 201-243.

Ginott, Haim G. *Between Parent & Teenager.* New York: Avon Books (1969).

———. *Teacher and Child: A Book for Parents and Teachers.* New York: Macmillan (1972).

Glasser, William. *Schools Without Failure.* New York: Harper and Row (1969).

Goble, Frank G. *The Third Force: The Psychology of Abraham Maslow.* New York: Grossman (1970).

Gordon, Thomas. *T.E.T.—Teacher Effectiveness Training.* New York: Peter Wyden (1974).

Graubard, Allen. *Free the Children: Radical Reform and the Free School Movement.* New York: Vintage Books (1974).

Greenberg, Herbert M. *Teaching with Feeling: Compassion and Self-Awareness in the Classroom Today.* New York: Macmillan (1969).

Gross, Beatrice and Ronald Gross, eds. *Radical School Reform.* New York: Simon & Schuster (1970).

Gustaitis, Rasa. *Turning On.* New York: Macmillan (1969).

Hamachek, Donald E. *Encounter with the Self.* New York: Holt, Rinehart, and Winston (1971).

Harris, Thomas. *I'm Ok, You're Ok: A Practical Guide to Transactional Analysis.* New York: Harper & Row (1969).

Henderson, George and Robert F. Bibens. *Teachers Should Care: Social Perspectives of Teaching.* New York: Harper & Row (1970).

Hentoff, Nat. *Our Children Are Dying.* New York: Viking Press (1966).

Herndon, James. *How to Survive in Your Native Land.* New York: Simon & Schuster (1971).

———. *The Way It Spozed to Be.* New York: Viking Press (1966).

Holt, John. *Freedom and Beyond.* New York: Dutton (1972).

———. *How Children Fail.* New York: Pitman (1964).

———. *How Children Learn.* New York: Pitman (1967).

———. *The Underachieving School.* New York: Pitman (1969).

———. *What Do I Do Monday?* New York: Dutton (1970).

Howard, Jane. *Please Touch.* New York: McGraw-Hill (1970).

Jersild, Arthur T. *In Search of Self: An Exploration of the Role of the School in Promoting Self-understanding.* New York: Teachers College Press (1952).

———. *When Teachers Face Themselves.* New York: Teachers College Press (1955).

Jackson, Philip. *Life in the Classrooms.* New York: Holt, Rinehart, and Winston (1968).

Jones, Richard. *Fantasy and Feeling in Education.* New York: New York University Press (1968).

Jourard, Sidney. *The Transparent Self.* New York: Van Nostrand Reinhold (1964).

———. *Self-disclosure: An Experimental Analysis of the Transparent Self.* New York: John Wiley (1971).

Kirschenbaum, Howard, Rodney W. Napier, and Sidney B. Simon. *Wad-ja Get?: The Grading Game in American Education.* New York: Hart (1971).

Knoblock, Peter and Arnold P. Goldstein. *The Lonely Teacher.* Boston: Allyn & Bacon (1971).

Kohl, Herbert R. *The Open Classroom: A Practical Guide to a New Way of Teaching.* New York: Vintage Books (1969).

———. *36 Children.* New York: New American Library (1976).

Kozol, Jonathan. *Death at an Early Age: The Destruction of the Hearts and Minds of Negro Children in the Boston Public Schools.* Boston: Houghton Mifflin (1967).

Krathwohl, David R., Benjamin S. Bloom, and Bertram B. Masia. *Taxonomy of Educational Objectives: Handbook II, Affective Domain.* New York: David McKay (1956).

Lederman, Janet. *Anger and the Rocking Chair: Gestalt Awareness with Children.* New York: Viking Press (1973).

Leeper, Robert R., ed. *Humanizing Education: The Person in the Process.* Washington, D.C.: Association for Supervision and Curriculum Development (1967).

Leonard, George. *Education and Ecstasy.* New York: Delacorte Press (1968).

Lyon, Harold C., Jr. *It's Me and I'm Here! From West Point to Esalen: How a Rigid Overachiever Revolutionized His Life.* New York: Delacorte (1974).

Maltz, Maxwell. *Psycho-Cybernetics and Self-Fulfillment.* New York: Bantam Books (1973).

Marshall, Bernice S. *Experiences in Being.* Belmont, Calif.: Brooks-Cole (1971).

May, Rollo. *Love and Will.* New York: Norton (1969).

Menninger, William C. *Making and Keeping Friends.* Palo Alto, Calif.: Science Research Associates (1952).

Miles, Matthew. *Learning to Work in Groups.* New York: Teachers College Press (1959).

Morris, Van Cleve. *Existentialism in Education: What It Means.* New York: Harper & Row (1966).

Moustakas, Clark E. and Cereta Perry. *Learning to Be Free.* Englewood Cliffs, N.J.: Prentice-Hall (1973).

———. *Loneliness.* Englewood Cliffs, N.J.: Prentice-Hall (1961).

———. *The Authentic Teacher: Sensitivity and Awareness in the Classroom.* Cambridge, Mass.: Howard A. Doyle (1966).

———, ed. *The Self: Explorations in Personal Growth.* New York: Harper & Row (1956).

Napier, Rodney W. and Matti K. Gershenfeld. *Groups: Theory and Experience.* New York: Houghton Mifflin (1973).

Neill, Alexander S. *Summerhill: A Radical Approach to Child Rearing.* New York: Hart (1960).

Newman, Mildred, Bernard Berkowitz, and Jean Owen. *How to Be Your Own Best Friend: A Conversation with Two Psychoanalysts.* New York: Lark Publishing Co. (1971).

Perls, Frederick S. *Gestalt Therapy Verbatim.* Lafayette, Calif.: Real People Press (1969).

Postman, Neil and Charles Weingartner. *Teaching as a Subversive Activity.* New York: Delacorte Press (1969).

———. *The Soft Revolution: A Student Handbook for Turning Schools Around.* New York: Delacorte Press (1971).

Rogers, Carl R. and Barry Stevens. *Person to Person: The Problem of Being Human.* New York: Pocket Book (1971).

Romey, William. *Risk-Trust-Love.* Columbus, Ohio: Charles E. Merrill (1972).

Rosenthal, Robert and Lenore Jacobson. *Pygmalion in the Classroom: Teacher Expectations and Pupil's Intellectual Development.* New York: Holt, Rinehart and Winston (1968).

Rubin, Lewis J. *Facts and Feelings in the Classroom.* New York: Walker (1973).

Saylor, J. Galen and Joshua L. Smith, eds. *Removing Barriers to Humaneness in the High School.* Washington, D.C.: Association for Supervision and Curriculum Development (1971).

Shostrom, Everett. *Freedom to Be: Experiencing and Expressing Your Total Being.* New York: Bantam Books (1974).

———. *Man, the Manipulator: The Inner Journey from Manipulation to Actualization.* New York: Bantam Books (1968).

Silberman, Charles E. *Crisis in the Classroom: The Remaking of American Education.* New York: Random House (1970).

Silberman, Melvin L., Jerome S. Allender, and Jay M. Yanoff, eds. *The Psychology of Open Teaching and Learning: An Inquiry Approach.* Boston, Mass.: Little, Brown, and Company (1972).

Simon, Sidney B. *Caring, Feeling, Touching.* Niles, Ill.: Argus Communications (1976).

Tomkins, Silvan. *Affect-Imagery and Consciousness,* 2 vols. New York: Springer (1962-3).

Watts, Alan. *The Book: On the Taboo Against Knowing Who You Are.* New York: Random House (1972).

Wells, Harold C. and John T. Canfield. *About Me: A Curriculum for a Developing Self.* Chicago, Ill.: Encyclopedia Britannica Education Corporation (1971).

Articles Related
to
Humanistic Education

Adams, G.S., ed. "Humanizing Education." *Educational Horizons.* 52 (Fall 1973), pp. 2-38.

Anderson, R. A. "Humanized and Individualized Secondary School Program." *Theory into Practice.* 11 (February 1972), pp. 43-49.

Arnstine, D. "Knowledge Nobody Wants: The Humanistic Foundations in Teacher Education." *Educational Theory.* 23 (Winter 1973), pp. 3-15.

Aronson, Howard. "The Role of Attitudes About Languages in the Learning of Foreign Languages." *Modern Language Journal.* 57 (November 1973), pp. 323-327.

Bailey, R.P. "Comment: Education Yesterday and Today." *Today's Education.* 62 (November 1973), p. 65.

Bennett, R. V. "Curricular Organizing Strategies, Classroom Interaction Patterns, and Pupil Affect." *Journal of Educational Research.* 66 (May 1973), pp. 387-393.

Bessell, Harold. "The Content is the Medium: The Confidence is the Message." *Psychology Today.* (January 1968), pp. 32-35.

Blake, R. W. "I See You, I Hear You, You're OK: Humanizing the English Classroom." *English Journal.* 63 (May 1974), pp. 41-46.

Borton, Terry. "What Turns Kids On?" *Saturday Review.* (April 15, 1967), pp. 72-74.

Brennan, E. C. "Meeting the Affective Needs of Young Children." *Children Today.* 3 (July 1974), pp. 22-25.

Bridges, W. "Three Faces of Humanistic Education." *Liberal Education.* 59 (October 1973), pp. 325-335.

Broudy, H. S. "Humanism in Education." *Journal of Aesthetic Education.* 7 (April 1973), pp. 67-77.

Brown, G.I. "I Have Things to Tell: Confluent Education." *Elementary English.* 50 (April 1973), pp. 515-520.

Brown, G.J. and J.E. Rentschler. "Humanizing the Schools." *Contemporary Education.* 45 (Winter 1974), pp. 90-95.

Brown, H. D. "Affective Variables in Second Language Acquisition." *Language Learning.* 23 (December 1973), pp. 231-244.

Buchholz, E. S. "Proper Study for Children: Children and Their Feelings." *Psychology in the Schools.* 11 (January 1974), pp. 10-15.

Carney, Helen. "Students Make the Scene." *Modern Language Journal.* 57 (November 1973), pp. 335-340.

Carswell, E. M. "To Become Through Behaving." *Instructor.* 82 (February 1973), p. 18.

Christensen, Clay B. "Affective Learning Activities (ALA)." *Foreign Language Annals.* 8 (October 1975), pp. 211-219.

Combs, A. W. "Human Side of Learning." *National Elementary Principal.* 52 (January 1973), pp. 38-42.

Coopersmith, S. and R. Feldman. "Promoting Motivation Through Inter-Related Cognitive and Affective Factors." *Clarement Reading Conference Yearbook.* (1973), pp. 129-134.

DeWitt, G. "How to Identify Humanistic Teachers." *NASSP Bulletin.* 57 (December 1973), pp. 19-25.

Dinkmeyer, D. and K. D. Ogburn. "Psychologists' Priorities: Premium on Developing Understanding of Self and Others; DUSO Program." *Psychology in the Schools.* 11 (January 1974), pp. 24-27.

Disick, Renee. "Teaching Towards Affective Goals." *Foreign Language Annals.* 7 (October 1973), pp. 323-327.

Edman, M. L. "Can Children Achieve Humaneness?" *Educational Horizons.* 51 (Spring 1973), pp. 107-110.

Eldridge, M.S. "Effects of DUSO on the Self-concepts of Second Grade Students." *Elementary School Guidance and Counseling.* 7 (May 1973), pp. 256-260.

Esler, W. K. and J. Armstrong. "Humanistic Curriculum: Is It for Everyone?" *Clearing House.* 48 (November 1973), pp. 189-190.

Fantini, M. D. "Alternative Schools and Humanistic Education." *Social Education.* 38 (March 1974), pp. 243-247.

Filep, R. T. "Open Learning Systems: Toward Humanistic Educational Technology." *Educational Technology.* 13 (August 1973), pp. 42-43.

Franzwa, H. H. "Limitations in Applying Humanistic Psychology in the Classroom." *Today's Speech.* 21 (Winter 1973), pp. 31-36.

Gabriel, Toni. "Mind Expanding." *American Foreign Language Teacher.* 57 (Fall 1973), pp. 25-26.

Galyean, Beverly. "A Confluent Design for Language Teaching." *TESOL Quarterly.* 11 (June 1977), pp. 143-155.

Garner, H. G. "Mental Health Benefits of Small Group Experiences in the Affective Domain." *Journal of School Health.* 44 (June 1974), pp. 314-318.

Geiser, R. G. "Help Them to Learn About Themselves." *Teacher.* 90 (September 1972), pp. 27-28.

Gordon, Robert A. "Human Potential in the Foreign Language Conversation Class." *The Bulletin of the Pennsylvania Modern Language Association.* 54 (Fall 1975), pp. 25-26.

Grittner, F. M. "Barbarians, Bandwagons, and Foreign Language Scholarship." *Modern Language Journal.* 57 (September 1973), pp. 241-248.

Hamm, R. L. and D. G. Findley. "On Being Human: Guidelines for Teachers." *Contemporary Education.* 46 (Summer 1975), pp. 284-286.

Harrison, A., Jr. "Humanism and Educational Reform: The Need for a Balanced Perspective." *Educational Forum.* 38 (March 1974), pp. 331-336.

Heichberger, R. L. "Toward a Strategy for Humanizing the Change Process in Schools." *Journal of Research and Development in Education.* 7 (Fall 1973), pp. 78-85.

Helling, C. E. "Are Losers Essential to the Success of Winners? A Comment on Our Value System." *American Vocational Journal.* 49 (January 1974), p. 34.

Henderson, T. "Review of the Literature on Affective Education." *Contemporary Education.* 44 (November 1972), pp. 92-99.

Holcomb, R. F. "Don't Check Your Emotions at the Door." *School and Community.* 60 (March 1974), p. 36.

Howe, L.W. and L.J. Kraft. "Affective Education Guidelines." *NASSP Bulletin.* 58 (March 1974), pp. 37-43.

Hubbard, G. "Our Most Precious Possession." *Instructor.* 82 (April 1973), p. 12.

"Humanizing Process: Symposium." *NASSP Bulletin.* 60 (April 1976), pp. 1-38.

"Inside Out! Confluent Education." *Saturday Review of Education.* 1 (February 1973), p. 51.

Kagerer, R. L. "Toward an Affective Outcome of Higher Education: Analytical Objectivity Test." *Journal of Educational Measurement.* 11 (Fall 1974), pp. 203-208.

"Kids Learn Best When They Feel Good About Themselves." *Instructor.* 83 (April 1974), pp. 71-76.

Kneer, M. E. "How Human Are You? Exercises in Awareness." *Journal of Health, Physical Education, and Recreation.* 45 (June 1974), pp. 32-34.

Levine, E. "Affective Education: Lessons in Ego Development." *Psychology in the Schools.* 10 (April 1973), pp. 147-150.

Lyon, H. C., Jr. "Humanistic Education for Lifelong Learning." *International Review of Education.* 20 (No. 4, 1974), pp. 502-505.

Manning, M. "Open Education: A Way to Humanize." *Delta Kappa Gamma Bulletin.* 40 (Summer 1974), pp. 49-51.

McGill, W. J. "Prolegomenon to Humanistic Learning." *Liberal Education.* 60 (May 1974), pp. 249-257.

Messmore, M. "Curriculum of Today: A Foreshadowing of Tomorrow." *English Journal.* 63 (April 1974), pp. 37-41.

Morrison, D. W. "How to Experience Ideas." *Education.* 93 (April 1973), pp. 357-361.

Mosher, Ralph L. and Norman A. Sprinthall. "Psychological Education in Secondary Schools: A Program to Promote Individual and Human Development." *American Psychologist.* 25 (October 1970), pp. 911-924.

Muessig, R. H. and J. J. Cogan. "To Humanize Schooling." *Educational Leadership.* 30 (October 1972), pp. 34-36.

Myrick, R. D. and L. S. Moni. "Helping Humanize Education." *Elementary School Guidance and Counseling.* 7 (May 1973), pp. 295-299.

Nash, P., ed. "Humanistic Education: Symposium." *Journal of Education.* 157 (May 1975), pp. 3-69.

———. "Humanistic Education: Symposium." *Journal of Education.* 157 (August 1975), pp. 3-58.

O'Brien, C. R. and J. R. Johnson. "Humanistic Emphasis in Adult Education." *Adult Leadership.* 24 (April 1976), pp. 242-244.

Ohlsen, M. M. "Focus on Issues: Affective Education." *Contemporary Education.* 44 (January 1973), p. 194.

Ray, H. "Media and Affective Learning." *American Annals of the Deaf.* 117 (October 1972), pp. 545-549.

Ruth, L. "Way Things Shouldn't Be." *English Journal.* 62 (May 1973), pp. 817-824+.

Schrag, F. "Learning What One Feels and Enlarging the Range of One's Feelings." *Educational Theory.* 22 (Fall 1972), pp. 382-394.

Splittgerber, F. and R. Trueblood. "Accountability and Humanism." *Educational Technology.* 15 (February 1975), pp. 22-26.

Swick, K. J. "Affective Readiness for the Classroom Teacher." *Reading Improvement.* 11 (Spring 1974), pp. 32-33.

———. "Need for Creating Productive Attitude Climates for Learning." *Education.* 93 (February 1973), pp. 305-308.

"Teaching with Affect." *Elementary English.* 51 (March 1974), pp. 435+.

Travers, E. X. "How Human Is Your Classroom?" *Today's Education.* 64 (November 1975), pp. 66-67.

Wagner, T. "All Is Quiet But Not All Is Well in Suburbia." *Phi Delta Kappan.* 57 (April 1976), pp. 542-544.

Washington, K.R. "Self-concept Development: An Effective Educational Experience for Inner-City Teachers." *Young Children.* 29 (July 1974), pp. 305-310.

Willers, J. C. "Humanistic Education: Concepts, Criteria, and Criticism." *Peabody Journal of Education.* 53 (October 1975), pp. 39-44.

Winkeljohann, R. "Children's Affective Development Through Books: ERIC/RCS Report." *Elementary English.* 51 (March 1974), pp. 410-414.

Withrow, F. "Humanistic Education and Technology." *American Annals of the Deaf.* 117 (October 1972), pp. 531-537.

Wolfe, D. E. and L. W. Howe. "Personalizing Foreign Language Instruction." *Foreign Language Annals.* 7 (October 1973), pp. 81-90.

Wolfe, D.E., L.W. Howe, and M. Keating. "Clarifying Values Through Foreign Language Study." *Hispania.* 56 (May 1973), pp. 404-406.

Yarcott, G. "Mad, Sad, or Distinctly Frustrated?" *Educational Review.* 25 (February 1973), pp. 90-105.

Index